Mastering Magento 2

Second Edition

Maximize the power of Magento 2 to create productive online stores

Bret Williams

Jonathan Bownds

BIRMINGHAM - MUMBAI

Mastering Magento 2

Second Edition

First published: May 2012

Second published: June 2016

Production reference: 1220616

Published by Packt Publishing Ltd.
Livery Place
35 Livery Street
Birmingham B3 2PB, UK.

ISBN 978-1-78588-236-4

www.packtpub.com

Credits

Authors
Bret Williams
Jonathan Bownds

Reviewer
Andre Gugliotti

Commissioning Editor
Wilson D'souza

Acquisition Editor
Aaron Lazar

Content Development Editor
Arun Nadar

Technical Editor
Vivek Pala

Copy Editor
Pranjali Chury

Project Coordinator
Ritika Manoj

Proofreader
Safis Editing

Indexer
Monica Ajmera Mehta

Graphics
Jason Monteiro

Production Coordinator
Melwyn Dsa

Cover Work
Melwyn Dsa

About the Authors

Bret Williams, for over 20 years, has engineered the creation of hundreds of websites, including many profitable e-commerce properties and several Internet firsts. Beginning with version 1.3 of Magento CE, Bret began an odyssey of becoming one of the foremost experts on leveraging Magento to build successful online businesses. Today, as CEO of novusweb llc, Bret continues to provide e-commerce management services from his office in Austin, Texas. Bret authored the wildly popular *Mastering Magento*, and he is the co-author of *Magento 2 Administrator's Guide* (Packt Publishing) with his wife and business partner, Cyndi. His company also owns `MageDaily.com`, a Magento news and reviews blog, and `MageRevolution.com`, which sells Magento enhancements.

I would like to extend his sincere thanks to the team at Packt Publishing for helping bring this book to life. I am also thankful to Jon Bownds for being a great writing partner and source of in-depth technical knowledge about Magento 2. Magento—the company and people—are to be commended for creating an extraordinary platform for building e-commerce businesses that succeed. Last, but certainly not least, I would like to thank my wife of 36 years, Cyndi, for allowing me the time and environment to write.

Jonathan Bownds is an e-commerce professional living in the sunny climes of Austin, Texas. He got his start working in technology around 1998, and he promptly gravitated toward Linux, system administration, security, and open source projects. He's been embroiled in something related to one of these topics ever since.

He is currently a partner at Praxis Information Science (www.praxisis.com), a web development company that specializes in tackling interesting Magento problems and helping merchants make a go of it in the wild and woolly frontier of e-commerce.

Beside work, he enjoys spending time with his wife and two boys, playing tennis, reading, and in an ongoing search for the best breakfast taco in Texas.

I would like to thank Bret Williams for the opportunity to work on this book, and his invaluable guidance during the entire process. In addition, I'd like to thank Packt Publishing for their deft editorial guidance, and Magento for creating the most flexible e-commerce platform available. Last but not least, I'd like to thank my wife, Shana, and kids, Sebastian and Maxwell, for their support and inspiration.

About the Reviewer

Andre Gugliotti is a Brazilian author, writing about e-commerce and working on internet business since 2004. He is a specialist in building and maintaining online stores and helping companies and entrepreneurs to achieve success. He also teaches teams on e-commerce subjects and give lectures in Brazil or abroad.

www.PacktPub.com

eBooks, discount offers, and more

Did you know that Packt offers eBook versions of every book published, with PDF and ePub files available? You can upgrade to the eBook version at www.PacktPub. com and as a print book customer, you are entitled to a discount on the eBook copy. Get in touch with us at customercare@packtpub.com for more details.

At www.PacktPub.com, you can also read a collection of free technical articles, sign up for a range of free newsletters and receive exclusive discounts and offers on Packt books and eBooks.

https://www2.packtpub.com/books/subscription/packtlib

Do you need instant solutions to your IT questions? PacktLib is Packt's online digital book library. Here, you can search, access, and read Packt's entire library of books.

Why subscribe?

- Fully searchable across every book published by Packt
- Copy and paste, print, and bookmark content
- On demand and accessible via a web browser

Table of Contents

Preface   **ix**

Chapter 1: Planning for Magento   **1**

  Defining your scope   **2**

    Project requirements   2

      Requirements checklist   3

    Planning for users   3

      Staff   4

      Customers   4

    Assessing technical resources   5

  Technical considerations   **6**

    Hosting provider   6

    In-house hosting   7

      Servers   7

    The best of both worlds   8

      Setting up a local test installation   8

  Global-Website-Store methodology   **9**

    Global   10

    Website   11

    Store   11

  Planning for multiple stores   **12**

    Using multiple domains for effective market segmentation 12

    Using multiple businesses to keep finances separate   13

    Using multiple languages to sell globally   14

  Summary   **15**

Chapter 2: Installing Magento 2   **17**

  How hosting effects installation   **17**

    Understanding types of hosting   17

    Successful hosting guidelines   18

    Avoiding the PCI headache   20

Keys to a successful installation	**22**
Avoid the bleeding edge	23
Take your time	23
Install the sample data	23
Setting up Magento stores	**24**
Planning your categories	26
Disabling the cache	28
Set up websites, stores, and store views	29
Nginx versus Apache	33
Configuring Apache	33
Configuring Nginx	36
Configuring Magento	37
Configuring base URLs	38
Using localization to sell globally	40
Language files	40
Manually translating labels	42
Converting currencies	45
It begins with the base currency	45
Let Magento automatically convert currencies	46
Strategies for backups and security	**50**
Backend backups	50
File structure backups	52
Keep it secure	53
Summary	**53**
Chapter 3: Managing Products	**55**
Catalogs and categories	**55**
Creating categories	56
General information tab	57
Display Settings tab	59
Custom Design tab	61
Category Products tab	61
Re-ordering categories	62
Special categories	62
Managing products the customer focused way	**65**
The simple product type	65
The complex product types	66
Configurable product type	66
Grouped product type	69
Bundle product type	69
Virtual product type	71
Downloadable product type	71
Attributes and attribute sets	72
Attribute types	74
Creating attribute sets	81

Creating products **85**
　The new product screen 85
　　Creating a simple product 86
　　Creating a configurable product 89
　　Creating a grouped product 93
　　Creating bundled products 94
　　Creating a downloadable product 96
　　Creating a virtual product 97
Managing inventory **97**
　Low stock notifications 98
　Product reports 98
Pricing tools **99**
　Pricing by customer group 99
　Quantity-based pricing 100
Autosettings **101**
Related products, up-sells, and cross-sells **102**
　Related products 103
　Upsell products 104
　Cross-sell products 104
Importing products **105**
　The shortcut to importing products 105
Summary **107**
Chapter 4: Designs and Themes **109**
The Magento theme structure **110**
　Theme files and directories 113
　The concept of theme inheritance 114
　　Configuring a parent theme in theme.xml 115
　　Overriding static files 115
　　Overriding theme files 116
Default installation of design packages and themes **117**
Installing third-party themes **119**
Inline translations **121**
Working with theme variants **122**
　Assigning themes 124
　Applying theme variants 125
　Scheduling a theme variant 125
Customizing themes **126**
Customizing layouts **126**
　Expertly controlling layouts 130
　　Using the reference tag to relocate blocks 132
　Customizing the default layout file 133
Summary **134**

Chapter 5: Configuring to Sell — 137

The sales process — 138
  The Magento sales process — 138
  Managing backend orders — 140
    Convert orders to invoices — 143
    Creating shipments — 144
Payment methods — 145
  PCI compliance — 146
  Classes of payment systems — 147
    Off-site payment systems — 147
    On-site payment systems — 148
  PayPal — 149
    PayPal all-in-one payment solutions — 149
    PayPal payment gateways — 150
    PayPal Express — 150
  Braintree — 151
  Check/money order — 151
  Bank transfer payment — 151
  Cash on delivery payment — 151
  Zero subtotal checkout — 151
  Purchase order — 152
  Authorize.net direct post — 152
Shipping methods — 152
  Origin — 154
  Handling fee — 154
  Allowed countries — 155
  Method not available — 155
  Free shipping — 155
  Flat rate — 156
  Table rates — 156
    Quantity- and price-based rates — 157
    Save your rate table — 158
    Table rate settings — 158
    Upload rate table — 159
  Carrier methods — 159
Managing taxes — 160
  How Magento manages taxes — 160
  Creating tax rules — 161
  Importing tax rates — 166
  Value added tax configurations — 166
  Setup VAT taxes — 167

Transactional e-mails	**172**
Create a new header template	174
Assign e-mail header and footer	175
Create new e-mail template	176
Summary	**178**
Chapter 6: Managing Non-Product Content	**179**
The Magento content management system	**179**
Pages	180
Customizing a CMS page	182
Creating a CMS page	186
Using blocks and widgets	189
Adding a page link	190
Using variables	195
Using widgets to insert content onto site pages	199
Summary	**201**
Chapter 7: Marketing Tools	**203**
Customer groups	**203**
Creating a customer group	204
Promotions	**205**
Creating a catalog price rule	205
Creating cart price rules	209
Adding the new rule	211
Defining the rule's conditions	214
Defining the rule's actions	217
Modifying the rule's labels	220
Generating coupon codes	221
Testing the rule	223
Newsletters	**223**
Subscribing customers	224
Creating newsletter templates	224
Scheduling your newsletter	226
Checking for problems	227
Managing your subscribers	227
Using sitemaps	**228**
Adding a sitemap	228
Optimizing for search engines	**230**
Using meta fields for search engine visibility	230
Meta fields in Magento	231
SEO checklist	232
Summary	**233**

Chapter 8: Extending Magento — **235**

  Magento Connect — **236**
    Searching Magento Connect — 236
    Why developers create free extensions — 237
  The new Magento module architecture — **238**
  Extending Magento functionality with Magento plugins — **240**
  Building your own extensions — **243**
    Whether others have gone before — 243
    Your extension files — 243
      Step one — 244
      Step two — 244
      Step three — 245
      Step four — 246
      Step five — 246
      Step six — 247
  Summary — **249**

Chapter 9: Optimizing Magento — **251**

  Exploring the EAV — **252**
    Entity — 252
    Attribute — 253
    Value — 254
    Putting it all together — 254
    The good and bad of EAV — 256
    Making it flat — 256
  Indexing and caching — **257**
    Indexing — 257
      Flat or no flat — 258
      Reindexing — 258
    Caching — 258
      Core caching — 259
      Full page cache — 260
      The impact of caching — 260
      Managing caching — 260
  Caching in Magento 2 – not just FPC — **261**
  Tuning your server for speed — **261**
    Deflation — 262
    Enabling expires — 263
    Increasing PHP memory — 263
    Increasing the MySQL cache — 264
    Using the Nginx server — 264
    Using Varnish cache — 264

Using a CDN   265
Summary   **266**
Chapter 10: Advanced Techniques   **267**
  Setting up a staging environment   **267**
   A simple approach   268
   The basic staging setup   268
   Don't be tempted to skip   269
  Version control   **269**
  Magento cron   **276**
   Magento cron jobs   276
   Triggering cron jobs   278
   Tuning Magento's schedules   281
    Setting your frequency   281
    Creating compatible settings   282
  Backing up your database   **283**
   The built-in back-up   283
   Using MySQLDump   284
   Setting a cron for back-up   284
  Upgrading Magento   **285**
   Obtaining Magento Marketplace keys   286
   Upgrading your Magento installation   287
  Summary   **289**
Chapter 11: Pre-Launch Checklist   **291**
  A word about scope   **292**
  System configurations   **292**
   SSL   292
   Base URLs   292
   Administrative base URL   293
   Reducing file download time   293
    Merging JavaScript files   294
    Merging CSS files   294
   Caching   294
   Cron jobs   294
   Users and roles   294
  Design configurations   **295**
   Transactional emails   295
   Invoices and packing slips   295
   Favicon   296
   Placeholder images   296

404 and error pages 296
Search engine optimization **297**
Meta tags 297
Analytics 297
Sitemap 297
Sales configurations **297**
Company information 298
Store e-mail addresses 298
Contacts 298
Currency 299
General sales settings 299
Customers 299
Sales emails 300
Tax rates and rules 300
Shipping 301
Payment methods 301
Newsletters 301
Terms and conditions 301
Checkout 302
Product configurations **302**
Catalog 303
Storefront panel 303
Product reviews 305
Product alerts 305
Product alerts run settings 305
Product image placeholders 305
Recently viewed/compared products 306
Price 306
Layered navigation 306
Category top navigation 306
Search engine optimizations 306
Catalog search 307
RSS feeds 308
Maintenance configurations **308**
Backups 308
Summary **308**
Index **311**

Preface

Since its launch in late 2007, Magento has become the most widely used open source e-commerce platform. The growth of the system was fueled by its ability to be extended and customized to meet almost any online retailing need. Thousands of developers and store owners have built profitable B2C and B2B implementations.

However, it's no secret that the learning curve to master Magento can be intense. With power comes a degree of complexity. To meet this need for Magento 1.x, one of the authors, Bret Williams, wrote the very successful *Mastering Magento* for Packt Publishing in 2012. The book helps thousands of readers navigate Magento.

Magento has released the long-awaited version 2. This version introduces a completely revamped code architecture, admin user interface, and better workflows. Version 2 is truly a completely new version.

Therefore, it stands to reason that Magento users will need to learn how to maximize this improved platform. *Mastering Magento 2* satisfies this need while following much of the same easy-to-learn, information-rich format of the first book.

With *Mastering Magento 2*, author Bret Williams has teamed with eminent Magento developer and technical architect, Jonathan Bownds. The combination of these long-time Magento experts brings a full-circle approach to truly mastering the world's most powerful open source platform for online sales.

What this book covers

Chapter 1, Planning for Magento, introduces you to Magento 2 with a discussion of its technical considerations, its multistore methodology, and how to apply this key feature to your plans for multiple stores.

Chapter 2, Installing Magento 2, provides keys to ensure that you have a successful Magento 2 installation as well as guidance to plan your categories, backups, and security.

Chapter 3, Managing Products, teaches you about how Magento manages products and categories.

Chapter 4, Designs and Themes, explores the new Magento 2 theming structure and shows you how to customize your store for your brand.

Chapter 5, Configuring to Sell, covers the entire sales process, including payment systems, shipping methods, taxes, and transactional e-mails.

Chapter 6, Managing Non-Product Content, discusses the Magento content management system that helps you create pages and layouts to communicate your brand.

Chapter 7, Marketing Tools, covers the various Magento features that work to drive more business — and repeat business — to your store.

Chapter 8, Extending Magento, dives into the powerful extendibility of the platform, including how to build your own Magento 2 extensions.

Chapter 9, Optimizing Magento, takes an in-depth look at the core Magento 2 data architecture and how you can tune your Magento store for maximum speed.

Chapter 10, Advanced Techniques, guides more technical readers through processes that improve Magento reliability and stability.

Chapter 11, A Pre-Launch Checklist, provides an easy-to-follow checklist to use when taking a new Magento 2 store online.

What you need for this book

Store owners using this book to learn Magento 2 should have an installed version of Magento 2 to work with. Developers should have a development environment capable of supporting a Magento 2 installation:

- A Unix operating system (Linux, MacOS X)
- Composer
- Apache 2.2 or 2.4, or Nginx 1.8.x web server
- PHP 5.5, 5.6 or 7.0.2
- MySQL 5.6.x

Developers are also required to have a good working knowledge of PHP, object-oriented programming, and MVC architecture.

Who this book is for

Mastering Magento 2 was crafted for anyone who will use Magento 2, whether it's as a store owner or developer. The book was designed specifically for those with little or no prior experience with Magento. Packt Publishing provides additional books by experienced authors to cover more specific Magento topics in even greater detail. This book provides the reader with a solid, functioning foundation to successfully use Magento 2.

Conventions

In this book, you will find a number of text styles that distinguish between different kinds of information. Here are some examples of these styles and an explanation of their meaning.

Code words in text, database table names, folder names, filenames, file extensions, pathnames, dummy URLs, user input, and Twitter handles are shown as follows: "Open the .htaccess file in a text editor."

A block of code is set as follows:

```
SetEnvIf Host www\.[domain] MAGE_RUN_CODE=[code]
SetEnvIf Host www\.[domain] MAGE_RUN_TYPE=[type]
SetEnvIf Host ^[domain] MAGE_RUN_CODE=[code]
SetEnvIf Host ^[domain] MAGE_RUN_CODE=[type]
```

When we wish to draw your attention to a particular part of a code block, the relevant lines or items are set in bold:

```
[default]
exten => s,1,Dial(Zap/1|30)
exten => s,2,Voicemail(u100)
exten => s,102,Voicemail(b100)
exten => i,1,Voicemail(s0)
```

Any command-line input or output is written as follows:

```
cd <your Magento install dir>/bin
./magento setup:rollback (full path to backup filename from var/backups directory)
```

New terms and **important words** are shown in bold. Words that you see on the screen, for example, in menus or dialog boxes, appear in the text like this: "Click on **Default Category** shown on the left side of the edit area."

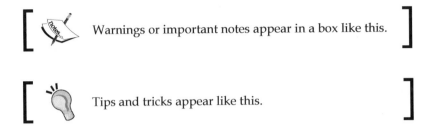

Warnings or important notes appear in a box like this.

Tips and tricks appear like this.

Reader feedback

Feedback from our readers is always welcome. Let us know what you think about this book—what you liked or disliked. Reader feedback is important for us as it helps us develop titles that you will really get the most out of.

To send us general feedback, simply e-mail `feedback@packtpub.com`, and mention the book's title in the subject of your message.

If there is a topic that you have expertise in and you are interested in either writing or contributing to a book, see our author guide at `www.packtpub.com/authors`.

Customer support

Now that you are the proud owner of a Packt book, we have a number of things to help you to get the most from your purchase.

Errata

Although we have taken every care to ensure the accuracy of our content, mistakes do happen. If you find a mistake in one of our books—maybe a mistake in the text or the code—we would be grateful if you could report this to us. By doing so, you can save other readers from frustration and help us improve subsequent versions of this book. If you find any errata, please report them by visiting `http://www.packtpub.com/submit-errata`, selecting your book, clicking on the **Errata Submission Form** link, and entering the details of your errata. Once your errata are verified, your submission will be accepted and the errata will be uploaded to our website or added to any list of existing errata under the Errata section of that title.

To view the previously submitted errata, go to https://www.packtpub.com/books/content/support and enter the name of the book in the search field. The required information will appear under the **Errata** section.

Piracy

Piracy of copyrighted material on the Internet is an ongoing problem across all media. At Packt, we take the protection of our copyright and licenses very seriously. If you come across any illegal copies of our works in any form on the Internet, please provide us with the location address or website name immediately so that we can pursue a remedy.

Please contact us at copyright@packtpub.com with a link to the suspected pirated material.

We appreciate your help in protecting our authors and our ability to bring you valuable content.

Questions

If you have a problem with any aspect of this book, you can contact us at questions@packtpub.com, and we will do our best to address the problem.

1
Planning for Magento

It's not difficult to download Magento 2. With some hosting companies, it only takes a simple request or "one-click" to do an initial installation of this powerful e-commerce platform. The question now becomes, "where do you go from here?"

Before you even download and install Magento, it's important that you take some time to plan. The temptation to dive right in and get your feet wet is strong – especially for those of us who enjoy exploring new technologies. However, this is perhaps the primary reason why many people abandon Magento even before they get off the ground. Not only are there lots of wonderful features and configurations to tackle, there are significant installation issues to consider even before you download the installer.

[Avoid the "uninstall-reinstall" syndrome. Plan your installation before you install and you're less likely to have to start all over again at a later date.]

In this chapter, the following topics will be covered:

- How to form a plan for your Magento installation
- How to analyze and research your hosting alternatives
- How Magento's powerful Global-Website-Store methodology gives you tremendous power to run more than one website in a single installation
- How to plan for multiple languages, business entities, and domains

Defining your scope

There are three important areas to consider when defining your e-commerce project:

- Your project requirements (What do you want to accomplish?)
- Your users (Who will be using your Magento installation? What are their roles and capabilities?)
- Your technical resources (What are your own skills? Do you have others on whom you will rely?)

It is never wise to skimp on defining and analyzing any of these, as they all play crucial roles in the successful implementation of any e-commerce project (or any web project). Let's look at each of them in detail.

Project requirements

Magento is a powerful, full-featured e-commerce platform. With that power comes a certain degree of complexity (one very good reason to keep this book handy!). It's important to take your analysis of how to leverage this power one step at a time. As you discover the many facets of Magento, it's easy to become overwhelmed. Don't worry. With proper planning, you'll soon find that Magento is quite manageable for whatever e-commerce project you have in mind.

It is very likely that your e-commerce project is ideal for Magento, particularly if you intend to grow the online business well beyond its initial design and configuration – and who doesn't? Magento's expandability and continued development insures that, as an open source platform, Magento is the ideal technology for both start-up and mature stores.

When considering Magento as a platform, here's what Magneto offers that makes it shine:

- Large numbers of products, categories, and product types.
- Multiple stores, languages, and currencies sharing the same product catalog.
- The ability to add features as needed, whether obtained from third parties or by your own efforts.
- Large, involved developer community, with thousands of experienced developers around the world. You are now a member of that community and able to share your questions and experiences through forums and blogs hosted by Magento and others, such as MageDaily.com.
- Robust, yet usable user interface for administering your store.

Where you might find Magento to be more than required is if you have only a small handful of products to offer or expect very few sales.

If you think that Magento might be too complicated to use as an e-commerce platform, think again. Power always involves some level of complexity. With *Mastering Magento 2*, we feel the challenge of using Magento will quickly become an appreciation for all the ways you can sell more products online.

Requirements checklist

How are you going to be using your Magento installation? This list will help you focus on particular areas of interest in this book. Answer these questions, as they pertain to your single Magento installation:

- Will you build more than one online store? How many? Will each store share the same products or different catalogs?

- Will you build different versions of stores in multiple languages and currencies?

- What types of products will be offered? Hard goods? Downloadable? Subscriptions? How many products will be offered?

- Will products be entered individually or imported from lists?

- How many customers do you expect to serve on a monthly basis? What is your anticipated growth rate?

- Are there particular features you consider to be "must-haves" for your stores, such as social marketing, gift certificates, newsletters, customer groups, telephone orders, and so on?

Whatever you can conceive for an e-commerce store, it can almost always be accommodated with Magento!

Planning for users

The second stage to defining your scope is to think about "users" – those who will be actually interacting with Magento: customers and store staff. These are people who have no technical expertise, and for whom using the site should be straightforward and intuitive.

Designers and developers may use Magento's administration screens to configure an installation, but it's the ones actually interacting with Magento on a daily basis for which designers and developers must plan. As you use this book to craft a successful Magento store, always keep the end-user in mind.

Who are your users? Basically, your users are divided into two segments: staff and customers.

Staff

Staff refers to those who will be using the Magento administration screens on a daily basis. Magento's administration screens are elegant and fairly easy to use, although you'll want to pay close attention to how you create user permissions, as described in *Chapter 2, Installing Magento 2*. Some users won't need access to all the backend features. By turning off certain features, you can make the administration area much more user-friendly and less overwhelming. Of course, regarding staff managers, additional permissions can give them access to reports, marketing tools, and content management sections. In short, as you work with staff, you can fine tune their back-end experience and maximize their effectiveness.

One key staff user should be designated as the "Administrator". If you're the one who will be responsible for managing the Magento configurations on an ongoing basis, congratulations! You now have at your fingertips the power to adjust your online business in ways both significant and subtle. You also have in front of you the guidebook to give you a full appreciation of your capabilities.

For store administrators, *Packt Publishing* offers a companion book, *Learning Magento 2 Administration*. This book, authored by Bret and Cyndi Williams, is the perfect training and reference book for your staff.

Customers

There are several types of **customers**, and they are based on their relationship to the vendor: retail and wholesale. Among these customers, you can also have customers that are members of the site – and therefore privy to certain pricing and promotions – both on the retail and wholesale level. You can also subdivide wholesalers into many other levels of manufacturers, jobbers, distributors, and dealers, all operating through the supply chain.

Magento has the ability to handle a variety of different users and user types, including all the ones mentioned above.

The one caveat to consider when scoping users is that if you are going to use a single Magento installation to operate more than one business – which can certainly be done – you cannot create unique permissions for staff users which restrict them to managing the content, customers, and orders of any one business.

Assessing technical resources

As reviewed in the Preface, there are basically three different types of people who will be involved in any Magento installation: the Administrator, the Designer, and the Developer. Which one, or ones, are you?

As a complete, installable platform, make sure you have sufficient technical resources to handle all aspects of web server configuration and administration. It is not uncommon to find one or maybe two people tackling the installation, configuration, and management of a Magento installation. The web industry is well populated with "Jacks-of-all-Trades." As you analyze your own technical abilities, you may find it necessary to hire outside help. These are the disciplines that can help you maximize your Magento success:

- **User interface design**: Even if you use one of the many themes available for Magento stores, you will find the need to adjust and modify layouts to give your users a great online experience. Knowledge of HTML, CSS, and JavaScript is critical, and the use of these across multiple browser types means maximum accessibility. As we'll learn in this book, specific knowledge of the Magento design architecture is a plus.

- **PHP**: Many people setting up a Magento store can avoid having to work with the underlying PHP programming code. However, if you want to expand functionality or significantly modify layouts, the ability to at least navigate PHP code is important. Furthermore, a familiarity with programming standards, such as the model-view-controller methodology used in Magento coding (explained in *Chapter 6, Managing Non-Product Content*), will increase your ability to modify and, when necessary, fix code.

When hiring a developer for your Magento store, make sure you find someone with specific experience with Magento 2. The new architecture and coding standards require particular knowledge. Magento provides a list of certified Magento developers at `http://www.magentocommerce.com/certification/directory`. Be sure to inquire about Magento 2 qualifications.

- **Sales processes**: Selling online is more complex than most newcomers imagine. While it appears fairly simple and straightforward from the buyers point of view, the backend management of orders, shipping, payment gateways, distribution, tracking, and so on requires a good understanding of how products will be priced and offered, inventory managed, orders and returns processed, and shipping handled. Businesses vary as much by how they sell their products as they do by the product categories they offer.

- **Server administration**: From domain names and SSL encryption to fine-tuning for performance, the management of your Magento installation involves a thorough understanding of how to configure and manage everything from web and mail servers to databases and FTP accounts. In addition, PCI compliance and security is becoming an increasingly important consideration.

> Fortunately, many Magento-friendly hosting providers offer assistance and expertise when it comes to optimizing your Magento installation. In *Chapter 9, Optimizing Magento*, we explain ways you can perform many of the optimization functions yourself, but don't hesitate to have frank discussions with potential hosting providers to find out just how much and how well they can help you with your installation.
>
> If you choose to host the installation on your own in-house servers, note that Magento does require certain "tweaks" for performance and reliability, which we cover in *Chapter 9, Optimizing Magento*.

Technical considerations

You have assessed the technical knowledge and experience of yourself and others with whom you may be working, now it is important that you understand the technical requirements of installing and managing a Magento installation.

Hosting provider

If you're new to Magento, I certainly recommend that you find a capable hosting provider with specific Magento experience. There are many hosting companies that provide hosting suitable for Magento, but far fewer who invest resources toward supporting their clients with specific Magento-related needs. Keep these points in mind as you research possible hosting candidates:

- Do they provide specific Magento support for installing and optimizing? (You'll learn how to do that in this book, but if you're hesitant to do it yourself, find a provider who can help.)

- Can they provide PCI compliance? (If you're going to accept credit cards online, you'll be asked by your merchant account provider to be "PCI" compliant. We'll cover this in *Chapter 5, Configuring to Sell*.)

- Are they a Magento Partner? (The Magento website lists companies who they have designated as "Solution Partners." While this is a good place to start, there are many other hosting providers who are not official partners, but who do an excellent job in hosting Magento stores.)

- Do they have links to client sites? (If Magento stores are properly optimized, and the servers are fast, the websites will load quickly.)

In-house hosting

You may already be hosting PHP based websites, have a robust server setup, or manage racked servers at a hosting facility. In these instances, you might well be capable of managing all aspects of hosting a Magento installation. In this book, you will find considerable information to help you configure and manage the server aspects of your Magento installation. We do repeat the advice that if you're new to Magento, an experienced hosting provider could be your best friend.

Servers

Due to Magento's complex architecture, your servers should be powerful. The architecture, indexing, and caching schemas of Magento require considerable resources. While we will attack these issues in *Chapter 9, Optimizing Magento*, the more horsepower you have, the better your store will perform.

To host your own Magento installation, your server must have the following *minimum* requirements:

- Linux x86-64 operating system.
- Apache 2.2 or 2.4, or nginx 1.8+. The apache `mod_rewrite` module must be enabled.
- MySQL 5.6 (Oracle or Percona).
- PHP 5.5.10-5.5.16 or 5.6.0, with these extensions:
    - PDO_MySQL
    - Mbstring
    - Mcrypt
    - Mhash
    - SimpleXML

- ° Curl
- ° Xsl
- ° gd, ImageMagick 6.3.7+, or both
- ° soap
- ° intl
- ° bc-math (only for Enterprise Edition)
- ° openssl

- SSL Certificate for secure administration access on production servers. Self-signed certificates are not supported.
- **Mail transfer agent (MTA)** or an SMTP server.

Magento 2 can also use **Redis** 3.0 or **Varnish** 3.5/4.x for page caching and **memcached** for session storage.

The best of both worlds

Most Magento Community users we know (and there are lots!) opt for a hosted solution. Even with our own experience managing web servers, we too use a third-party hosting provider. It's easier, safer, and in most cases, far less expensive than duplicating the same degree of service in-house.

However, we do enjoy installing and testing open source platforms in-house, rather than setting up another hosting account. This is especially true when working with new platforms. Setting up an in-house installation can also allow you to test modifications, extensions, and updates before installing them on your live production server.

Setting up a local test installation

You can set up a complete Magento environment with PHP and MySQL on your own desktop computer or a local server in your office. In *Chapter 10, Advanced Techniques*, we'll provide detailed instructions for several different methods that can be used to install Magento on a local machine.

Global-Website-Store methodology

Now you're probably itching to install your first Magento store. In fact, you probably have done that already and have been fumbling through the vast labyrinth of configuration menus and screens. If you're like so many first-time Magento installers, you might feel ready to uninstall and reinstall; to start all over.

Most of the time, this "restart" happens when users try to take advantage of one of Magento's most powerful features: managing multiple stores. It seems easy when you look at the **store management** screen until you begin setting up stores, configuring URLs, and assigning specific configurations to each frontend website.

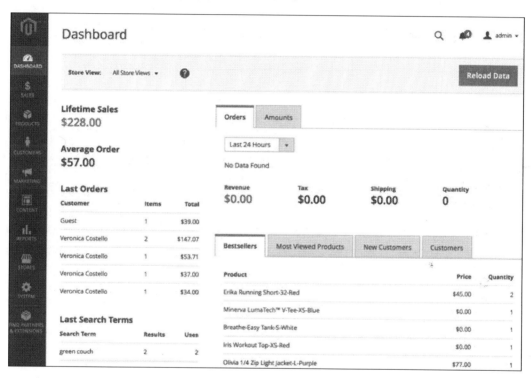

Before you begin laying out your master plan for the various websites and stores you intend to create (and even if you're only beginning with one website), you need to master the Magento methodology for multiple stores. Magento describes this as "**GWS**," which stands for "Global, Website, Store." Each Magento installation automatically includes one of each part of this hierarchy, plus one more for "Store View."

The following diagram shows how each part of **GWS** is related to one another:

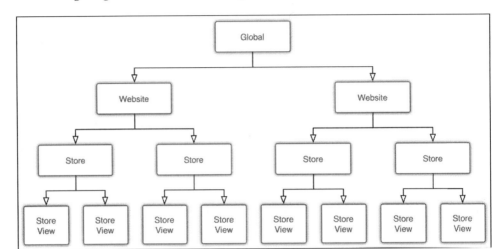

Global

Global refers to settings (for example, stock management rules) and values (for example, product price) for the entire installation. Throughout your Magento installation, you'll find **Global** displayed next to various form fields.

In terms of installation planning, your *Global* considerations should include:

- Will customers be shared among all sites? You can elect not to give customers the ability to register for one website and automatically be registered to all others.

- Can I allow any user with Admin permissions to see all orders and customers from all websites and stores within the single installation? Without modification, Magento does not allow you to set up Admin users by limiting them to certain websites and stores. If an Admin user can see orders, they can see all orders for all customers.

- Will all stores within an installation use the same rules for managing inventory? Inventory rules, such as whether stock is to be managed or whether backorders are allowed, are system-wide choices. (These choices can be changed, in some cases, at the product level, though that does mean paying careful attention to how products are configured and managed.)

In general, we recommend that you consider a single Magento installation only for multiple websites and stores that are similar in concept. For example, if your online business is selling drop-shipped furniture through several differently branded websites, then a single Magento installation is ideal. However, if you have two or more different businesses, each with a different product focus, company name, banking, and so on, it is best to use a separate Magento installation for each discrete business.

Website

The **website** is the "root" of a Magento store. From the website, multiple stores are created that can each represent different products and focus. However, it is at the website level that certain configurations are applied that control common functions among its children stores and Store Views.

As described above, one of the most important considerations at the website level is whether or not customer data can be shared among websites. The decision to share this information is a *Global* configuration; however, remember that you cannot elect to share customer data among some websites and not others: it's an all or nothing configuration.

If you do need to create a group of websites among which customer data is to be shared, and create other websites among which the data is not to be shared, you will need more than one installation of Magento.

Store

What can sometimes be confusing is that "**Store**" for Magento is used to describe both a store structure as well as a Store View. When configuring your hierarchal structure, "Store" is used to associate different product catalogs to different stores under a single "Website," whereas "Store Views" can be created to display a "Store" in multiple languages or styles, each with their own URL or path. Each Store View can be assigned different themes, content, logos, and so on.

Yet, throughout Magento's many administration screens, you will see that "Store" is used to define the scope of a particular value or setting. In these instances, entered values will affect all Views under a Store hierarchy. We know this can be confusing; it was to us, too. However, by following the processes in this book, you'll quickly come to not only understand how a Store and Store View is referred within Magento, but also appreciate the tremendous flexibility this gives you.

Perhaps the best way to consider Stores and Store Views is to learn that a View is what your website visitor will see in terms of language, content and graphics, while Store refers to the data presented in each view.

Planning for multiple stores

How you utilize **GWS** in your particular case depends on the purpose of your Magento installation. With GWS, you have an enormous number of configuration possibilities to explore. That said, your configuration planning would generally fall within three major categories: multiple domains, multiple businesses, and multiple languages. Of course, in the real world, a Magento installation may include aspects of all three.

It's important to realize that Magento allows you to drive your e-commerce strategy according to your own business and marketing goals, rather than conforming to any limitations according to what your e-commerce platform might or might not be able to deliver.

Using multiple domains for effective market segmentation

It's becoming more popular in e-commerce to create multiple storefronts selling the same or similar products, each having a different domain name, branding design, and content. In this way, merchants can extend their marketing by appealing to different market segments, not just having one website trying to satisfy all consumers.

For example, let's assume you want to sell shoes online. You have a great distribution source where you can source all kinds of shoes, from dress to casual, running to flip-flops. While you can certainly have a comprehensive, "all types available" online shoe store, you might elect to secure different domain names focused on different segments of the shoe market. www.runningshoes4you.com would cater to joggers, while www.highheelsemporium.com features designer-quality dress shoes for women.

In Magento, you would create one website but create at least two stores, one for each of your domains. You might also create a third as an overall retail store for all your shoes. Each store could either share the same product catalog or each have its own separate catalog. By having all stores assigned to the same website, you have the ability to control certain configurations that apply to all stores. For example, if all the stores belong to the same retailer, as in this example, all would offer the same payment methods, such as `PayPal.com` or `Authorize.Net`. Most likely, the shipping methods you offer would be the same as well as your policies for returns and shipping.

In short, if all the domains belong to the same retail business, it may make sense to have one website with multiple stores, rather than to create entire website-store hierarchies for each product-focused domain. As you can see in the following diagram, this makes for a slimmer, more manageable structure:

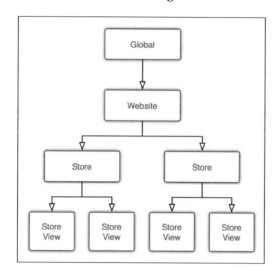

Using multiple businesses to keep finances separate

In contrast, if your installation will be used to manage multiple businesses, you will need to create multiple websites. The reason for this is that actual, separate business entities will have separate payment system accounts (for example, PayPal, credit card merchant accounts, shipping), and therefore need to be able to segregate these between different websites.

To extend our example, let's assume your shoe retailer also owns a sideline business selling women's sportswear. This other business exists under a separate legal entity (for example, corporation, partnership), and therefore has different bank accounts, distributors, and customers. With Magento, you should create separate websites for each, even if they are to share certain products.

For instance, the sportswear site might also feature women's casual shoes, which are also offered by the shoe website. The same product can be assigned to multiple product catalogs (and therefore different stores) even if the catalogs belong to separate businesses. And somehow, through a complex database architecture, Magento succeeds in keeping all this straight for you. Amazing.

Remember that Magento 2 does not allow you to give back-end user permissions based on the website. Permissions can only be set at the Global level.

Using multiple languages to sell globally

Even among some of Magento's top competitors in the open source e-commerce arena, very few provide the ability to create multiple language views of a website. Multiple language views are not simple matters for several reasons:

- All site content, including links, instructions, error messages, and so on must be translated to the intended language.

- The platform must seamlessly provide multiple language selection and, if possible, intelligently provide the appropriate language to the website visitor based on their geographical location.

- Multiple languages can also infer the need to provide product prices in multiple currencies. Conversion rates vary almost minute-by-minute. Daily swings in conversion rates can affect profitability if the amounts shown online are not updated.

Magento has several tools to help you create multiple languages and currencies for retailers wanting to sell globally (or just provide multiple languages to users within a single country), which we will tackle in *Chapter 2, Installing Magento 2*. It all begins with creating multiple views for a given store.

In our example, our running shoe website needs to be available in both English and French, so you would create two views within the running shoe store, one for each language. In your Magento-powered website, you can easily include a small drop-down selector which allows a visitor to choose their preferred language based on the views you have created.

In fact, in most Magento theme designs, this dropdown is automatic whenever there are multiple views created for any given store.

 Another interesting use of multiple views could be to segment your customer market within a store. For example, if you wanted your shoe store to have a different overall look for men versus women versus children, you could create multiple views for each customer segment, and then allow the visitor to choose their desired view.

Summary

The power of Magento can also be a curse, particularly if you're like many of us: eager to jump in and begin building an online store. However – and this comes from the experience of investing lots of hours – taking a moment to understand the scope of your undertaking will make navigating the intricacies of Magento a much more rewarding experience.

In this chapter, we outlined the key areas to consider when planning our Magento installation. We also learned about the powerful Global-Website-Store methodology for managing multiple web stores in a single installation. In addition, we looked at the possibilities of introducing multiple languages, businesses, and domains for effective market segmentation.

As we go forward in this book, we'll learn how each decision we make in installing, configuring, and managing Magento traces back to what we covered in this chapter. In the next chapter, we will be taking your plans from this chapter and applying them to a new Magento installation.

2

Installing Magento 2

Now that you've got your plan in hand from *Chapter 1, Planning for Magento*, it's time to now take the leap and install **Magento 2 Community**. While some hosting providers will install Magento for you, or provide installation assistance, Magento makes installation fairly easy. There are a few points to pay attention to, but if you follow the steps in this chapter, you'll be up and running with Magento in quick order.

In this chapter, we will learn about the following topics:

- Installation strategies to improve Magento performance
- How to configure multiple websites and stores
- Strategies for backups and security

How hosting effects installation

If you own and operate your own servers, and your server meets the requirements for installing Magento, you're all set to go. However, for most people installing Magento Community, the quest to install Magento on an appropriate hosted server is vital to insuring that their Magento stores run quickly and securely.

Understanding types of hosting

Hosting plans range from a few dollars to hundreds of dollars per month, depending mainly on the type of server configuration you have. For most hosting providers, hosting is divided into three distinct categories:

- For small beginner Magento stores, a **shared server** is a great way to start. In essence, you are sharing the server with other hosting clients. However, expect to outgrow this if your store begins to handle more than about 5,000 visitors each day.

- Another option is a **virtual machine (VM)**, commonly referred to as a **cloud server.** With a VM, the operating system is entirely abstracted from the underlying hardware, allowing the user a greater degree of control. The server can be turned on or off, and new servers can be provisioned in an automated matter. Virtual machines typically feature utility billing, so users of a VM will pay based on usage metrics, which can represent significant cost savings. It is worth noting that the management of a virtual machine requires significant technical sophistication. For this reason, the best option for a beginner merchant is to work with a hosting provider that provides a managed service for virtual machines configured to run Magento optimally.

- The most expensive solution is a **dedicated server**. As the name implies, you are renting a standalone computer server solely dedicated to your needs. No other clients are sharing your machine, so you will have full use of the resources of the machine. However, with most hosting providers, little, if any, support is provided to help you configure or troubleshoot the server. This is because dedicated server users are generally well versed in server configurations. In addition, having a dedicated machine means you could conceivably configure it in such a way that the hosting support team would not be able to understand or modify your settings.

Successful hosting guidelines

In our own evaluations of hosting providers for our Magento installations, we found prices and configurations varied quite widely. Through it all, though, we have been able to establish some basic guidelines that you should consider when surveying possible hosting providers:

- If you've never managed a server, begin with a shared server plan. Choose a hosting provider that provides strong customer support and includes tools for handling your server configuration, such as cPanel, DirectAdmin, and Plesk, web-based server management systems, and phpMyAdmin, a web-based tool for managing your MySQL database. Confirm with the hosting company that they will help you upgrade to a VM when necessary.

- If you plan on taking credit cards directly in your Magento store (beyond using PayPal or Google Checkout), you'll need to get an SSL certificate (see the following information box) to protect your customer's information. Additionally, SSL encryption is used when your customer logs in to review their order history. Find out up front what fees are charged for SSL Certificates, including installation. You can buy SSL certificates elsewhere, but it usually incurs an installation fee by the hosting provider. The easiest way is to have the hosting provider order and install the SSL certificate for you. A basic SSL certificate costs as little as $15-25, although $50 including installation is not uncommon. Avoid hosting providers that charge more than $50. The SSL charge is an annual fee.

Secure Socket Layer (SSL) certificates

When you visit a website to shop, you may find that when it comes time to checkout, the URL in your browser changes from `http://www.domain.com` to `https://www.domain.com`. This means that any information you submit on a form is encrypted, or scrambled, before being sent to their web server. SSL encryption protects everything from credit card numbers to online banking transactions. To achieve this security, the web server has two security "keys," a private and public key. When you visit a secure web page, the public key is sent to your browser and is used to encrypt your data. When received by the web server, the private key is used to decrypt the data. Therefore, only data processed by a matching public and private key set can be read and processed by the server.

These keys are issued by means of an SSL certificate, which is issued by one of a select few "root" certificate issuers. You can purchase SSL certificates from a number of vendors, but they all get their certificates from the same issuers. To get an SSL certificate, you have to provide business information and prove you own the domain you wish to secure. Furthermore, your hosting provider has to generate the private key to submit with the SSL certificate application.

See the next section, *Avoiding the PCI headache*, for ways to avoid the need for securing an SSL certificate. It's not difficult to obtain, but it is an annual fee that you may not need to incur.

- Ask about Magento experience. Any hosting provider can allow you to install Magento but it pays – especially if you're new to Magento – to use a hosting provider that exhibits specific experience of hosting Magento sites. This will come in handy if you ever need assistance troubleshooting your server configuration. Some hosting providers even provide "one-click" installers that alleviate the need to download Magento and upload it to your hosting server. In fact, we strongly encourage you to look for this feature, as it will help you understand the rest of this chapter!

- As with SSL certificates, if you intend on taking credit cards using your own merchant account, you will, at some point, be "scanned" to check for PCI compliance. **PCI (Payment Card Industry)** compliance means that your server meets stringent criteria to protect cardholder information. Even if you don't store actual credit card information (and you shouldn't!), if you allow customers to directly enter credit card information on your website, your server has to be impervious to hackers and other vulnerabilities that could expose the card information. Your hosting provider should configure their systems for PCI compliance and agree to help you resolve any scans, which are conducted by your merchant account provider, that reveal any security vulnerabilities. See the next section for more information about PCI compliance.

- Don't forget about backups, either. Make sure your hosting provider performs regular backups of their servers, at least on a daily basis. As dependable as servers generally are these days, a fatal crash is not impossible. What is their procedure for restoring crashed servers? What is their process for restoring your files and databases if you need to revert to a previous version?

Avoiding the PCI headache

To counter the continued threat of hackers stealing credit card and personal identity information from servers on the Internet, the credit card industry adopted a standard that every merchant is required to adhere to if they take credit card information online. If you intend on securing a merchant account to take major credit cards, you are required to be PCI compliant in terms of how your online store is configured and operated.

As little as six years ago, small online retailers doing fewer than 10,000 transactions per year could simply answer a self-questionnaire attesting that they did not store unencrypted credit card numbers on their servers or databases. For the vast majority of small business online retailers, this questionnaire was simple and precluded the need to take extra steps to provide the highest level of server security.

That is no longer the case. All of our merchant clients are scanned quarterly by their merchant account providers to make sure their web sites are without security vulnerabilities. In every case, these scans report one or more vulnerabilities which, when more fully evaluated, usually uncover "false positives," meaning the vulnerabilities described don't actually exist or cannot be resolved based on the server operating system or software used but don't present any real security threat.

Nevertheless, each scan must be analyzed and a response to every supposed vulnerability provided. This is taking more and more time from both our clients, ourselves as the designer of their store, and the hosting companies we use to actually host our clients' sites. Even hosting providers who are PCI compliant will receive false positives that must be resolved. In short, PCI compliance is becoming an increasing burden on merchants of all sizes.

There are ways you can manage your PCI compliance, though, that will ease this burden:

- **Don't take credit cards on your web site**: Instead of taking credit cards directly on your **Checkout** page in Magento, offer PayPal Express and/or Google Checkout to your customers (there are many others, especially for global businesses, such as iDeal and CarteBlue; Magento includes PayPal and Google Checkout functionality as part of its default installation). When they're ready to pay, they will be taken to the PayPal or Google servers to enter their payment information. Of course, this may not be preferred, as there is some drop off from customers who are redirected to third-party payment providers, plus the fees charged by PayPal and Google may be more than you'd pay if you had your own merchant account. However, if you don't take payment information on your own server, you won't have PCI compliance requirements.

- **Find a true PCI compliant hosting provider**: Most hosting providers who cater to Magento installations have undergone the rigors of PCI compliance. In most cases, you can provide a statement of PCI compliance from the hosting provider to your merchant account provider that will satisfy their needs.

For the purposes of our initial installation, we will use a basic hosting configuration. *Chapter 9, Optimizing Magento,* will help you enhance your configuration to handle higher load and visitor capacities.

I know you're wanting to ask, "but who do *you* use for hosting?" It's okay; given our experience with Magento, everyone asks us for a recommendation.

First, let me say there are several good companies that are fully capable of providing fast servers and who invest resources in knowing and supporting their Magento clients. You can find a list of companies who have taken steps to be an approved hosting partner with Magento at `http://www.Magentocommerce.com/partners/find/hosting-partners/`.

For our clients, however, we use a company based in Pennsylvania called MageMojo (`www.magemojo.com`). MageMojo specializes only in Magento installations: they don't promote hosting any other solutions. In addition, their plans are a blend of a shared and virtual machine configuration: the benefits of a true, dedicated server at the cost of a shared server account. The servers also use solid-state hard drives which, from our experience, noticeably increase the speed of our Magento sites. Plus, each account comes with a one-year free SSL certificate. MageMojo also handles all Magento installations, performance tuning, server management, and upgrades for you at no extra cost.

Keys to a successful installation

Magento has made the installation process a reasonably easy-to-follow affair. Since you've probably completed at least one installation before (and who hasn't tried Magento out-of-the-box?), you're familiar with the process.

However, you can make the installation more successful just by adhering to the following battle-tested advice.

If you have never installed Magento before, it is not all that difficult. For assistance, there are a number of great resources, including the Packt book, *Magento 2: Beginner's Guide*. The Magento website also has an installation wiki (`http://devdocs.Magento.com/guides/v2.0/install-gde/bk-install-guide.html`).

Avoid the bleeding edge

If your Magento installation is to go live in short order, you should always avoid installing the latest, greatest version of Magento (or any other platform, for that matter). As a best practice, we never use any version where the third version number ends in zero, such as version 1.6.0, 1.5.0, and so on. Although the platform or software creators have gone to great pains to debug the software before release, until a new version meets the challenges of the real world, you can count on a number of unforeseen bugs popping up. Avoiding "zeros" works with operating systems, software applications, and, yes, e-commerce systems.

However, if you're drooling over the new features of version Y.0, plan for installing version X.8 and upgrading to Y.1 when it becomes available. Do a bit of research to find out what experiences people are having when upgrading from X to Y as well, so you'll be prepared.

As we write this book, Magento 2 is at version 2.0.2. Because this is an early release, it's very important to be comprehensive in testing your store. Make sure you've added the types of inventory you plan to carry and tested the user behavior you expect to see on the site.

Take your time

The complex power of Magento, which we cannot overstate, means that installing and configuring can be lengthy processes. You can't install Magento one day and be ready to sell tomorrow. Successful e-commerce involves a long list of to-do's, from payment methods, shipping methods, products, content, e-mail templates, forms, and so on and so on. We will cover all important aspects in this book, all of which deserve your attention and consideration.

Install the sample data

While installing sample data takes a bit of work, the benefit conferred by having it in place is considerable, and we'd strongly suggest starting your installation with sample data in place. We usually leave the sample data installed for quite some time, even as we begin configuring and adding the actual store information, as the data provides us with great reference examples.

 For more information on installing the sample data, see
http://devdocs.Magento.com/guides/v2.0/install-gde/install/sample-data-after-Magento.html.

Setting up Magento stores

As we discussed in *Chapter 1, Planning for Magento,* Magento leads the open source community in its ability to manage multiple websites and stores within a single installation. This is an often overlooked power of Magento. It is also one of the more complex configuration issues.

To help illustrate how to configure multiple stores in Magento, let's set up an example. As shown in the following table, we are going to build two online businesses, each with their own categories and products, and one with three Store Views. The following table shows the GWS relationship of this example:

Business focus	Types of product	Domain	Language
Sportswear	Apparel	www.AcmeSportswear.com	English
Sportswear	Apparel	www.AcmeSportswear.fr	French
Sportswear	Apparel	www.AcmeSportswear.de	German
Furniture	Furniture	www.AcmeFurniture.com	English

If these are your planned stores, your next decision is how to set up your websites. As we discussed in *Chapter 1, Planning for Magento,* websites are generally considered to be separate business entities in which all subordinate stores share common configurations for such things as payment gateways, shipping, and inventory management.

In considering your planned stores, you could choose to operate all stores within a single website, such as in the following image:

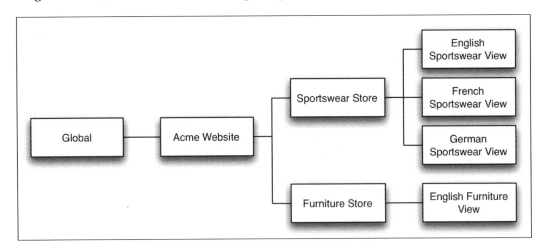

Alternatively, you could set up your Magento configuration so that the sportswear business operated as a separate website from the furniture business:

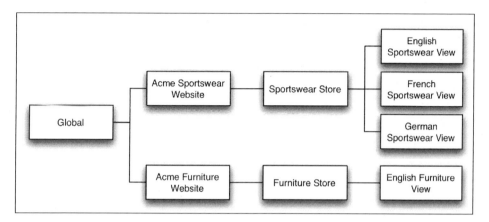

Finally, you could also conceivably create separate websites for each of the various stores.

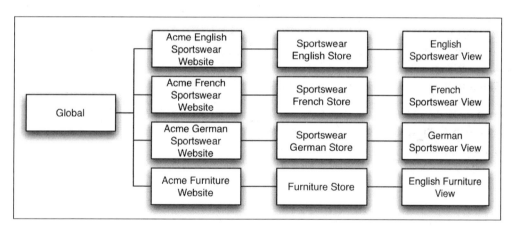

Understandably, you may find the differences subtle, but they can have consequences regarding how you operate your stores within a single Magento 2 installation. Your ultimate choice should be based on flexibility. For maximum configuration choices for any given store, you should create a website for each store. However, it can become a considerable chore to maintain configurations across multiple websites, especially if they really share all the same configurations.

For this book, we're going to focus on the second hierarchy shown before. This will best illustrate the power of Magento's GWS methodology and, to be honest, is probably the most logical choice for the example stores we're considering.

Planning your categories

Before creating your multiple stores, you need to plan your product category structure. In the Magento GWS hierarchy, Websites are assigned to root categories. Root categories are not shown to your visitors, but rather act as the top level under which all your subsequent categories reside.

Categories versus catalogs

There can be some confusion when using the terms categories and catalogs. This is due to the fact that Magento uses root categories as a synonym for catalogs. To keep this straight, a catalog is all the products within one group, represented by the group's root category. Any level below the root category is what we will call categories throughout this book.

The following image shows the category hierarchy of the sample data you may have installed during installation:

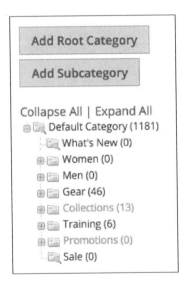

While Magento names the top sample data category, **Default Category**, you can use any name you wish. The categories at the next level below the **Root Category** are the top-level categories which will usually appear on the navigation bar on the site.

To accomplish our example configuration, we need to rename the **Default Category** and create a new root category:

1. Click on **Default Category** shown on the left side of the edit area.
2. In the **Name** field, change **Default Category** to **Sportswear**.

3. Click on **Save Category** in the upper right-hand corner of the screen (a red button).

Our next step is to create the additional **Root Category** we will use for our furniture catalog:

1. Click on **Add Root Category**.
2. In the **Name** field, enter **Furniture**.
3. Select **Yes** for **Is Active**.
4. Click on **Save Category**.

If you want, you can add subcategories within these root categories, but for the purposes of creating multiple stores, it is not necessary at this point.

You may be asking at this point, can multiple Websites share the same root category? The answer is yes. Due to the extensiveness of the GWS hierarchy, you can use the same product catalog for more than one business or website. For example, you might be creating multiple business entities, each selling the same products, but with separate payment gateways, store owners, and so on. While you could create duplicate catalogs with the same products, you can also use one catalog for both businesses. With GWS, you can control pricing, availability, and many other product attributes for each business. We'll be discussing categories and products in more detail in *Chapter 3, Managing Products*.

Disabling the cache

While we will discuss caching more fully in *Chapter 9, Optimizing Magento*, as you build your stores, categories, CMS pages and more, you should turn off the Magento cache so your changes will appear immediately in your new store. In fact, any time you make changes to your Magento store, it's helpful to turn off the Magento cache.

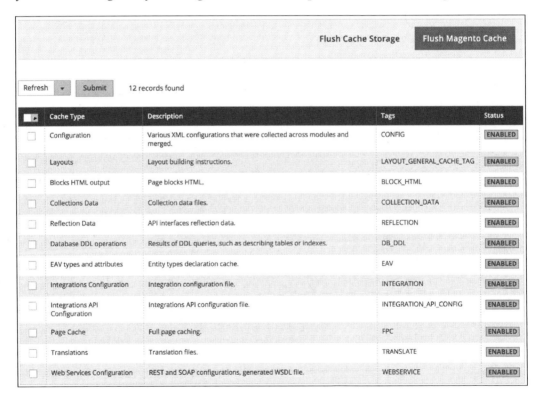

To disable the Magento cache, follow these steps:

1. Go to **System | Cache Management** in your Magento backend.
2. Using the **Mass Actions** drop-down menu (the checkbox at the top of the first category), choose **Select All**.
3. Select **Disable** in the **Actions** drop-down menu.
4. Click on the **Submit** button.

Set up websites, stores, and store views

Next, let's go to **Stores | All Stores** in your Magento backend. The following screenshot shows the sample data configuration:

First, let's change the name of the default website to coincide with our planned hierarchy:

1. Click on **Main Website**.
2. Change the **Name** to **Sportswear Website**.
3. If you wish, you can also change code to any lowercase word (with no spaces), such as **sportswear**.
4. Click on **Save Website**.

Next, let's create the furniture website:

1. Click on **Create Website**.
2. Enter **Furniture Website** for **Name**.
3. Enter **furniture** for **Code**.
4. Click on **Save Web Site**.

Your **Stores** panel should now look like this:

Next, let's create the stores for our example:

1. Click on **Create Store** at the top of the screen.
2. Make sure that **Furniture Website** is chosen in the **Web Site** dropdown menu.
3. Enter **Furniture Store** for **Name** (you can use any name you wish).
4. Choose **Furniture** for the **Root Category** to assign the product catalog containing your furniture products to this store.
5. Click on **Save Store**.

Now, let's rename the sportswear website store:

1. Click on the **Main Website Store** link in the **Stores** panel.
2. Change the **Name** to **Sportswear Store**.
3. Click on **Save Store**.

Now, let's stop a moment to review what we just did:

*   We created two websites, one for each business (sportswear and furniture)
*   Then, we created two stores (sportswear and furniture)

But wait! The example shows four stores; sportswear is to have three stores, one each in English, French, and German.

Since all the sportswear stores will sell the same products, just in different languages (and, most likely, currencies), there really is only one sportswear store. There will be, as we'll create next, three store views. This is where the store/store view nomenclature can get a tad confusing. Think of stores as analogous to different physical stores in different cities. Store views are different *entrances* to those stores. In our example, we have one store with different entrances for English-speaking, French-speaking, and German-speaking customers.

At this point, our **Manage Stores** screen should look like this:

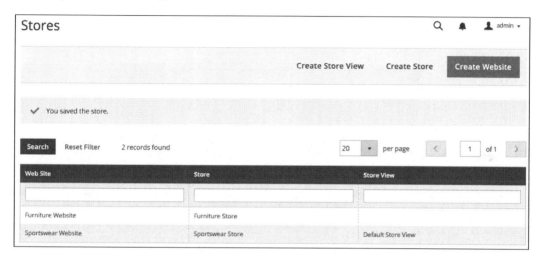

Finally, we will create our necessary store views:

1. Click on **Create Store View** at the top of the **Stores** panel screen.

2. Choose **Furniture Store** for **Store**.

3. Enter **Furniture English View** for **Name** (you can use whatever name you wish).

4. Enter a lowercase **Code**. You can use underscores ("_") as well, but no spaces or other characters other than letters and numbers.

> We often use a language abbreviation in the code, such as `furniture_en` for Furniture, English. You can, of course, use `furniture_english`, or if you're not going to create multiple languages, simply use `furniture` or `furniture_store`.

5. Choose **Enabled** for **Status,** unless you don't want the store view active for any reason.

6. Click on **Save Store View**.

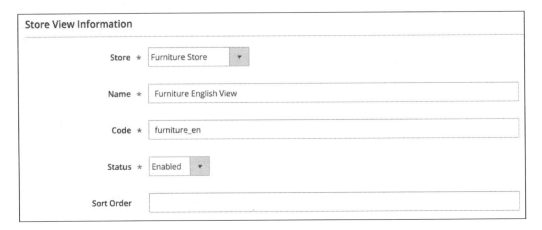

Now we can turn our attention to creating the first store view for our sportswear store:

1. Click on **Default Store View** shown in the list of stores.
2. Update the **Name** to something such as **Sportswear English View**.
3. You can leave the **Code** as **default**, but for consistency's sake, you may want to change it to **sportswear_en** or similar.
4. Click on **Save Store View**.

 As with the website code, consult your developer if you're working on a live Magento installation before changing.

To create the additional sportswear store views, use the same technique you used to create the **Furniture English Store View**, substituting the appropriate language nomenclature where appropriate (for example, sportswear_fr, sportswear_de, for French and German respectively).

When completed, your **Stores** panel should look as follows:

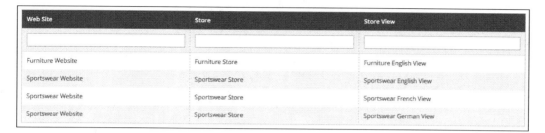

Web Site	Store	Store View
Furniture Website	Furniture Store	Furniture English View
Sportswear Website	Sportswear Store	Sportswear English View
Sportswear Website	Sportswear Store	Sportswear French View
Sportswear Website	Sportswear Store	Sportswear German View

You have now created four new store views for two stores of two websites.

Nginx versus Apache

Before our stores are "reachable" by visitors, you'll have to undertake one additional bit of work, specifically, setting the `mage_run_code` and `mage_run_type` variables for the webserver. Traditionally, nearly all Magento hosting has used the Apache web server. The Nginx web server has been gaining popularity of late, however, and has reached something of a critical mass when it comes to hosting Magento. For this reason, we'll be including multistore webserver configurations for both Nginx and Apache.

Configuring Apache

The most popular method for configuring multiple stores in Magento is modifying the `.htaccess` file. It's also possible to configure multiple stores using Apache's **virtual host declaration**, so we will cover both methodologies here.

Modifying the .htaccess file

The `.htaccess` file resides at the root of your Magento installation directory. This important file controls access to the directory, as well as setting certain parameters for handling HTTP requests from visitors to your site.

For our purposes, we need to add additional code that will direct requests to the proper online store.

 Before editing the `.htaccess` file, it is always a good practice to make a copy as a backup in case you need to revert to the original.

Open the .htaccess file in a text editor. We are going to add our code at the *end* of this file.

To assign domains to your different sites, the following is the template to use:

```
SetEnvIf Host www\.[domain] MAGE_RUN_CODE=[code]
SetEnvIf Host www\.[domain] MAGE_RUN_TYPE=[type]
SetEnvIf Host ^[domain] MAGE_RUN_CODE=[code]
SetEnvIf Host ^[domain] MAGE_RUN_CODE=[type]
```

This code is telling your web server to analyze an incoming URL based on the domain name and then to tell Magento which website or store to deliver to the visitor:

- [domain]: This is your host domain, such as acmefurniture.com. By specifying both with and without the "www," we are accepting URL requests with or without the leading "www."

- [code]: This is the code value you entered when you created the websites and store views in the previous process.

- [type]: This is the type of code you entered, either website or store (meaning store view).

Therefore, for our example configuration, we add the following to our .htaccess file:

```
SetEnvIf Host www\.acmefurniture.com MAGE_RUN_CODE=furniture_en
SetEnvIf Host www\.acmefurniture.com MAGE_RUN_TYPE=store
SetEnvIf Host ^acmefurniture.com MAGE_RUN_CODE=furniture_en
SetEnvIf Host ^acmefurniture.com MAGE_RUN_TYPE=store
SetEnvIf Host www\.acmesportswear.com MAGE_RUN_CODE=sportswear_en
SetEnvIf Host www\.acmesportswear.com MAGE_RUN_TYPE=website
SetEnvIf Host ^acmesportswear.com MAGE_RUN_CODE=sportswear_en
SetEnvIf Host ^acmesportswear.com MAGE_RUN_TYPE=website
```

Naturally, you're wondering why the sportswear site used a different configuration approach:

- If you are going to use one domain name for multiple store views, use website as the [type]. For our example, all visitors will go to www.acmesportswear.com but will have the opportunity to switch from English to French using a drop-down menu in the header. In fact, by setting both languages with one domain, and a [type] of website, Magento will automatically add the language, or store view, drop-down menu selector:

- If, on the other hand, you will have different URLs for each language (for example, www.acmeoutdoor.com and www.acmeoutdoor.fr), then you would add a .htaccess configuration for both, setting the [type] to store.

Temporary URLs

When you first install Magento, you may not be ready to point actual, live domains to your new stores. You can use this same configuration for other URL variations, such as teststore1.domain.com, teststore2.domain.com, and so on, subdomains of your actual domain; or you could be more descriptive: english.domain.com and french.domain.com. Later, when you're ready to "go live," you can re-configure your .htaccess file to process the live domains.

Modifying the virtual host declaration

The **virtual host declaration** is found in different spots in different distributions of Linux. It's typically named httpd.conf or httpd-vhosts.conf and looks like this:

```
<VirtualHost *:80>
    ServerName [domain]
    DirectoryIndex index.php
    ErrorDocument 404 /404.php
    DocumentRoot /var/www/html/Magento
    SetEnv MAGE_RUN_CODE = [storecode]
    SetEnv MAGE_RUN_STORE = [store or website]
    ErrorLog /var/www/html/logs/error_log
    TransferLog /var/www/html/logs/access_log
    <Directory /var/www/html/html/Magento>
        AllowOverride all
        Options -MultiViews
        Options -indexes
    </Directory>
</VirtualHost>
```

The emboldened lines in the virtual host are the ones responsible for multistore routing. After you've made this change, you'll need to restart the Apache server.

Configuring Nginx

To do this, we'll need to modify the Nginx configuration file, typically located in the /etc/ directory (for example, /etc/nginx.config). Because Nginx doesn't support .htaccess files, the best way to map multistore variables is to use the HTTPMapModule.

Modifying the nginx.config file

The HTTPMapModule should be enabled by default, so all you're going to do is add the following text to your /etc/nginx.config file:

```
map $http_host $magesite {
   [domain].com [storecode];
}
```

After this map has been set up, you will then add the $magesite variable to your server declaration as a fast CGI parameter, like this:

```
fastcgi_param MAGE_RUN_CODE $magesite;
fastcgi_param MAGE_RUN_TYPE [store or website];
```

After making these changes, you'll have to restart the Nginx webserver for them to take effect. If these changes seem daunting and you're using an experienced Magento hosting partner, such as MageMojo, you can request these changes to be made for you.

Alternately, because you may not be able to make these changes in some environments, shared servers being one example, you may choose to modify the index.php file. While this approach is generally frowned upon, you may have no other option.

Modifying the index.php file

Personally, we prefer modifying the .htaccess or nginx.config files instead of the index.php file. For one thing, updates to Magento that may modify the index.php file will not affect your configuration. For those of you who are not familiar with PHP programming language, modifying the .htaccess is also easier. That said, some prefer modifying index.php, particularly if they have other modifications to make. To each his own: use the method with which you feel most comfortable.

As stated earlier, an alternative method to adding configurations to the .htaccess or nginx.config files is to modify code in the index.php file in the Magento root using a PHP case statement. The same principles apply in terms of type (website or store).

To configure the index.php file, you need to perform the following steps:

1. Open the index.php file in the text editor of your choice.
2. Find Mage::run($mageRunCode, $mageRunType); in the code (the last line).
3. Insert the necessary code right before this line.

The format for creating the PHP case statement is as follows:

```
switch($_SERVER['HTTP_HOST']) {
  case '[domain]':
  case 'www.[domain]':
    $mageRunCode = '[code]';
    $mageRunType = '[type]';
  break;
}
```

As with the .htaccess file, [code] refers to the website or store view code used when creating your websites and views, while [type] is either website or store. In our ongoing example, our index.php file would be modified as follows:

```
switch($_SERVER['HTTP_HOST']) {
  case 'acmefurniture.com':
  case 'www.acmefurniture.com':
    $mageRunCode = 'furniture_en';
    $mageRunType = 'store';
  break;
}
switch($_SERVER['HTTP_HOST']) {
  case 'acmesportswear.com':
  case 'www.acmesportswear.com':
    $mageRunCode = 'sportsweawr_en';
    $mageRunType = 'website';
  break;
}
```

Configuring Magento

Finally, we need to return to our Magento backend and tell Magento to use our domain names as base URLs. Base URLs are what Magento uses to provide a complete URL path for the website pages it delivers to your visitors.

For example, if a visitor enters `http://acmefurniture.com` in their browser and arrives at your store, we can configure Magento to always convert that to the fuller `http://www.acmefurniture.com` for that request and all others afterwards. Additionally, we can set a different base URL for secure SSL connections, such as `http://secure.acmestores.com`, in cases where we might be sharing an SSL Certificate among multiple stores, as we'll see in this section.

In our example, we are also creating three store views with different languages and, for our discussion, multiple currencies. Let's get going!

Configuring base URLs

To begin, go to **Stores** | **Configuration** | **General** | **Web** in the Magento backend. At the top-left of the screen is a drop-down menu labeled **Store View**. This determines at what level – global, website, or store view – the configuration changes we make will have an effect. Everything we change at the global level will affect all website and store view levels, unless we make another change at those levels: Website changes negate global settings and store view changes negate both global and website configurations. Not all settings can be changed at all levels; however, Magento notes to the right of each setting field the depth at which settings can be changed.

At this point, you should be at the global level (**Store View** should be showing **Default Config**). There are two important global-level settings to consider, both under the **Url Options** (yes, for some reason, Magento spells URL as "Url") section in the center:

- **Add Store Code to Urls** is necessary if you are going to use a shared SSL or if you need to pass a URL that distinguishes one store from another. For example, for `acmesportswear.com`, requests for the English language site would look like `http://www.acmesportswear.com/sportswear_en/page.html`. Requests to the French language version would look something like `http://www.acmesportswear.com/sportswear_fr/page.html`. It is not necessary to use this feature to normally accommodate multiple languages of a single URL, though. In addition, using this feature can cause certain complications with outside services.

- **Auto-redirect to Base URL** set to **Yes (302 Found)**, means that requests that come to the server in one manner will be rewritten to your preferred – or Base – URL. For single-store setups, this can help prevent 404 not found errors by redirecting such requests to your base URL. However, for multi-store configurations, this should be set to **No**.

After setting these values, click **Save Config**, and let's move on to setting the base URLs:

1. Set the **Store View** to the store view you wish to edit. In our example, let's set it to **Sportswear English View** under **Sportswear** (you'll notice that **Sportswear Store** is dimmed in this menu; we can't really change settings for a **Store**, only a **Store View**).

2. Open the section titled **Base URLs** in the panel.

3. For our sportswear store, enter `http://www.acmesportswear.com/` for **Base URL** (always include the trailing "/" at the end of the URL).

 Remember to de-select the **Use Website** checkbox to the right of the **Base URL** field in order to change the field's value.

4. Click on **Save Config**.

5. For our electronics store, change the **Current Configuration Scope** to **English** under **Sportswear**.

6. Once the page refreshes, enter `http://www.acmeelectronics.com/` for the **Base URL** in the **Unsecure** section.

7. Click on **Save Config**.

8. Since our outdoor sites are sharing the same URL, change the **Current Configuration Scope** to **Outdoor Products**, the website scope level.

9. For the **Unsecure Base URL**, enter `http://www.acmeoutdoor.com/`.

10. Click on **Save Config**.

11. Go to **System | Cache Management** and click on **Flush Magento Cache**.

12. Go to **System | Index Management**. Click on the checkbox to the left of **Catalog URL Rewrites**, and then click on the **Submit** button in the top-right corner. This will force Magento to rewrite all the catalog URLs according to your configuration.

Congratulations! You've now completed a process that's widely unknown and misunderstood in the Magento community. Yet by understanding this process, you will find yourself swimming with ideas about how to leverage this power to create multiple sales channels and ways of hosting multiple stores in a single Magento installation.

Using subdirectories for stores

If you want to use subdirectory paths in your store URLs, rather than the store code which may be less SEO friendly, you can create subdirectories in your root Magento directory for each store (for example, `furniture`, `electronics`, `outdoor`, `great-furniture`, `cheap-electronics`, `outdoor-products`, and so on) and place a copy of the `index.php` and `.htaccess` files in each directory. Instead of adding store codes to URLs (see above), simply use the full directory path for the base URLs. For example, if your subdirectory for furniture is `/great-furniture`, use `http://www.acmefurniture.com/great-furniture/` for the **Unscure Base Url**. Because Nginx doesn't support `.htaccess` files, this option isn't available when using it as a web server. There are ways to do this using rewrite rules in the server declaration, but they are beyond the technical scope of this chapter.

Using localization to sell globally

In our example configuration, we have set up one store with an English-language store view, a French-language store view, and a German-language store view. The standard installation of Magento Community only includes the English language for the United States. Therefore, to have the French language store display the content in French (or any other language we desire), we have to install the language **localization** files for French. Furthermore, we can assign different currencies to each language site so that visitors can view prices in a related currency.

Language files

The Magento community has created localization files for over 80 languages, translating as many as 15,000 words throughout the Magento files. Many languages remain incomplete, but the more popular languages, such as French, German, and Chinese, are at or near 100% complete. These language files are bundled with the default build of Magento 2.0. Additional instructions on creating language packs can be found here: `http://devdocs.magento.com/guides/v2.0/frontend-dev-guide/translations/xlate.html`.

Creating translation dictionaries and language libraries is an involved process, however, and is beyond the scope of this book. To enable existing language packs, use the following instructions:

1. In the Magento backend, go to **Stores** | **Configuration** | **General**.

2. Select **Sportswear French View** under **Sportswear Store** in the **Store View** drop-down menu.

3. In the settings panel, click on **Locale Options**.

4. By default, the **Use Website** checkbox will be checked next to the **Locale** drop-down menu. Uncheck this box.

5. Select **French (France)** in the **Locale** drop-down menu.

6. Change any other store-level settings you wish. You may, for example, wish to use kilograms as the weight unit for your French-language store.

7. Click on **Save Config**.

Now, when we go to our sample data store and select **Sportswear French View** from the drop-down at the top of the screen, some of the content on the site is in French, as shown in the following screenshot (of course, the images are not updated; you will have to create new images with translated copy):

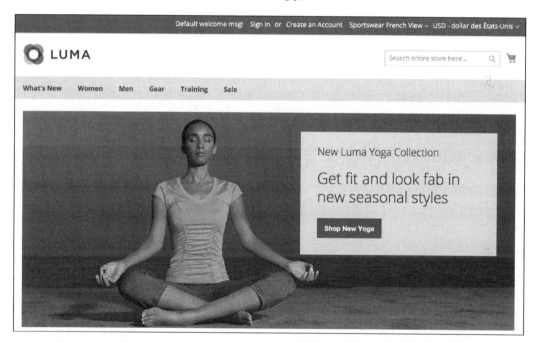

You'll also notice that there are many English labels, as well. Localization does not translate *all* your content, it simply substitutes certain names and labels as configured in the `translate.csv` file you uploaded to your Magento installation.

Manually translating labels

So, how do you manually translate the remaining information? Let's take the category names as an example. In our sportswear store, we see the six top level categories (under **Products | Categories**): **What's New, Women, Men, Gear, Training,** and **Sale**. For our French store, we'd like those translated to Quoi de Neuf, Femmes, Hommes, Équipement, Entraînement, and Vente respectively (we don't speak French well, so you might personally prefer different labels than these).

The first way to translate these categories is to change the actual name of the category in the **Manage Categories** area of the backend:

1. Go to **Products | Categories**.
2. Select the appropriate store view (for example, **Sportswear French View**) in the **Store View** drop-down menu.
3. Select the category you wish to translate (for example, **What's New**) in the category hierarchy.
4. Enter the term you wish to display for the chosen store view (for example, **Quoi de Neuf**).
5. Click on **Save Category**

Now when we view the French language version of the sportswear store, we see the renamed category in the top navigation bar, as shown in the following screenshot:

Switch back to **Sportswear English View**, and you'll once again see **What's New** as the top category name.

This method is useful for translating product names and page content as well.

To change other labels on the site – if we don't like the terms used by the localization package or if there are other labels that need to be translated – we'll use the second method, called **Inline Translation**. For this example, we'll change the term **Checkout** in the **French language Sample Data** site to the possible French equivalent of Terminez L'achat (complete the purchase):

1. In the Magento backend, go to **Stores** | **Configuration** | **Developer**.
2. Select your desired store view in the **Current Configuration Scope** drop-down menu (for example, **Sportswear French View**).

> You can also activate **Inline Translation** at the global or website level and make your translation changes by selecting the appropriate store view on the frontend of your store.

3. Find the center section titled **Translate Inline**.

> Using inline translation means anyone visiting the page can change your titles. You should only use **Inline Translation** if your store is off-line.

4. Deselect **Use Website** next to the **Enabled for Frontend** drop-down menu.
5. Select **Yes** in the drop-down.
6. Click on **Save Config** and refresh your Magento cache.

When you return to your storefront, you'll see small dotted borders around words which can be edited right on the page.

1. Change to the store view you wish to translate on your store frontend. For our example, we're using the sportswear French view.

2. Roll your mouse over the word **Sign In** and click on the small book icon that appears just below the word. A pop-up will appear like this:

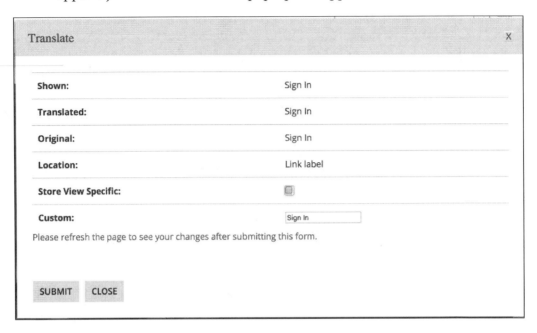

The top half of the screen allows you to change the tag attributes for the link, which is what will appear when the mouse hovers over the link.

The bottom part of this screen is what will actually appear on the screen.

1. Select the checkbox labeled **Store Specific View** so your change will apply only to the specific store view on which you're working.

 If you wish to change the text across all your store views, leave this checkbox unselected. This can be useful if you wish to change a label across all websites and store views. You will need to enable **Inline Translation** at the global or website level as well.

2. For **Custom**, enter **Se Connecter**.

3. Click on **Submit**.

4. Refresh your browser. Checkout has now been replaced by **Se Connecter**.

Use *CTRL + F5* (Windows) or *Command + R* (Mac) to easily refresh your browser window.

Remember to return to **Stores | Configuration | Developer** and turn off **Inline Translation** when you're finished.

Converting currencies

To continue our French setup, we want to show prices in Euros. Again, Magento provides multiple means of accomplishing this.

The process of configuring your installation to handle multiple currencies follows this flow:

1. Establish your base currency and its scope. You can have different base currencies for each website within your installation (but not store view).

2. Select the additional currencies in which your site will be available: what currencies will you be using in your stores?

3. Designate the default displayed currencies for specific stores.

4. Configure automatic currency conversions, if so desired, or manually adjust prices for any additional currencies.

It begins with the base currency

The base currency is the currency in which you operate your business. If you're a US business, you most likely operate in US Dollars. That means your transactions with payment gateways and shipping calculations are in US Dollars. Any automatic currency conversions you establish will be based on US Dollars. Likewise, if your base currency is Euros, all your monetary calculations will be based on Euros, even if you choose to display prices to your visitors in Pounds Sterling or Fijian Dollars.

To begin, let's assume that the US Dollar will be our base currency, but we will be allowing both Dollars and Euros to be used on our French language store:

1. Go to **Stores | Configuration | Catalog**.
2. Select **Default Config** for the **Store View** at the top of the screen.
3. Click on the panel titled **Price**.
4. Change the **Catalog Price Scope** to **Website**.
5. Click on **Save Config**.

We have now allowed the ability to adjust our available currencies at the website level, rather than the overall global level. If you know your base currency will always be the same throughout your installation, you can leave this set to global:

1. Go to **Stores | Configuration | Currency Setup**.

2. Select all the various currencies you would like to have allowed in the stores within our installation, as a default, in the **Allowed Currencies** selection field. For our purposes in this example, we only want **US Dollar** selected.

3. Change the **Base Currency** and **Default Display Currency** to reflect your preferred choices. For our example, we'll leave them as is: **US Dollar**.

The **Allowed Currencies** are set up under **Stores | Configuration | System** in the center section titled **Currency**. By default, Magento pre-selects all *current* currencies. The others are obsolete currencies but are available to you should you find a need to display prices in these currencies.

Next, we need to change the default currency of the French language store:

1. Go to **Stores | Configuration | Currency Setup**.

2. Select **Sportswear French View** in the **Store View** drop-down menu.

3. In the center section, select **British Pound Sterling, Euro, Japanese Yen**, and **US Dollar** in the **Allowed Currencies** selection field (we're adding a couple of extra ones for illustrative purposes).

4. Choose **Euro** in the **Default Display Currency** drop-down menu.

5. Click on **Save Config**.

Let Magento automatically convert currencies ·

Now, if that little piece of the process didn't impress you with the depth of its flexibility, the following should: **automated currency conversions**.

One of the features of Magento is its ability to automatically and periodically set a conversion rate between currencies that will be used to calculate prices at various allowed currencies. Magento calls upon a third party service called Webservicex to provide the conversion rates.

To set up periodic currency conversions:

1. Go to **Stores | Configuration | Currency Setup**.
2. Select **Default Config** in the **Current Configuration Scope** drop-down menu.
3. Click to open the center panel: **Scheduled Import Settings**.
4. Change **Enabled** to **Yes**.
5. Select a **Start Time** (most likely, you will want a time late at night or early in the morning to prevent prices from changing during your busiest shopping periods; it might surprise some shoppers!).
6. Select a **Frequency**. **Daily** is fine, but if you want less frequent updates, choose **Weekly** or **Monthly.**
7. Enter an e-mail address for whomever would like to receive any email alerts if the currency conversion update fails.
8. Click on **Save Config.**

Next, let's set the initial conversion rates:

1. Go to **Stores | Currency Rates**.
2. The first record on this screen is labeled **USD** on the left. The remaining fields, one for each allowed currency, are blank (the **EUR** field may have a value set with the sample data).
3. To initiate the first currency conversion update, click on **Import**.
4. Now the fields are filled and displaying the rate at which 1 US Dollar converts.
5. Before these can take effect, though, click on **Save Currency Rates.**

Based on your settings for the automatic updates, these figures will change every day, week, or month. After manually updating currency rates, flush your Magento cache.

Let's take a look at what we have accomplished. Go to the sample data front-end site in English and, using the category navigation at the top, go to the **Women | Tops | Jackets** category. The page should look like this:

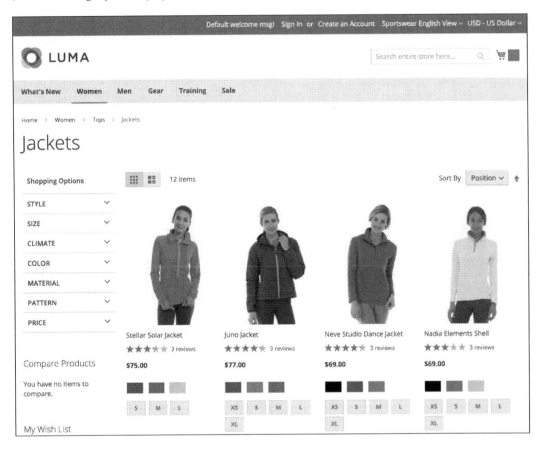

Change the language of the site to French, *et d'observer* the difference in the page:

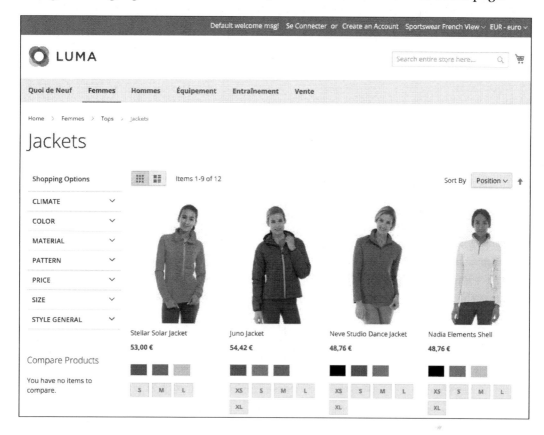

As you can see, on the French site, there is an added currency selector at the top of the left column and the product prices are shown in Euros, rather than Dollars. Since we configured the system to allow more than one currency in the French site, the currency selector automatically appears and will display all allowed currencies (Euros and Dollars).

Strategies for backups and security

If you're a seasoned developer or webmaster, you certainly have protocols in place for protecting your work, from daily backups to fail over servers. If you're a designer or site administrator, your back-ups are managed by your hosting provider or system administrator; you probably don't think much about back-ups on a daily basis.

However, with any complex configuration, a failure or mistake can still lead to hours and hours of lost time. Daily system backups are only good for what was done up to the time the backup was made. If you've worked with us in these first two chapters, you've already made a significant number of changes and configurations that, if you had to go back to yesterday's system backup, could take you hours to re-create.

We like to have backups, backups, and more backups, all along the way. Without interfering with how your systems are backed up, allow us to suggest some hard-learned strategies for working with Magento.

Backend backups

Under **Stores** | **Configuration** | **Advanced** | **System**, you can schedule backups of your Magento system at regular intervals with ease.

In addition to this, one time backups can be created from **System | Backups**:

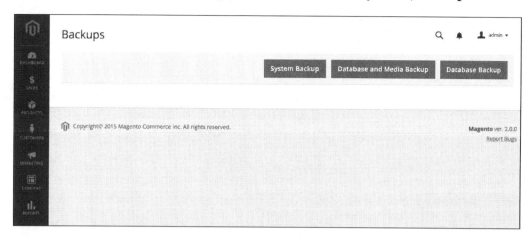

The backup utility has been significantly improved in Magento 2. The utility now includes complete backups of the relevant file system and database, with the option to just back up the database or the database and media as well.

If you're fond of the command line or have issues with the user interface, it's also possible to back the entire system up using the Magento binary from the command line. We've included an example:

```
cd /var/www/html/public_html/bin/ (magento bin directory)
[user@host bin]$ ./magento setup:backup --code --db --media
Enabling maintenance mode
Code backup is starting...
Code backup filename: 1450365584_filesystem_code.tgz (The archive can be
uncompressed with 7-Zip on Windows systems)
Code backup path: /var/www/public_html/var/backups/1450365584_filesystem_
code.tgz
[SUCCESS]: Code backup completed successfully.
Media backup is starting...
Media backup filename: 1450365584_filesystem_media.tgz (The archive can
be uncompressed with 7-Zip on Windows systems)
Media backup path: /var/www/public_html/var/backups/1450365584_
filesystem_media.tgz
[SUCCESS]: Media backup completed successfully.
DB backup is starting...
DB backup filename: 1450365584_db.gz (The archive can be uncompressed
with 7-Zip on Windows systems)
```

```
DB backup path: /var/www/public_html/var/backups/1450365584_db.gz
[SUCCESS]: DB backup completed successfully.
Disabling maintenance mode
```

Running the system backup saves the following:

- The Magento filesystem (excluding the `var` and `pub/static` directories)
- The `pub/media` directory
- The Magento 2 database

Also new is the ability to restore to a backup previously created using the utility. The backups created are stored in the `var/backups` directory and can be restored at any time from the command line. To restore a backup, you can use the `magento setup:rollback` command. Here's an example:

```
cd <your Magento install dir>/bin

./magento setup:rollback (full path to backup filename from var/backups
directory)
```

Be careful about both backing up and restoring your Magento instance, as it will put the store into maintenance mode if you select this option (which you should) and impact your ability to take orders whether you're in maintenance mode or not. The creation and restoration of a backup should be scheduled for a low traffic time when it's acceptable for the site to be offline.

File structure backups

What about your actual Magento files on the server? Again, your system backups should prevent any major losses on this front. However, we make it a general practice to download the full installation onto our computer using an FTP client. Periodically, we use an FTP program to synchronize or merge the online store files with my local files, so we're up to date with what is on the server.

A more secure method of uploading and downloading files to a server is to use **SFTP (Secure File Transfer Protocol)**, a common method allowed by almost all hosting providers.

The reason we do this is that if we want to make changes in the code files, a theme's CSS file, or edit an image, we first make a duplicate of the original file. Then, we make the changes we want to make to the original copy and upload it to the server. If we have somehow made a fatal error and need to recover quickly, we can simply copy the contents of the copy we made earlier, paste it into the original copy and upload it again to the server, and we're back in business.

Keep it secure

As with system backups, those responsible for your servers are most likely taking steps to prevent physical access to your hard drive and files.

 Periodically, Magento issues patches designed to address discovered vulnerabilities. As with any software, it is very important that you keep your Magento installation up to date in order to maintain the safest shopping experience for your customers.

The security we're most concerned with in terms of our work as Magento administrators is that of user access. Under **System**, you can set up roles and users. Generally, we establish the following roles:

- Sales, with access to orders, promotions, and customers
- Product management, with access to catalogs and products
- Marketing, with access to customers, CMS, promotions, newsletters, and reports
- Management, with access to everything other than the system configuration tools

And as for us, the administrators, we usually create other users in our organization with full privileges should any of us be on vacation or sick.

The one caveat about users and roles which you should be aware of is that Magento does not allow you to assign permissions based on website or store view. Unfortunately, a user with sales access has permission to view all orders and all customers. This is a feature of Magento Enterprise Edition, but not in the Community Edition, on which this book focuses.

Summary

Boy, we covered a lot in this chapter! Yet despite all the screen captures and instructions, you most likely found the configuration processes not as daunting as first imagined. The sophistication of Magento requires a certain degree of complexity.

In this chapter, we implemented our planned multi-store configuration, learned how to configure our stores for multiple languages and currencies, and covered some basic practices for insuring our work against loss.

Next, we begin the process of creating our category and product infrastructure. After all, the reason we're here is to sell products!

3
Managing Products

After successfully installing Magento, you can now take on the task of creating and configuring your store. You could begin by crafting the design that reflects your store's brand, or you could start configuring the many settings that will direct how your customers will interact with your online store.

However, selling online really boils down to the products you are selling. Additionally, many of Magento's configurations are dependent on the products you're offering and how they are arranged into categories.

Therefore, when we create a new Magento-powered store, we begin at the root, so to speak: the products.

In this chapter, we will tackle:

- Creating categories
- Managing products and attributes to help your customers shop more easily
- Setting up reviews, tags, and feeds to help promote your products
- Importing products en masse

Catalogs and categories

The use of the terms **catalogs** and **categories** in Magento used to be a bit confusing, as Magento tended to use these terms with some inconsistency. In Magento 2, the distinction is better defined.

In Magento, the catalog is the full collection of products within your Magento installation. Looking under **Products | Catalog** in the backend, you can view all your products regardless of to which Website or categories they may be assigned.

Categories in Magento 2 are just that: categories of products. Let us delve a bit deeper into this.

Creating categories

In *Chapter 2, Installing Magento 2*, we created the root categories needed for our new stores. Now, we need to learn how to create sub-categories that will allow us to assign products and display them in logical groups on our store.

For our furniture store, we want to create a new subcategory for sofas:

1. Go to **Products** | **Categories** in your Magento backend.
2. Click on **Furniture** in the list of categories on the left.

 You must first click on the parent category before creating a subcategory (although you can always drag and drop categories to re-position them if you need to later).

3. Click on **Add Subcategory**.
4. For **Name**, enter Sofas.
5. Set **Is Active** to Yes.
6. Click on **Save Category**.

This is how the additional subcategory would then appear:

You can, of course, add additional subcategories, as well as subcategories of subcategories. But, before you go to too much trouble building a huge category hierarchy, be sure to read through the section on *Attributes and Attribute Sets* later in this chapter.

Let's now explore the other panels and fields in the category detail screen.

 Don't be afraid to experiment! While this book provides a considerable amount of detail and helpful advice, the power of Magento can only truly be appreciated the more you work with it. Test various setting combinations. You may well come up with a particular configuration that helps you better connect with your shoppers.

General information tab

As you will noticed, there are only two required fields when creating a category (**Name** and **Is Active**). But others, as shown below, on this tab are important as well.

- **URL Key**: Once you create a category, Magento will automatically create a unique URL Key. This becomes the path for your category, such as www. acmefurniture.com/sofas.html. The sofas part is the URL Key. If you create more than one category with the same name, Magento will create unique keys by adding an incremental number, such as "sofas-1," "sofas-2." You can rename this to any value you wish, and in some cases, it may have more *SEO value* for you to enter a key such as "cheap-sofas" or "living-room-sofas." If you change the key of an existing category, you can select **Create Permanent Redirect for old URL** and Magento will create the necessary **URL rewrites** so that anyone still trying to view your category with the old URL Key will be automatically re-routed to the new path.

- **Description**: In the front end of your store, the **Description** tab will appear at the top of the category page, giving you the ability to describe the category to shoppers, as well as adding more SEO rich content. The field has a very basic WYSIWYG editor. However, you can access a WYSIWYG editor with considerably more features by clicking on **WYSIWYG Editor**. A panel will slide from the right with the enhanced field.

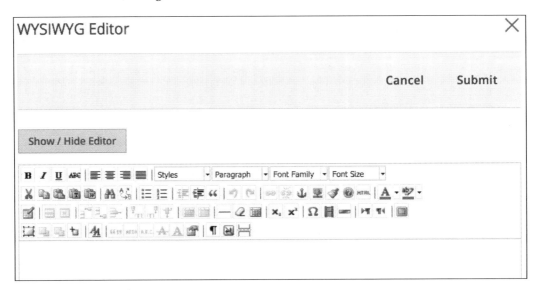

- **Image**: You can upload an image to appear at the top of the category. Your theme design may dictate how and where this image is displayed.

- **Page Title**: The page title shown at the top of a web browser window — this is also displayed as the title of your category in Google search results — is automatically created according to how you configure your store settings. However, you can override your default settings by entering a value here.

 Page title defaults are configured under **Stores | Configuration | General | Design | HTML Head**.

- **Meta Keywords**: Modern search engines don't use meta keywords for determining page rankings or content. However, if you want to enter keywords here, you may enter them inserting a comma between each keyword or phrase.

- **Meta Description**: In Magento, the meta description that is added to the header of your page for search engines to use is automatically taken from the **Description** field. However, Google only displays approximately the first 160 characters of a description. You may want to compose a different description here for that purpose.

- **Include in Navigation Menu**: You will most likely want a category displayed in your main navigation menu. However, there are instances where you may not want the category listed. For example, as discussed later under the section, *Special Categories*, you may want to create a Featured category that displays products in a special location on your site, but is not listed in the main menu.

Display Settings tab

As you build out your category schema, you may decide that you don't want products displayed on all category pages. For example, a top-level "Furniture" category might display graphics for each subcategory (for example, "Sofas", "Chairs", "Tables"). However, within those subcategories, you probably do want to display the list of products available. Let us have a look at the various attributes within this tab:

- **Display Mode**: In *Chapter 6*, *Managing Non-Product Content*, we'll explain about **static blocks** — content that can be used as desired within your site. You can elect to show products, a static block, or both products and a static block.

> Unless your theme is configured otherwise, the description and image you add in the **General Information** tab will still show even if you choose **Products only** for **Display Mode**.
>
> Why use a static block if you can simply add a category description? Good question, and one we're often asked. Static blocks are very useful for displaying the same content in many places. For instance, you may want to use a static block to regularly display a new product announcement or discount. By using a static block, you can update this information in one place and have it instantly appear throughout your site wherever it is referenced.

- **CMS Block**: If you do choose to display a static block, you can choose the block to show within this drop-down menu.

- **Is Anchor**: Later in this chapter, we will explore attributes and how you can use them in **filtered navigation**. If you want your category page to show layered navigation for the products within the category (if products are shown), set this to **Yes**, as shown in the following screenshot:

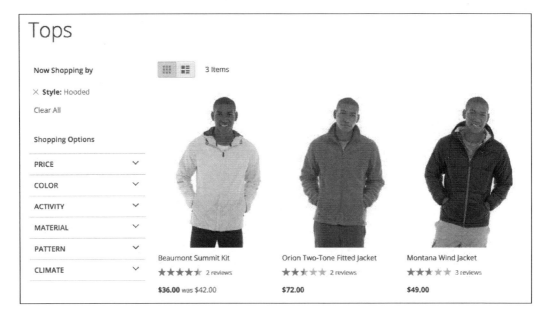

- **Available Product Listing Sort By**: By default, Magento allows products to be sorted by position, name, and price. Position is managed within the **Category Products** tab (this will be explained a bit later). You can choose which of these sorts to include.

- **Default Product Listing Sort By**: You can also choose which sort you wish to use by default when a customer first views a category page.

- **Layered Navigation Price Step**: Based on your configurations, Magento will automatically calculate the price steps shown in the layered navigation sidebar. You can override this by entering the steps you wish to show by entering the amounts separated by commas (for example, "0,50,100,500").

Default price step configurations are in **Stores | Configuration | Catalog | Catalog | Layered Navigation**.

Custom Design tab

In this tab, you can control specific display configurations for your category.

- **Use Parent Category Settings**: You can choose to have any subcategory use the same display settings as its parent category.

- **Apply To Products**: Setting it to **Yes** will apply any applicable design settings to products shown within the category.

- **Custom Theme**: If you have another theme you wish to apply to a category — perhaps a holiday-focused theme — you can choose that theme in this field.

- **Active From/Active To**: These date fields, if filled in, allow you to control the dates on which any custom theme will be applied.

- **Page Layout**: Depending on the capabilities of your theme, you can choose an alternative layout scheme for the category. Your choices include one column, two columns with either left or right sidebar, three columns, or empty (this requires the definition of your own page layout using XML).

- **Custom Layout Update**: You can enter custom XML code to alter the display of your category page.

[For more on themes, see *Chapter 4, Designs and Themes*.]

Category Products tab

When you create products in your Magento store, you can assign the product to a category. Alternatively, you can assign multiple products to a category within this tab. Use the search features to find your products.

- **Selection Column**: The first field at the top of the column allows you to search for products that are (**Yes**), are not (**No**), or either (**Any**) assigned already to your category. For example, if you want to identify products not already assigned to your category, select **No**.

- **Search Fields**: The empty fields at the top of the other columns allow you to enter a search criteria for further filtering your search results.

Once you have identified the products you wish to add, select the ones you wish to add. Be sure to click **Save Category** in order to complete your assignments.

Re-ordering categories

We mentioned it earlier, but it deserves repeating: you can re-arrange the order of your categories — and how they will appear in navigation menus — by dragging and dropping your categories in the sidebar display. The order in which they appear can be set differently for each website or store view.

 Re-arranging categories is a very intensive computing operation owing to the work that Magento has to perform in order to update its data tables and re-index. If you intend to make several changes, you may want to disable caching until you complete your work, although each change may still take some time. *Be patient*. After each re-arrangement, make sure Magento has completed its work before making the next change. Otherwise, your data tables may become "confused."

Special categories

Magento provides some inherent tools for grouping products for special display purposes. For example, by designating **New From** and **New To** dates in the **Advanced Settings | Autosetting** panel of a product detail screen, as shown in the following screenshot, Magento will display a product within a **New Products** block if today's date falls within the range of these dates.

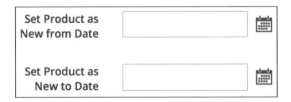

However, in some cases, you may want to display groups of products for other reasons. It's not uncommon to show **Featured** products on an e-commerce website. You might even want to show products grouped by family or purpose.

Let's take the case of creating a **Featured** products section for our homepage. Let's also assume that you don't want **Featured** as a category in your navigation bar just as a "special" category.

1. Go to **Products | Categories** in your Magento backend.
2. Click on the root category under which you wish to create your special category.
3. Click on **Add Subcategory**.

4. In the center part of the screen, enter the following values:

    ◦   **Name: Featured**
    ◦   **Is Active: Yes**
    ◦   **Include in Navigation Menu: No**

5. Click on the tab at the top labeled **Category Products**.

6. Find the product you wish to add to this category and check the box in the left-most column.

7. Click on **Save Category**.

8. After the screen refreshes, note the ID number of the category at the top of the screen, as shown in the following screenshot (in this example, the category ID is **43**):

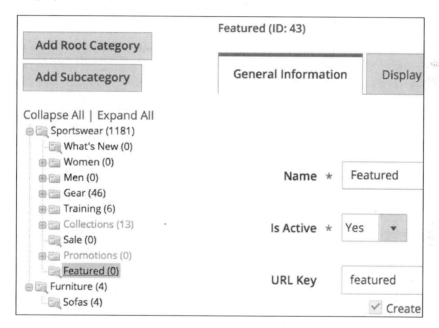

You've now created a new category called **Featured** and added some products. Now we need to add a block to the homepage that will display your **Featured Products**.

1. Go to **Content | Pages**.

2. Select to edit the home page for the store you wish to update.

3. Click the side tab labeled **Content**.

4. If the WYSIWYG editor is showing, click on **Show/Hide Editor** to reveal the HTML code.

5. Find in the code where you want to put your **Featured Products** section and position the cursor there.

6. Click the **Insert Widget** button.

7. For **Widget Type**, select **Catalog Product List**.

8. Add a custom title.

9. Once this is done you should see something similar to the following block notation in the content pane:

```
{{widget type="Magento\CatalogWidget\Block\Product\ProductsList"
title="Featured" products_count="10" template="product/widget/
content/grid.phtml"}}
```

10. Click **Save Page** (or **Save and Continue Edit**).

When you view the homepage, you should see a section displaying the featured items you assigned to this special category:

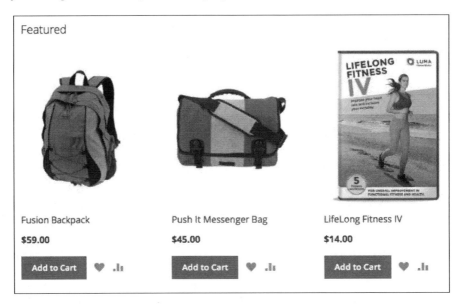

Furthermore, you can access this category and its products by appending the name of your special category to your store URL. For example, to see the entire **Featured** product category, you can go to http://www.yourstoredomain.com/featured. html.

In *Chapter 6, Managing Non-Product Content*, we'll go into more detail about blocks and how to use them in creative ways, giving your online store more features and functionality.

Managing products the customer focused way

The heart of any online store is the selection of products offered to visiting customers. Yet, as simple as that may sound, creating online stores to present the vast array of products and product types has proven to be one of the most challenging quests for platform programmers.

If all stores sold each product as an individual item without different colors, sizes, or add-ons, e-commerce would be much simpler. But that's not how the real world works. If you sell t-shirts (the classic example for this discussion), you might sell each color as a separate item, especially if you only offer a few shirts. However, it would make shopping very cumbersome to your customers if you also had each size of each color listed as a separate product.

People shop by product style, then decide upon variations such as size and color. To reflect this shopping "workflow," we need to create products in our store that are presented in the most convenient and logical manner possible.

The simple product type

If you shop online for a golf putter, you could well find a list of putters sold online where each style is a separate product. The individual putter products would be considered **simple products**.

In Magento, we think of a simple product as one for which there is a single **stock keeping unit (SKU)**, or if the putter has a SKU of PUT1234, then we would build it in Magento as a simple product.

Simple products can have **custom options**, though. For instance, we could offer this putter in different shaft lengths, but with a simple product, we cannot manage inventory for each option. Therefore, if we are stocking each putter in different shafts, then we would need to create simple products for each **variant**.

Variant is a common term used in e-commerce to describe related variations of a product. For example, a t-shirt that comes in small, medium, and large would be referred to as having three variants; each size would be a variant of the t-shirt.

The preceding figure illustrates a simple product. It has no other sizes or colors and is not a bundle or group of products.

Simple products in Magento become the basis for all other tangible complex product types, which we'll discuss in the next section. The important concept to learn here is that all tangible products begin with the simple product.

The complex product types

When two or more simple products are combined in a single product representation, we are creating a **complex product type**. In Magento, we also consider virtual and downloadable products as "complex" because of the additional considerations needed to manage non-tangible products.

Configurable product type

Perhaps the most popular complex product type is the **configurable product type**. This type is used when you sell an item that comes in different sizes, colors, and so on. The most common example is clothing.

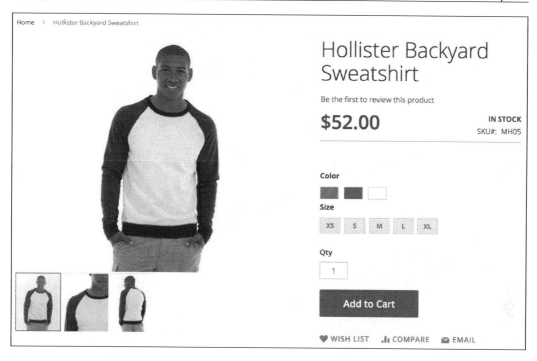

As shown in the preceding screenshot, this sweatshirt comes in three different colors and five different sizes. In Magento, there are actually two ways you can build out this product:

- You can build a simple product and create options for the colors and sizes
- You can build simple products for each combination of color and size (for example, Red-Small, Red-Medium, White-Small, and so on) and present all the variations as a single configurable product

The key to which method to use boils down to how you answer the following questions:

1. Do you need to track inventory for each variant?
2. For all the colors and sizes of this item, will any of the possible combinations not be available (for example, you might not be able to source White-XL sweatshirts)?

If you answer Yes to either question, then you should use a configurable product. You cannot track inventory on **Custom Options** (which we'll go into in more detail later in this chapter), and for whatever **Custom Options** you create, customers will be able to choose all possible combinations.

Configurable products also give you tremendous content versatility as well. For example, in the sweatshirt product (included in the Magento 2 Sample Data), as the customer selects a different color, the main image changes to that of the associated simple product image.

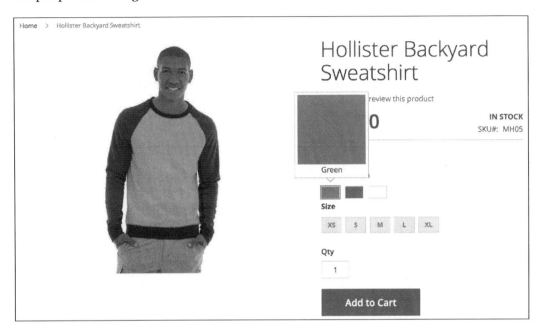

Additionally, the stock available for each combination selected is shown to the customer. Any associated simple product that is not available will be indicated, as shown in the following screenshot: when **Red** is selected, the **XL** size is not available.

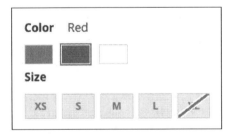

As we'll see when we create a configurable product type later, Magento 2 introduces new tools for rapidly creating the needed variants.

Grouped product type

Sometimes it's helpful to display several different products as a related group to make it easier for customers to choose one or more products. The grouped product type associates simple or virtual product types into one complex product.

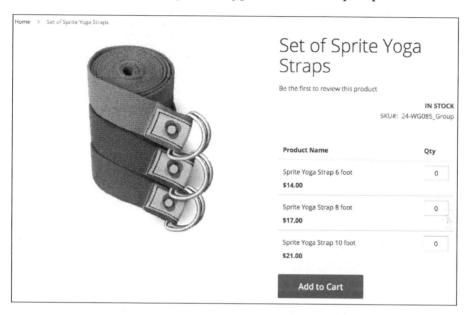

As shown in the sample Yoga Straps, the customer can choose any quantity of any of the products, which exist as simple products in your catalog. Each product chosen will appear separately in the customer's shopping cart.

 Keep in mind that a grouped product cannot use simple products that have **Custom Options**.

Bundle product type

A complex product similar to the grouped product is the bundle product type. It is similar in that it associates simple or virtual products that do not have **Custom Options**, but different in that you can create a *base collection* of products for the bundle and set a price for the combined items. You can also create additional options for the user to choose and allow the pricing to be determined *dynamically*.

If it's the latter, the product listing will show a range of pricing based on the least expensive and most expensive possible configurations. There's a lot of versatility to the bundle product type.

Although not completely supported, the bundle product can be used to create what is often called a **kit**. As we use this term, it refers to the assembling of various individual products into a single presented product, usually priced at a discount from the sum of the individual product prices. Let's explore a possible scenario to better understand the concept of a kit.

We have a client who sells dictation-related products. He wants to combine a digital recorder that retails for $500 with a transcription kit that retails for $400 and offer this combined "kit" for a special discounted price of $800, saving the customer $100 if purchased separately. In addition, he needs to maintain inventory counts for both items, so that if one goes out of stock, the bundle is, therefore, not in stock.

Using a bundle product, our client can build this kit — or bundle — assigning its special price, yet maintain each one separately for inventory and shipping purposes.

> The big "issue" with using the bundle product type for kits is that, by default, the customer must still click to **Customize** the bundle before adding it to their cart. Even though you may not have any options available for the customer, this extra step is still required. Look for innovative developers to create modifications that will modify this behavior.

Virtual product type

Just as the name implies, a virtual product type is an intangible product. Typical virtual products include subscriptions, memberships, and warranties.

Unlike tangible products, virtual products have no shipping weight and no shipping options will appear during the checkout process, unless a tangible product is also included in the customer's order.

Downloadable product type

We live in a world of digital distribution. Books, music, and software are more commonly downloaded today than sent on CDs or — anyone remember these? — floppy disks.

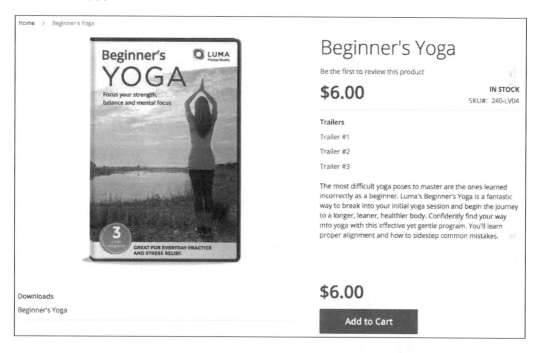

In Magento, you can sell and distribute digital products using the **downloadable product type**. When customers purchase the product, they are emailed links to files on your server or on another server. Customers can also access their downloadable products when they log into their account in your store.

With a downloadable product, you can set the maximum number of downloads you will allow a customer and whether the link is "shareable" with others.

Attributes and attribute sets

Before diving into the creation of products, we need to explore a very important — and powerful — feature of Magento: product attributes. We have yet to find another common platform that provides the level of sophistication for product attributes as well as Magento.

Every field related to a product is called, in Magento, an attribute. The description, price, weight, and SKU are attributes. In fact, all the fields that appear by default on a product detail screen are attributes.

But the real power comes in those attributes when you can add to your product screens to capture more granular aspects of your products, such as color, size, kHz, and screen size. Obviously, not all attributes are relevant to all products. For instance, t-shirt size would not be applicable to your furniture products. Fabric would not be a useful attribute for computer monitors, and that's where Magento really shines!

If you view the **More Information** tab under the **Sample Data** product Montana Wind Jacket, for example, you will see four attributes listed.

Each of these relevant attributes helps your customers get a better understanding of your products. You can certainly include this information in your product description field, but by creating attributes your customers can use them for comparison purposes, and it makes it easier for you to make sure you have included all product specifications when creating new products in your store.

Furthermore, attributes can be used to create the **layered navigation** that appears in the sidebar on your category pages (if **Is Anchor** is set to **Yes**; see *Chapter 4, Designs and Themes*).

 Only certain attribute types can be used in layered navigation: Multiple Select, Dropdown, Price, Visual Swatch, and Text Swatch. See the next section for more information on attribute types.

In your Magento 2 backend, go to **Stores | Product** (under the **Attributes** group heading).

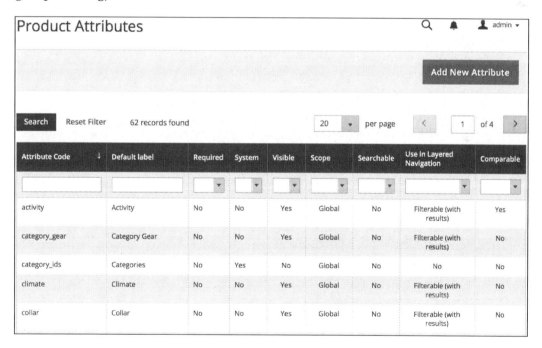

Here, you will see a listing of all the product attributes, both default and user-added, that are available for your products.

To use attributes for creating products, you create attribute sets (also referred to as product templates in Magento 2) to group attributes into meaningful sets relevant to the various products you are offering. We'll explore attribute sets in a moment, once we learn how to create individual attributes.

Attribute types

Before we begin building or editing product attributes, let's learn about the different attribute types accommodated in Magento 2. Each has its own considerations and features.

Attributes are considered name-value pairs, meaning that for each attribute there is a name, such as "Size," and one or more values, such as "Small, Medium, Large." The values you need for each attribute — and how you wish to use the attribute — is what helps you determine the type of attribute to create.

- **Text field**: As the name implies, this attribute allows you to enter any text information you wish to describe the feature.

- **Text area**: Similar to a text field, the text area field allows for a larger entry. Plus, you can use the WYSIWYG editor to style the content, insert HTML tags, or use other editing features.

- **Date**: You might have a product with a release date (such as a music album) or another date-specific feature. Use the date field to allow you to easily input a date using a pop-up calendar.

- **Yes/No**: As the name implies, it allows you to simply choose between "Yes" and "No" as values. This might be useful for question type features, such as "Includes Power Cord?" or "Eligible for Extended Warranty?"

- **Multiple select**: This field type presents you with a list of choices for the attribute. You can choose one or more from the list. You have full control over the items in the value list (as we'll see a bit later in this section).

- **Dropdown**: Similar to the multiple select, except that you can only choose one from a list of possible choices.

- **Price**: You can create additional price fields for your products in addition to the Price, Special Price, Tier Prices, and Cost fields already in Magento. While additional price fields aren't used during the checkout process, you could create fields to present prices for other reasons, such as "Compare At" or "Sold in Stores At."

- **Media image**: You can add additional image fields to your products in addition to the base, small, and thumbnail images. You can exclude this new image from the thumbnail gallery or allow it to be included.

- **Fixed product tax**: If you have a product that has a fixed tax amount, you could use this attribute type. The values entered would be included in any tax reporting or display based on your general tax settings (see *Chapter 4, Designs and Themes*).

- **Visual swatch**: A new feature in Magento 2, this field allows you to present the attribute as a color or image, such as a texture or cloth.

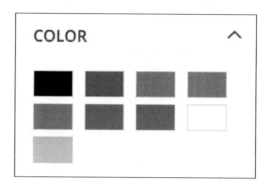

- **Text swatch**: This new Magento 2 attribute type displays text as a button. You could use this for things such as shoe sizes or kHz.

Selecting an attribute type

Before you begin creating attributes, it's important to understand the implication of using one attribute type over another. Each type has its own particular abilities.

The one ability that is usually the most important is whether or not the attribute can be used in layered navigation (as described earlier). For an attribute to be used as a layered attribute, it has to have fixed values. Magento indexes attributes and it makes sense that it cannot provide layered navigation on free-form fields. Therefore, if you wish to use an attribute in layered navigation, it must be a multiple select, dropdown, price, visual swatch, or text swatch attribute type. Eligible attribute types can also be designated for use in the layered navigation of search results.

Another ability commonly considered for attributes is whether the attribute will be used when customers compare products. In the comparison display, only those attributes chosen for comparison will be shown side-by-side. All attribute types, except for media image and fixed product tax, are eligible for use in comparisons.

Creating an attribute

We're going to create a new attribute to use for our furniture products called "fabric," which will help us learn how to add new attributes. We want to use this value in layered navigation and for comparison purposes.

To begin, click **Add New Attribute** at the top of the attribute list.

> As with many configurations in Magento, the availability of certain fields and choices is often determined by other field choices. If some fields we discuss are not visible, it may be due to a previous choice.

Attribute properties

On the first panel, you'll find the following fields:

- **Default label**: Regardless of what you wish to have the attribute labeled as on your store (which we'll discuss a bit later), you can name it for your backend use. In our example, we would enter Fabric.

- **Catalog Input Type for Store Owner**: Use this to select the type of attribute you wish to create (see the previous section for more on attribute types).

- **Values Required**: If you wish to require that a value be entered or selected, choose Yes.

- **Update Product Preview Image**: For applicable attribute types, this will allow the main product image on a catalog listing page to display the related swatch value (applies only to the backend catalog listing).

- **Use Product Image for Swatch if Possible**: When using swatches in configurable products, the product will display the swatches as selectors. When a swatch is selected, the main image can be replaced with the base image of the associated product.

Manage options

This section will only appear if you select **Multiple Select** or **Dropdown** as your attribute type (**Catalog Input Type for Store Owner**). For these attribute types, you have to provide the possible value choices. Let's take t-shirt size as an example. If you use a **Dropdown** type, you can enter all possible size choices — make sure they're presented and spelled as you would like them to appear.

To create an option, click on **Add Option**. Enter the value you want for the option in the **Admin** column. If you want different displayed values for your multiple stores, enter those into the other fields. Any store views without a value will use the admin column value.

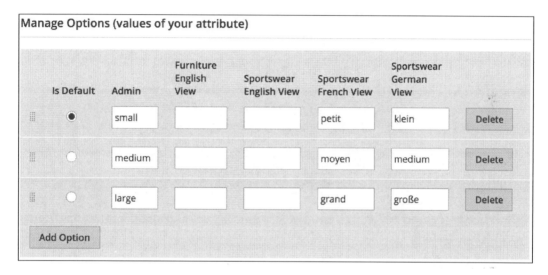

Once you have more than one value, you can choose which will be the default value when creating a new product by clicking the **Is Default** radio button. You can also re-arrange the order of the values by clicking and dragging the handle on the left end of an option row.

Manage Swatch

If you choose a Visual or Text Swatch attribute type, this section will be available. Adding swatch options works very similarly to the **Options** described before, except that you are working with swatches instead of option values.

Visual swatches are configured by selecting either a color value or uploading an image of the swatch. Using the down-arrow menu, select **Choose a Color** to reveal a color selector pop-up. You can move your mouse across the color spectrums, enter RGB or HSB numerical values, or enter a hexadecimal value to choose your color. Once you make your selection, click the small, round rainbow-colored button in the lower right-hand color of the selector.

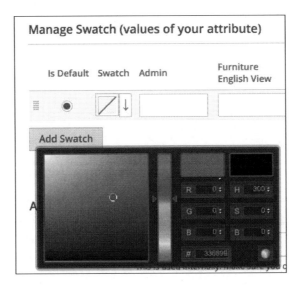

If you choose **Upload a File** for your swatch, you can select a swatch image on your computer to upload.

If you use swatch images, try to create your swatches so that they're big enough to display enough texture, if that's important. For layout quality, your swatches should all be the same size.

Text swatches will display the values you enter as a "button." The swatches will show all available values and if any are out of stock or not available, it will appear as crossed out.

Advanced attribute properties

Expand this panel to reveal the following field choices:

- **Attribute Code**: This is an internal code used by Magento (and perhaps your developer if they customize your installation). Similar to a URL path, the key should be all lowercase and not include spaces. If you don't enter one, Magento will create one automatically.

- **Scope**: Use this to decide whether the entry should apply to all products at the Global, Website, or Store level. For instance, if you select Global, then whatever is entered in your attribute for a product will apply at all scope levels and cannot be changed at the website or store level.

- **Default Value**: If you want to have a default value displayed when the field is presented in a product edit screen, enter it here.

- **Unique Value**: There may be certain times you want a value to only apply to one product.

- **Input Validation for Store Owner**: You can have Magento validate whether a value entered meets certain requirements: decimal number (such as 12.43 — a number with a decimal point), integer value (for example, 2 or 77 — no decimal point), email address, a URL (web address containing "http" or "https"), letters (a through z), or letters and numbers (a-z and 0-9). If the entry does not match the validation selection, the user will receive an error message.

- **Add to Column Options**: You can elect to have an attribute appear in the list of products when viewing the catalog.

- **Use in Filter Options**: In addition, you can allow the backend user to filter listed products using your new attribute.

Managing labels

By default, your attribute will be named by the value you enter in the **Default** label field. However, if you want to display the name of your attribute on your store frontend, you may want to supply alternatives for each of your store views. For instance, if you create an attribute called "screen size," you will probably want to translate it for stores you build in other languages.

Storefront properties

This is the section that allows you to affect how your attribute can be used by your customers.

 As noted earlier, different attribute types will determine what properties may or may not be available.

- **Use in Search**: When customers search for products on your site, you can include the values of this attribute as a search value. For example, you may have customers that often search for "halogen light bulbs." If all your products have "halogen" in their title, no problem, but what if many of your products do not include "halogen" in the title? You could create an attribute called "Bulb Type" with "halogen" as one of the values. By setting this attribute field to Yes, if someone searches for "halogen light bulbs," products with this attribute set to "halogen" would be included in the search results.

- **Comparable on Storefront**: You can select attributes to be included in the side-by-side product comparisons for your customers.

- **Use in Layered Navigation**: For applicable attribute types, you can choose to use them in the frontend layered navigation.

- **Use in Search Results Layered Navigation**: Likewise for layered navigation in search results.

- **Position**: If you do use an attribute in layered navigation, you can command its position relative to other attributes by entering a number in this field. Attributes will be shown in ascending order (lowest to highest) according to this field.

- **Use for Promo Rule Conditions**: As we will discuss in *Chapter 8, Extending Magento*, you can construct discounts and promotions based on the values of attributes for which this field is set to Yes.

- **Allow HTML Tags on Storefront**: For applicable attribute types, you can allow the use of HTML tags in the field value. For instance, you might want to bold part of a value, such as Contains EPA-Approved cleaners.

- **Visible on Catalog Pages on Storefront**: Setting to Yes will display this attribute on the product detail page.

- **Used in Product Listing**: Depending on your theme, setting this to Yes may allow the attribute to be shown on the category listing pages.

- **Used for Sorting in Product Listing**: Also dependent on your theme, this may allow your attribute to be included as a sorting criteria, much as price, position and name are used by default.

Creating attribute sets

In order to have attributes available for use when creating a product, it should belong in an **attribute set**. Attribute sets also allow you to make available similar attributes across similar products.

To view existing attribute sets, go to **Stores | Attribute Sets**.

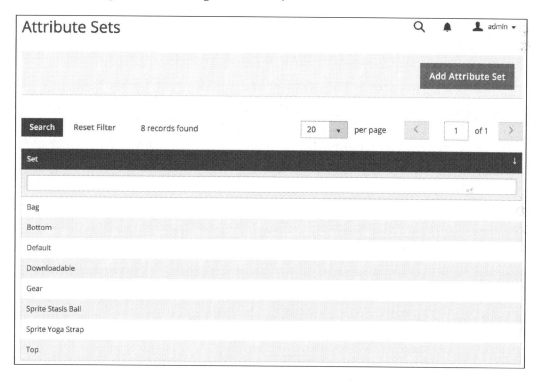

Each existing attribute set (the default will appear if you have not created any sets) contains attributes assigned to that set. Let's create a new attribute set for our furniture products.

For this exercise, we have already created one new attribute: fabric.

1. To begin creating our new attribute set, click on **Add Attribute Set**.

2. On the first screen, enter the name of your attribute set as you would like it to appear in the backend (your customers will never see attribute sets).

3. If you wish, you can base your new set on an existing attribute set, which can help reduce your configuration time if an existing set has most of the attributes you wish to use. For our example, we're going to select **Default**.

4. Click on **Save** to advance to the next screen.

5. To add **fabric** to our new attribute set, we need to drag it from the right **Unassigned Attributes** column and place it where we want it to appear on the **Product Detail** screen. We can place and move attributes into any order or group within the attribute set. A "Group" is noted by the folders in the **Groups** column.

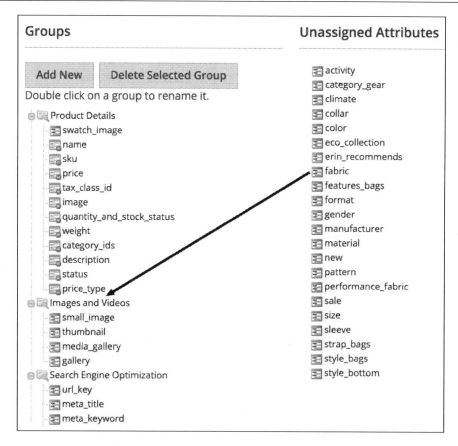

Groups   **Unassigned Attributes**

Add New Delete Selected Group	activity
Double click on a group to rename it.	category_gear
Product Details	climate
swatch_image	collar
name	color
sku	eco_collection
price	erin_recommends
tax_class_id	fabric
image	features_bags
quantity_and_stock_status	format
weight	gender
category_ids	manufacturer
description	material
status	new
price_type	pattern
Images and Videos	performance_fabric
small_image	sale
thumbnail	size
media_gallery	sleeve
gallery	strap_bags
Search Engine Optimization	style_bags
url_key	style_bottom
meta_title	
meta_keyword	

Attributes marked with a "Do not enter" icon cannot be removed from attribute sets. These are required fields for products. All others can be added or removed as needed.

6. If you wish, you can create additional groups within an attribute set by clicking **Add New** at the top of the **Groups** column.

7. Click **Save** to commit your new attribute set.

We often create a group within an attribute set to contain special, related attributes. For instance, we could create a group called "Furniture Specifications" and drag "fabric" and any other new, related attributes into this new group, as seen in the following screenshot. This can help focus attention on these special attributes when creating or editing products. The order and groups of attributes have no effect on the front end presentation nor will they change any programmatic aspects of Magento 2.

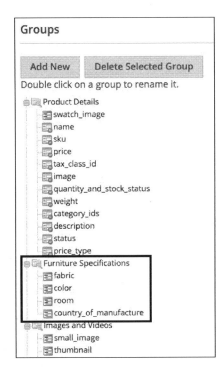

Now that we have created a new "Furniture" attribute set, we can add additional attributes as needed to help describe our furniture offerings. We can also use this attribute set when adding new furniture products so we have just the attributes related to our needs.

A new and powerful feature of Magento 2 is the ability to add existing attributes within the **Product Edit** screen. This means that as you create products, you can add attributes you need without having to leave your current work. These attributes will also be added to the attribute set you have applied to your current product, which means the attribute will also be added to all products using the same attribute set.

Creating products

Now that we've discussed the various Magento product types, let's go over the process of creating a new product in the Magento 2 backend. While there are some differences based on product type, the overall process and options are very similar.

The new product screen

After you go to **Products | Catalog** in the backend, you will see a list of the products in your catalog. In the upper right-hand corner is an orange button, titled **Add Product**. If you click on **Add Product**, you can create a simple, configurable, virtual, or downloadable product. For all types — including the bundled and grouped product types — you can also click the button menu (the down arrow on the right side of the button) and choose a specific product type.

The configurable, virtual, and downloadable product types can be created simply by changing settings within the simple product detail panel. For example, you can start with a simple product, add configurations, and the product type will automatically change to a configurable product type.

As we go through the product creation process, you'll learn that Magento has really upped their game in Magento 2, making it much easier for you to manage your products. For instance, you can start out adding all the various t-shirt styles you sell as simple products, and then go back and create the various size and color variants within those products. In Magento 1.x, you could not change the type of an existing product without first deleting the product, then re-adding it.

So, let's begin by building a simple product and then exploring how to create the other complex product types. For our example, we'll start with a red couch.

Creating a simple product

To begin, click on **Add Product** button on the **Products | Catalog** screen.

We're going to fill in the fields in the **Product Details** section as follows:

- **Name: Couch**
- **SKU**: C1234
- **Price: 599.99**
- **Tax Class: Taxable Goods**
- **Quantity: 100, In Stock**
- **Weight: Yes, 200 lbs**
- **Categories: Sofas**
- **Description: Beautiful, comfortable and stylish. Our Acme sofa is the perfect couch for formal or casual decór. Durable, yet supple microfiber fabric will last for years.**
- For the **Images and Videos** section, we're going to upload an image of a red sofa we have taken from sample data provided in earlier Magento versions.

Save your product now before proceeding.

Next, we want to click the small down arrow to the right of **Default** at the top of the screen and type **Furniture** to select the **Furniture Attribute Set** we created earlier.

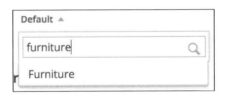

After the screen refreshes, you'll see an additional attribute group you created in the left sidebar, and any attributes you added to the attribute set will be available to you.

In the **Furniture Specifications** panel, we will enter the following values:

- **Fabric**: microfiber
- **Color**: Red
- **Room**: Living Room
- **Country of Manufacture**: United States

Under the **Websites** panel, we need to select **Furniture Website** so that the new product will appear in the stores within the furniture website.

We're going to leave all the other settings as they are for now and click on **Save**.

When we view the product on the website and click on the **More Information** tab, we can see the values of the attributes we have selected.

For attributes to appear on your product detail screen, as shown in the preceding screenshot, you must set **Visible on Catalog Pages on Storefront** to **Yes** in the **Attribute** properties.

Creating a configurable product

Let's say we have our couch available in three colors: red, blue, and green. How would we present all three choices as a single product yet allow the customer to select their desired color?

The simplest way would be to add colors as an option in our simple product. However, if we manage inventory separately for each color (let's say we have 100 red, 50 blue, and 30 green sofas in the warehouse), we have to, in essence, create three simple products and *associate* them to a single configurable product.

To do that, we have two options: auto-create the associated products from the configurable product or create the three individual simple products then associate them to a new, configurable product.

First, let's try method one using the couch simple product we just created:

1. Open the **Product Edit** screen in the backend and scroll down to the bottom panel titled **Configurations**. Expand this panel.

2. Click on **Create Configurations**. A new screen will appear from the right side of your browser window. A step-by-step navigation will appear at the top to note your progress in creating the associated products.

3. The next step is to select one or more attributes that will determine the product variants. In our case, we have different sofas based on color. If we have sofas of different colors and fabrics (three colors and two fabrics would produce six possible combinations), we could select both attributes. For now, we will only select **Color** and click on **Next**.

4. Now, we get to select all the different colors we wish to use. We will select **Blue**, **Green**, and **Red** for our example. Click on **Next** to proceed.

5. In Step 3, we have some choices to make regarding our images, prices, and quantities. As per our example, we will select **Apply unique images by attribute to each SKU** for **Images**; **Apply single price to all SKUs** for **Price** (all sofas are the same price); and **Apply unique quantity by attribute to each SKU** for **Quantity**. As we make our choices, we have the opportunity to add images and note quantities, since we elected to manage these uniquely for each variant. We will also be able to enter the price common to all sofas (in our case, $599.99). Click on **Next** when you have completed this step.

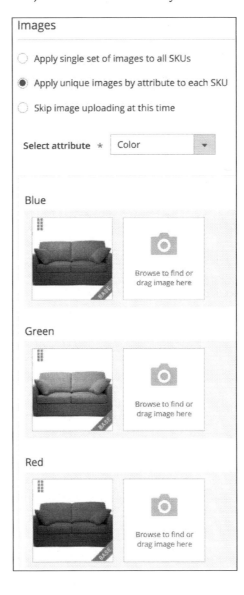

First, you are allowed to choose whether to use the same images for all variants, or assign unique images to each. As with any of these choices, you can also opt to skip this for later.

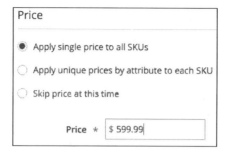

Alternatively, within the **Price** box, you can assign the same or unique prices to all variations.

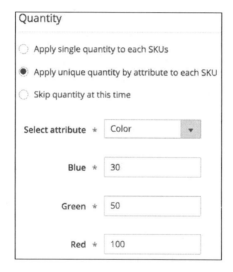

Finally, if you wish, you can assign inventory quantities for the associated products.

6. On the final step, you will be able to review your variants to make sure you have them as you wish. When you're satisfied, click **Generate Products**.

7. The overlay will disappear and you will see your new variants listed in the **Configurations** panel. Here, you can modify the **Name** and **SKU** fields for each variant to meet your needs. Once you have completed this, click on **Save** to complete creating your configurable product.

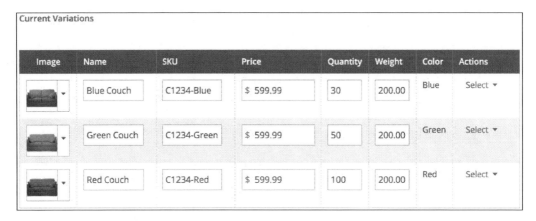

Having completed creating the configurable product, the product on the frontend now displays the color swatches for each variant (and removes the **Color** field from the **More Information** tab contents). As you click on each swatch, the main image will also change to reflect the image you uploaded for the particular variant.

In the backend, under **Products | Catalog**, you'll find four products now: the **Configurable Product** and the three new associated **Simple Products**.

	ID ↑	Thumbnail	Name	Type	Attribute Set	SKU	Price	Quantity
☐	2055		Red Couch	Simple Product	Furniture	C1234-Red	$599.99	100.0000
☐	2054		Green Couch	Simple Product	Furniture	C1234-Green	$599.99	50.0000
☐	2053		Blue Couch	Simple Product	Furniture	C1234-Blue	$599.99	30.0000
☐	2052		Couch	Configurable Product	Furniture	C1234	$599.99	0.0000

Alternatively, if you already have the **Simple Products** added to your store, you can create the configurable product and add the associated products manually instead of creating them automatically, as we just did.

Creating a grouped product

If you have a collection of related products, such as yoga straps (included in the Magento 2 Sample Data set), you can present them as a group. Customers can then select which individual items they want by entering a quantity for each associated product.

To create a grouped product, choose **Grouped Product** in the **Add Product** dropdown menu, as shown in the following screenshot:

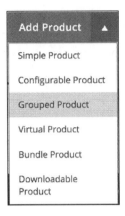

At the bottom of the **Product Details** screen, under **Grouped Products**, you add products to the group and any default quantity you wish to set (customers can always override any default).

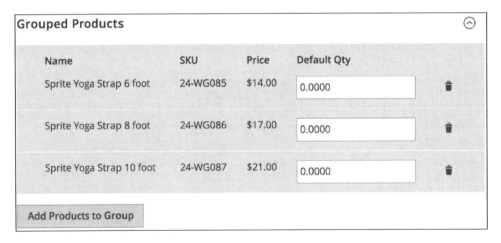

Grouped products are not really products at all but simply a *virtual* grouping of products you wish to present together.

Creating bundled products

Bundled products are similar to grouped products but with some differences. The biggest difference is that you are creating a bundle of products presented to the customer as one "set" or "bundle." Furthermore, you can configure the product so that the customer can select options of each product, if they wish.

Let's look at the **Sprite Yoga Companion Kit** product provided in the Magento 2 Sample Data. This is a bundle of yoga equipment that has been configured to include four required products: a Stasis Ball, a Foam Yoga Brick, a Yoga Strap, and a Foam Roller. Customers can select larger balls and longer straps. The price of the bundle is automatically calculated based on their selections.

When the customer clicks on **Customize and Add to Cart**, the choices available for the bundle are revealed.

First are the choices for the Stasis Ball:

As customers select alternative sizes, the total cost of the bundle will adjust accordingly.

Bundled products are created in two steps: creating the options for each bundle component, then attaching simple products to those options.

Simple products used in bundled products cannot have custom options. Remember, as with all complex product types, you can only associate simple or virtual products. Complex product types cannot be associated to other complex product types.

Let's build the **Sprite Stasis Ball** bundle option, as shown, in the **Product Detail** screen to illustrate this two-step process.

1. Under the **Bundle** panel, click on **Create New Option**.

2. For **Option Title**, we'll enter **Sprite Stasis Ball**.

3. We can allow the customer to make their selection using a drop-down menu, radio buttons, or a checkbox. You should use whatever you feel best communicates the choices to your customers. For our example, we're going to select **Radio Buttons**.

4. Our next step is to click on **Add Products to Option**. We can then use the search tools to find the products we want to add to this option. In our case, we're going to search for products with "Stasis Ball" in the title and "blue" in the SKU. We will check each product we want to attach to our option and click on **Add Selected Products**.

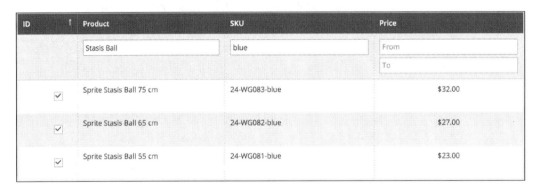

ID	↑	Product	SKU	Price
		Stasis Ball	blue	From
				To
	✓	Sprite Stasis Ball 75 cm	24-WG083-blue	$32.00
	✓	Sprite Stasis Ball 65 cm	24-WG082-blue	$27.00
	✓	Sprite Stasis Ball 55 cm	24-WG081-blue	$23.00

Once you have created your options and attached the associated products, you can save your product.

There are lots of great possibilities for how you can use bundled products in Magento. You should experiment, trying various configurations and settings to arrive at the ideal product setup for your needs.

Creating a downloadable product

In today's digital world, many online retailers offer files that can be purchased and downloaded, such as books, music, and software. Creating a downloadable product is achieved by attaching the files to the product. Once purchased, the customer will receive a link they can click to download their purchase to their computer.

Note that many downloadable products cannot be redeemed on mobile devices. Music, for example, may not always be able to be downloaded and played on a mobile device by clicking the redemption link. Please experiment and test your offerings so you know how to communicate any restrictions to your customers.

A downloadable product is created by making two initial selections:

- **Weight**: For the question "Does this have a weight?" you should select **No**.
- **Is this a downloadable Product?**: This box is checked to reveal the fields necessary to attach files that define your product.

In the **Downloadable Information** panel, there are two sections: **Links** and **Samples**. The **Links** section allows you to attach files that will be provided to customers once they purchase your products. The **Samples** section will provide linked files for shoppers to download as examples of what they will get when they buy the product. You can also use this section to attach files to promote the product.

When creating a downloadable product, you have controls over how easily it is for the customer to share their download link and how many times they can download their purchase. While these are not foolproof, they can help restrict the distribution of your digital products.

Creating a virtual product

A virtual product is just as it sounds: a product that doesn't actually exist, but can be purchased by the customer. Basically, a virtual product is one that has no weight and therefore cannot be shipped.

What kinds of product fall into this type? We've used the virtual product type for extended warranties, training courses, and hosting packages.

Managing inventory

If you sell actual products, you no doubt have inventory stock. Except in cases where you are having products drop-shipped from a distributor and have no means of monitoring inventory availability, you need to make sure you have enough inventory on hand to fulfill your orders. Furthermore, you may want to restrict customers' ability to order products that are out-of-stock — or, alternatively, allow customers to place backorders.

Magento has a host of configurations to help you establish your inventory rules and policies. Most can be overridden at the product level, too, giving you even more granular control over your product inventory needs.

 You can manage the individual inventory configurations of each product on the **Advanced Inventory** panel under **Advanced Settings**. These settings are very similar to the ones found in the **Stores** | **Configuration** | **Catalog** | **Inventory** panel.

The inventory configurations are covered in *Chapter 2, Installing Magento 2*. Here, let's discuss some additional tools in Magento that can help you manage your inventory.

Low stock notifications

One of the inventory configurations described in *Chapter 2, Installing Magento 2*, is that of **Notify for Quantity Below**. This value sets the threshold whereby Magento will send you an email notification if a product's inventory falls below this quantity. This notification will only come once each day for a given product. Using this feature can help you avoid running out of stock.

Product reports

Under the **Reports** menu in your Magento backend are several reports under the **Products** section. Use these reports regularly to help you monitor your inventory movements and plan your stock purchases. Let's have a look at these reports in brief:

 Before using reports, you may need to refresh Magento's statistics under **Reports** | **Refresh Statistics**.

- **Views**: This report shows the popularity of your products in terms of how often products are viewed by customers. If you have products that are often viewed but convert to few sales, you may want to evaluate pricing and content for possible improvements to encourage more sales.

- **Bestsellers**: Magento keeps track of the number of times products are sold and presents a list of these products to show you which are the most commonly purchased.

- **Low Stock**: With this report, you can list products that fall within a specified stock quantity. This is useful in planning your re-stocking purchases.

- **Ordered**: The ordered report shows for each given period (day, month, or year) how many of each SKU was purchased during the time span specified.

- **Downloads**: For downloadable products, this report shows how many times any digital file was downloaded by your customers.

Pricing tools

Many times we're faced with needing to manage special pricing for different customer groups or based on quantities purchased. Flexibility in pricing can help you meet the needs of your market and Magento gives you the tools necessary to accommodate those considerations.

Pricing by customer group

In *Chapter 4, Designs and Themes*, we learned how to create customer groups. You may, for instance, wish to offer discounted pricing for your wholesale customers — those who buy from you for resell to their customers. At the same time, you want to sell products at regular retail prices for your regular customers.

By creating a customer group — say "Wholesale" — and assigning select customers to that group, you can set up specific pricing for a product that will appear to customers who are logged into your store and are assigned to the particular customer group.

Let's use our green couch we created earlier as an example of how to configure pricing for a customer group. If we go to the **Product Detail** screen for this product and click on **Advanced Pricing** under the **Advanced Settings** menu in the left sidebar menu, we see a section called **Tier Price** (we will also refer to this section later when we discuss quantity-based pricing).

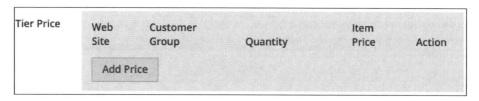

To add pricing for a customer group, click on **Add Price**. If we wish to set the price for this couch — normally selling for $599.99 — at $350.00 for our wholesale customer, we might configure this new entry as shown in the following screenshot:

Web Site	Customer Group	Quantity	Item Price	Action
All Websites [US ▼	Wholesale ▼	1 and above	350.00	Delete

With this configuration, any logged in customer who belongs to the wholesale customer group will see this couch priced at $350.00 on your store.

Quantity-based pricing

It's probably quite obvious now how you can create quantity-based — or **tiered**—pricing for your products using the same configuration tool. By adding additional pricing tiers and setting a new quantity value, you can create pricing that changes based on the number of items a customer purchases.

As an example, let's configure the pricing to show a price of $550.00 if a customer buys two-five couches and a price of $500.00 if they buy six or more. We will apply this to all customer groups.

[Be careful when using tiered pricing and multiple customer groups. Test your configurations carefully.]

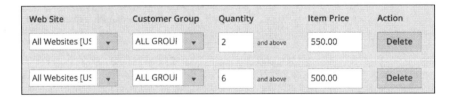

Web Site	Customer Group	Quantity	Item Price	Action
All Websites [US ▼	ALL GROU ▼	2 and above	550.00	Delete
All Websites [US ▼	ALL GROU ▼	6 and above	500.00	Delete

If we commit this pricing scheme, then when viewing the green couch in the store, we would see this pricing notice:

This notice may help stimulate higher purchased quantities by showing customers how much they can save buying more!

Autosettings

Before we leave our discussion of product creation and management, we need to discuss a special panel in the **Product Detail** screen: **Autosettings**. This panel is found in the **Advanced Settings** submenu.

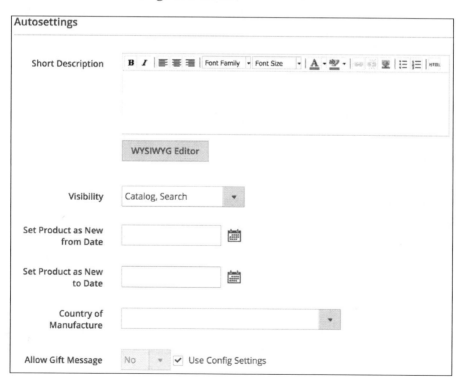

Let's go over the particular settings found on this panel. You'll find these can be valuable to your product presentation efforts.

- **Short Description**: The description you enter here will be used in category listings as a brief description of your product. In many themes, this description also appears at the top of the product detail page, usually below the title.

- **Visibility**: You can choose whether you want the product visible to customers within category listings (catalog), search results, or not at all. In our couch example, we might not want the individual color couches available outside of the configurable product; therefore, we would set this field to **Not Visible Individually**.

- **Set Product as New from Date/Set Product as New to Date**: In many themes, you can present new items in special display blocks or the word "New" might appear on the product listing. This trigger can be managed by setting from and to dates in these fields. If the current date falls within the dates used here (inclusive), then the product will be considered "New."

- **Country of Manufacture**: In our global economy, jurisdictions and regulations often require that a product's country of origin be presented to customers. This is not, by default, a required field, but you can use it to denote from where a product originates.

- **Allow Gift Message**: As described in *Chapter 2*, *Installing Magento 2*, you can allow customers to add gift messages to products purchased. These messages appear on the packing slip.

Related products, up-sells, and cross-sells

For each product you create in Magento, you have the opportunity to attract additional purchases from customers by linking products together. These crosslinks allow you to encourage shoppers to consider buying more products than the one they're reviewing. In the bricks-and-mortar world we're constantly bombarded with similar promotions. For instance, if you go into the grocery store, you'll often find small, red coupon machines hanging off the shelves, encouraging you by their flashing red light to pull a coupon out while you're reaching for the canned peaches you came for. Throughout the store, placards and banners promote "2-for-1" specials or "buy 1, get 1 free." The area around the checkout lane is crowded with magazines, razor blades, batteries and gum, put there to catch your eye just as you're about to leave the store.

In a similar fashion, Magento allows you, the store administrator, to encourage shoppers to spend more during their online visit using related products, up-sells, and cross-sells. All three types are managed within the **Product Detail** screen.

Each of the following product selling features are configured in the **Product Detail** screen under the **Advanced Settings** section. Each one has particular features and purposes.

Related products

Related products are those which you wish to present to customers as additional purchases to include when adding a viewed product to their shopping cart. In other words, if a customer is interested in product A, they may also want to purchase product B and product C at the same time.

As you can see, a customer may select one or more related items to include *with* the product they are currently viewing.

Upsell products

By contrast, upsell products are those to be considered as alternatives to the product the customer is viewing. That is, if the customer is interested in product A, they might instead consider product B. Not as an additional purchase, but instead of purchasing product A.

The manner in which related or upsold products are displayed on your store will depend on your theme. Consult your developer if you wish to change how these products are presented.

Cross-sell products

Cross-sell products are presented to your customer on the shopping cart page. For instance, if you want to encourage the purchase of an extended warranty, you could add it as a cross-sell product and it would be presented on the shopping cart. Your customer can add it to their order directly from the shopping cart.

Importing products

Creating products one-by-one is fine if you're only selling a few products, but many people choose Magento as a platform to sell hundreds and thousands of different products. Entering each product individually can take a long time, especially if you're writing unique product descriptions, uploading photos, and adding crosslinked products.

With Version 2.0.1, Magento has greatly improved the performance of product imports. In previous versions, importing thousands of products could take hours – literally. We once tried to import 19,000 products and the job took 20 hours to complete! The improvements to Magento importing have greatly decreased that time.

The shortcut to importing products

After spending hundreds of hours wrestling with the importing schemas of Magento over several versions of the platform, I'm happy to say that, starting with Version 2.0.1, there is one shortcut to helping you import products successfully.

Magento imports CSV files according to a specific layout scheme. Trying to configure an import file to accurately import a variety of different products, product types, attribute sets, and so on, will lead to many, many failed attempts as you try different ways of configuring the CSV to meet your needs. Therefore, my best advice is:

1. Enter at least one product into your store representing the different types (simple, complex, bundle, and so on) that you will be using.

2. Fully enter the data for each product, including all options. You don't have to upload images, however.

3. Go to **System | Import/Export | Export** in your backend.

4. Export a product CSV file to your computer using your browser (in previous Magento versions, this export would be placed on your server and you would have had to FTP to your server to retrieve it).

5. Open the downloaded CSV file in Excel or Numbers.

Now you can easily see how each type of product is configured in the export file. Using this format, you can easily add additional products, simply by following a similar pattern.

In the Magento 2.0.1 import interface, there is an option to download a sample file. This is a great step in the right direction and can be very helpful as a reference. Because this file only covers default products, though, we would suggest entering the type of product(s) you intend to sell into your store as described above to generate a more specific reference template.

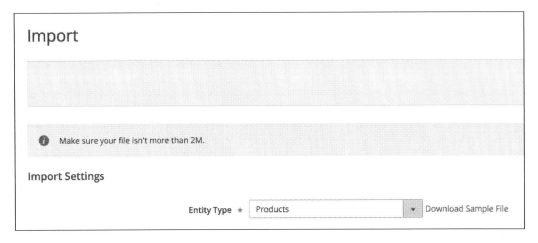

Notice that for products with various options, particularly configurable products, only the differences between each iteration are included on the rows below the main product row. Never repeat any other fields that are the same between variations. A unique SKU is required of each product, though. For configurable products, you'll need to include a **pipe delimited** list of the configurable SKUS and the attribute they vary by (in the example below, this is the **Color** attribute).

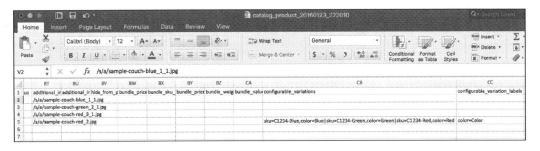

You don't need to worry about this for simple products, but if you do have a batch of configurable products it will really help to have a sample configurable product export file as a starting point.

To import images, you must upload the images to your server in the `/var/import` folder. If the `/var/import` folder doesn't exist, you can create it (or another of your directory) and specify it as part of the import process.

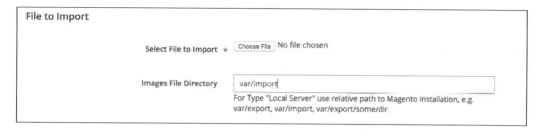

Put the name of the image file in the image columns of your import CSV file (don't include any path). Magento will pick the image out of the `/var/import` folder, resize it as needed, and store it within the `images/catalog` folder hierarchy. Never use capitals, spaces, or other strange characters in your image names; only the letters a through z, the numbers 0 through 9, and the underscore.

The most important thing to remember is to remove any unused columns before importing. For example, if you are not going to include categories in your import, leave that column out. This is especially important if you are re-importing or importing product updates. If you leave a column blank, then Magento will enter a blank value for that column in your product record. Oops!

Summary

Selling online begins with your products. Your products have to be presented well and in logical categories. Furthermore, Magento gives you additional, powerful tools for promoting your products to potential customers.

In this chapter, we learned how catalogs and categories relate to each other, and to your stores, and the different types of products that can be sold in a Magento store. We also went in-depth into how to create and manage attributes and attribute sets and discussed inventory management configurations. Finally, we learned a shortcut for configuring product imports.

Getting a handle on how the complexity of categories and products in Magento work is actually one of its greatest strengths and puts you in a better position to leverage the remaining topics in this book towards encouraging more sales from your visiting customers. Next, we turn our attention to grabbing attention: how to theme your Magento store.

4
Designs and Themes

Selling online, as with brick-and-mortar retailing, is more than simply having products to offer to customers. Buyers make purchases based on many things apart from the item itself. Customers want to understand the purpose of the retailer and have confidence that the seller is legitimate, safe, and honest. Corporations have spent billions over the years creating this understanding among their active and potential customers, through logos, design, copy, and service. Creating this understanding is called **branding**.

For an online store, branding is very important. However, unlike the offline shopper who drives to a store, parks, and enters the store to spend several minutes shopping; an online shopper may click to your online store, spend a few seconds to determine if they wish to remain, and leave to visit another website. Therefore, your store's brand—it's graphics, copy and function—must address the following in a matter of seconds:

- Does this online store have what I'm looking for? Can I easily find what they sell?

- Do I trust this seller if I've never heard of them before?

- Does the retailer make it easy for me to shop and purchase?

- Does it appear that the store owner is interested in helping me buy?

Magento gives you, or your client, the functional tools and systems to provide a powerfully rich shopping experience for your customers. It cannot, however, provide the branding aspects relating to design. You have to craft the outward appearance that will communicate to the potential buyer feelings of convenience, product selection, and security.

In this chapter, we will teach you:

- The Magento theme structure
- How to install third-party themes
- Creative translations
- Using theme variants
- How to customize themes to create your own unique look and feel
- Building theme packages

The Magento theme structure

In *Chapter 3, Managing Products*, we discussed the **Global-Website-Store**, or **GWS**, methodology. As we have learned, Magento allows you to customize many store aspects at some, or all, of the GWS levels.

The same holds true for themes. You can specify the look and feel of your stores at the Global, Website, or Store View levels (themes can be applied for individual Store Views relating to a store) by assigning a specific theme.

In Magento, a group of related themes is referred to as a design package. Design packages contain files that control various functional elements common among the themes within the package. By default, Magento Community installs one design package with two themes.

Themes within a design package contain the various elements that determine the look and feel of the site: layout files, templates, CSS, images, and JavaScript. Each design package must have at least one theme, but can contain other theme variants. You can include any number of theme variants within a design package and use them, for example, for seasonal purposes (such as holidays or back-to-school).

The following graphic shows the relationship between design packages and themes:

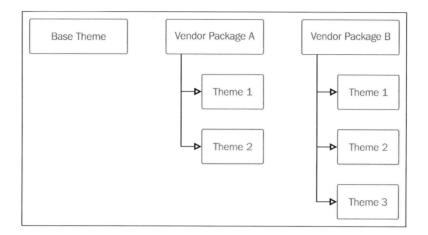

A design package and theme can be specified at the Global, Website, or Store levels.

Most Magento users will use the same design package for a website and all descendant stores. Usually, related stores within a website business share very similar functional elements, as well as similar style features. This is not mandatory; you're free to specify a completely different design package and theme for each store view within your website hierarchy.

A design package and theme can also be specified based on a per browser basis at the global and website level, by providing a **User-Agent Exception**. In the following example, the string for the Firefox browser is provided:

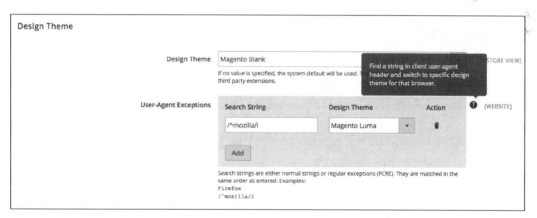

To be certain about the string used in the User-Agent Header, you can check `http://whatsmyua.com/` from the browser in question. This site will provide a very specific string you can use for the **Search String** field.

Magento 2 is a departure from Magento 1.x in that the `skin` directory used in Magento 1.x is absent, and the structure has been simplified. All files have been consolidated into one location, stored under the `/app` directory. Additionally, the `layout` and `template` directories from Magento 1.x have moved. Now, every module has its own `layout` and `template` directories in which you can access all template, layout, JS, and CSS/Less files.

Let's take a closer look at the new structure of a theme for Magento 2.0. The `theme` directory will typically include the files and directories visible in the following image:

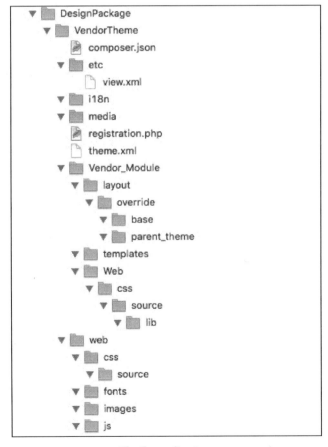

The theme directory

You may notice that in some default Magento 2.x builds, some themes are found in the `vendor/` directory. This indicates that a theme has been added via a composer dependency. We'll cover packaging your theme via composer later in the chapter. While Magento does check the `vendor/` directory for themes, you should never add a theme directly to this directory. When creating a new theme, always start in the `app/design/frontend/` directory.

Theme files and directories

In the new theme structure for Magento 2, all of the files related to design are in the preceding layout, under the `VendorTheme` directory. To clarify this new layout, we've provided a brief description of the role of each of the files and directories here:

- `/composer.json`: This file is not a required file, but you'll use it to describe the dependencies your theme has and metadata for your theme. This file is essentially for use if you intend your theme to be a `composer` package.

- `/etc/view.xml`: This file is required for a theme, but only if it doesn't already exist in a parent theme. We'll review parent themes later in this chapter as well. It includes information about product images and thumbnails.

- `/i18n`: This directory includes CSV translation files.

- `/media`: The `/media` directory contains a theme thumbnail, typically a screenshot of the theme that serves as a preview of the theme when it's being installed in the admin. This directory is required.

  ○ `/registration.php`: This file is required; it registers your theme within the system.

  ○ `/theme.xml`: Also mandatory, the `theme.xml` file declares the theme as a system component. It contains information about the theme like the theme name, the parent theme name, and so on.

- `/Vendor_Module`: This directory is the parent for module specific styles, and the naming convention is important. Magento will use it to determine which module it needs to apply the styles, layouts and templates to. If the module being overridden was the `Catalog` module, the directory would be `Magento_Catalog`. It is only required for modules that are being overridden.

  ○ `/Vendor_Module/layout`: This directory contains files that extend or establish module layouts. Layout files are XML that determines the position of blocks and containers on any given Magento page. We'll go into additional detail around layout files and the elements in them in the *customizing themes* section of this chapter.

- /Vendor_Module/layout/override/base: Files in this directory specifically override the default layouts for the module in question.

- /Vendor_Module/layout/override/parent_theme: Layout files in this directory specifically override the parent theme layouts for the module specified.

  - /Vendor_Module/templates: This directory contains template files that override either default or parent templates in place for this module. If there are custom templates for this module, they're stored in this directory as well. We'll review template files in greater detail in the *customizing themes* section.

- /web: This directory contains static files that can be loaded directly from the frontend. For example, if you wanted to reference a specific image, you could include it here, and you would be able to refer to it in a template file.

  - /web/css/source: This is the location where Less CSS configuration files for the theme are stored. Less is a CSS pre-processor that allows for variables and functions, making CSS for the theme more maintainable and extensible.

    - /web/css/source/lib: This directory contains files that extend or establish module layouts. Layout files are XML that determine the position of blocks and containers on any given Magento page. We'll go into additional detail around layout files and the elements in them in the *using themes to create your own look and feel* section of this chapter.

  - /web/fonts: This contains fonts specific to this theme. Everything in the web directory is static, so this folder is simply here for organizational purposes.

  - /web/images: This directory stores images specific to this theme.

  - /web/js: This location contains JavaScript specific to this theme. We'll talk more about how to insert JavaScript into a template in the *using themes to create your own look and feel* section.

The concept of theme inheritance

A very important aspect of Magento theming is the **fallback model**. Theme inheritance in Magento 2.x has been completely redesigned. The primary upshot of this is that unlimited fallbacks are supported and the default directory is no longer a part of the fallback mechanism.

The fallback order is slightly different for static assets (JavaScript, Less CSS, CSS) and templates, so we'll review both of these cases in detail. Before we explain the fallback order though, we'll need to begin with how parent themes are established in `theme.xml`.

Configuring a parent theme in theme.xml

This is new and central to the new theme fallback model. In any given theme, you have the option of identifying the parent theme. This is done in the `theme.xml` file, in the root directory of the theme. The following is an example of what text from a sample `theme.xml` file might look like:

```
<theme xmlns:xsi="http://www.w3.org/2001/XMLSchema-instance" xsi:noNam
espaceSchemaLocation="urn:magento:framework:Config/etc/theme.xsd">
    <title>Vendor Theme</title>
    <parent>Magento/luma</parent>
    <media>
        <preview_image>media/vendorpreview.jpg</preview_image>
    </media>
</theme>
```

As you can see, the parent theme is specified explicitly, and in this case it's the Magento Luma theme. That means that any files not found in the "Vendor Theme" theme will be pulled from the Luma theme. Any files not found there will, by default, be pulled from the Magento "Blank" theme, and if they're not found there, they'll be pulled from the module theme files.

Overriding static files

Static assets are content such as JavaScript files, CSS, images, fonts, and Less CSS files. Even though Less CSS files are not, technically speaking, static files, they produce the final CSS, so are categorized as such:

1. If the module context is not defined for a file, Magento will begin by checking the current theme's static files, in the `web` directory, `<theme_directory>/web/imagename.jpg`.

    ° If a match is not found there, it will recursively check the ancestor theme's static files until a theme with no parent is found.

    ° If there is still no match, Magento will check the library static view files in `lib/web/`.

2. If there is a module context established for a static file, the fallback is a little different. It will start with the current theme module's static files.

3. After this it will search for ancestors, again recursively, until a theme with no parent is found. Magento will then search module static files for the frontend area: `<module_dir>/view/frontend/web/`.

4. And finally the base area, `<module_dir>/view/base/web/`.

Overriding theme files

The fallback mechanism for theme files is simpler, because the module context is always known for them.

1. Magento starts by looking at the templates for the current theme in `<theme_dir>/<Namespace>_<Module>/templates`.

2. Next, Magento checks for ancestor templates until an ancestor with no parent is reached: `<parent_theme_dir>/<Namespace>_<Module>/templates`.

3. Finally, the module templates: `<module_dir>/view/frontend/templates`.

Here's a pictorial representation of the new fallback model in Magento 2.0. It's a little bit tricky, so we'll walk through each scenario represented here:

- In the case of **Vendor_Theme_1**, there is no parent declared in `theme.xml`, and there are no `module_override` files and there are no static override files. In this case, requests to the theme will fall back to the module theme files.

- In the case of **Vendor_Theme_2**, there is a module override, but no parent has been declared. Requests to the theme here will fall back to `magento_blank`, and subsequently the module theme files.

- **Vendor_Theme_3** and **Vendor_Theme_4** both have **Vendor_Theme_2** identified as a parent in the `theme.xml`, and have CSS overrides. In these cases, requests to the CSS will fall back to **Vendor_Theme_2**, and then `Magento_Blank`:

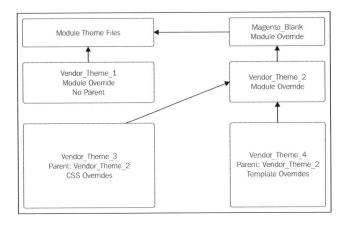

The fallback model is a tremendous shortcut for developers. When a new theme is created, it only has to contain those elements that are different from what is provided by the Parent or Module package files. For example, if all parts of a desired site design are similar to the Parent theme, except for the graphic appearance of the site, a new theme can be created simply by adding new CSS and image files to a new theme. Any new CSS files will need to be included in the local.xml file for your theme (we discuss the local.xml file later in this chapter). If the design requires different layout structures, only the changed layout and template files need to be created; everything that remains the same need not be duplicated.

If you're careful not to alter the magento_blank theme and default module theme files, then future upgrades to the core functionality of Magento will not break your installation. You will have access to the new improvements based on your custom design package or theme, making your installation virtually upgrade proof.

Default installation of design packages and themes

In a new, clean Magento Community installation, you are provided with the following design packages and themes:

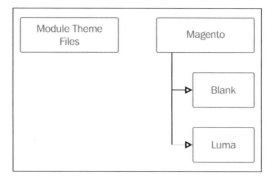

Depending on your needs, you could add additional custom design packages, or custom themes within the Magento design package:

- If you're going to install a group of related themes, you should probably create a new design package

- On the other hand, if you're only using one or two themes based on the feature of the Magento design package, you can install the themes within the Magento design package hierarchy

We like to make sure that whatever we customize can be "undone" if necessary. It's difficult for us to make changes to the core, installed files; we prefer to work on duplicate copies, preserving the originals in case we need to revert back. After re-installing Magento for the umpteenth time because we had altered too many core files, we learned this the hard way!

Your new theme hierarchy might now look like this:

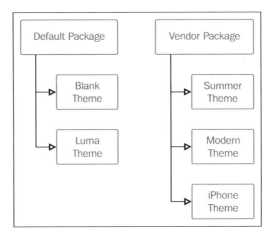

If you decide to use one of the installed default themes as the basis for designing a new, custom theme, duplicate and rename the theme to preserve the original as your fallback.

The Blank Theme

A default installed theme is called **Blank**. If the customization to your Magento stores is primarily one of colors and graphics, this is not a bad theme to use as a starting point. As the name implies, it's a pretty stark layout, as shown in the following screenshot. However, it does give you all the basic structures and components.

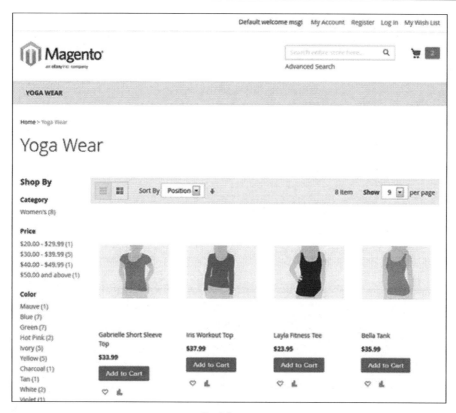

Stark layout

Installing third-party themes

In most cases, beginner level Magento users will explore the many available Magento themes created by third-party designers. While there are many free themes available, most are sold by dedicated designers.

Shopping for themes

One of the great good/bad aspects of Magento is third-party themes. The architecture of the Magento theme model gives knowledgeable theme designers tremendous abilities to construct themes that are virtually upgrade proof, while possessing powerful enhancements. Unfortunately, not all designers have either upgraded older themes properly or create new themes fully honoring the new 2.0 fallback model. If the older fallback model is still used for current Magento versions, upgrades to the base package could adversely affect your theme.

Therefore, as you review third-party themes, take time to investigate how the designer constructs their themes. Most provide some type of site demo. As you learn more about using themes, you'll find it easier to analyze third-party themes.

Most themes require that you install the necessary files manually, by FTP or SFTP, to your server. Every third-party theme I've ever used has included some instructions on how to install the files to your server. However, allow us to offer the following helpful guidelines:

- When using FTP/SFTP to upload theme files, use the merge function so that only additional files are added to each directory instead of replacing entire directories. If you're not sure your FTP client provides merge capabilities, or not sure how to configure for merge, you will need to open each directory in the theme and upload the individual files to the corresponding directories on your server.

- If you have set your CSS and JS files to merge under **Store | Configuration | Advanced | Developer**, you should turn merging off while installing and modifying your theme.

- After uploading themes or any component files (such as templates, CSS, images), clear the Magento caches under **System | Cache Management** in your backend.

- Disable your Magento cache while you install and configure themes. While not critical, it will allow you to see changes immediately instead of having to constantly clear the Magento cache. You can disable the cache under **System | Cache Management** in the backend.

- If you wish to make any changes to a theme's individual files, make a duplicate of the original file before making your changes. That way, if something goes awry, you can always re-install the duplicated original.

Inline translations

In *Chapter 2, Installing Magento 2*, we learned how to create Store Views in different languages. There's another very powerful tool available to store owners as well, whereby it's possible to provide translations manually. To enable the mode for editing/translating text, log into the administrative interface and visit **Store | Configuration | Advanced | Developer**. You'll see the option to translate inline, for the storefront and for the backend:

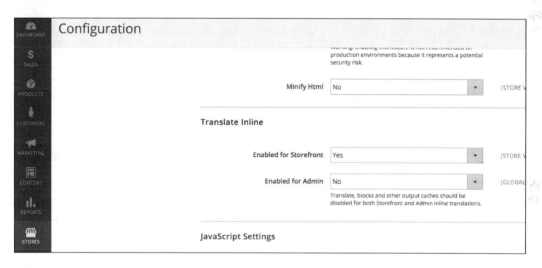

Enable this, and you'll be prompted to clear the cache, with a link to **System | Cache Management** to do so. Once the cache has been cleared, visit the front page of the site. You'll see red boxes around certain portions of the page. When you hover over these boxes, a dictionary will appear. When you click on this dictionary icon, you can provide inline translation that will be stored in Magento's translation database:

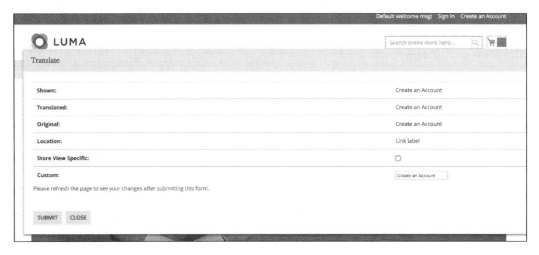

Working with theme variants

Let's assume we have created a new design package called `sportswear_package`. Within this design package, create a new theme and call it `sportswear_theme`. Our new design package file hierarchy, in `/app/design/`, might resemble the following hierarchy:

```
app/
    design/
        frontend/
            Magento/
                blank/
                luma/
            sportswear_package/
                sportswear_theme/
```

Because we want to use the blank theme as a starting point, the `theme.xml` in the root directory of our theme will look something like this:

```
<theme xmlns:xsi="http://www.w3.org/2001/XMLSchema-instance" xsi:noNa
mespaceSchemaLocation="../../../../../lib/internal/Magento/Framework/
Config/etc/theme.xsd">
    <title>Sportswear Theme</title>
    <parent>Magento/blank</parent>
    <media>
        <preview_image>media/preview.jpg</preview_image>
    </media>
</theme>
```

However, let's also take one more customization step here. We can create variations of a theme that are simply controlled by CSS and images by creating more than one skin. For "Sportswear", we might want to have our English language store in a blue color scheme, but our French language store in a green color scheme. We could take the sportswear_theme/ directory and duplicate it, renaming both for the new colors:

```
app/
  design/
    frontend/
      Magento/
        blank/
        luma/
      sportswear_package/
        sportswear_theme/
        sportswear_blue_theme/
        sportswear_green_theme/
```

Before we continue, let's go over something that is especially relevant to what we have just created.

For our sportswear theme, we created two skin variants: blue and green. However, what if the difference between the two is only one or two files? If we make changes to other files that would affect both color schemes, but which are otherwise the same for both, this would create more work to keep both color variations in sync, right?

Remember, with the Magento fallback method, if your site calls on a file, it first looks into the assigned theme, then the parent theme, the blank theme, and finally, the module-specific theme files. Therefore, in this example, you could use the sportswear_theme as a common parent to contain all files common to both blue and green. You would only need to include files or CSS impacting the color of these themes.

Assigning themes

As mentioned earlier, you can assign design packages and themes at any level of the GWS hierarchy. As with any configuration, the choice depends on the level you wish to assign control. Global configurations affect the entire Magento installation. Website level choices set the default for all subordinate Store Views, which can also have their own theme specifics, if desired.

Let's walk through the process of assigning a custom design package and themes. For the sake of this exercise, let's continue with our sportswear theme, as described earlier. If you recall from *Chapter 2, Installing Magento 2*, we created a sportswear website and store, with two Store Views for English and French:

Web Site	Store	Store View
Main Website	Main Website Store	Default Store View
Sportswear	active sportswear	English
Sportswear	active sportswear	french

We're going to now assign our sportswear theme to the sportswear **Website** and **Store View**. Our first task is to assign the design package and theme to the **Website** as the default for all subordinate **Store View**:

1. Go to **Stores | Configuration | Design** in your Magento backend.

2. In the **Current Configuration Scope** dropdown menu, choose **Sportswear**:

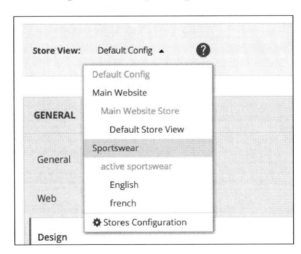

3. As shown in the following screenshot, enter the name of your design package, template, layout, and skin. You will have to uncheck the boxes labeled **Use Default** beside each field you wish to use.

4. Click **Save Config**:

The reason you enter **default** in the fields as shown above is to provide the fallback protection we described earlier. Magento needs to know where to look for any files that may be missing from your theme files.

Applying theme variants

Besides the obvious use of different themes within a package for different looks among Store Views, theme variants can be used to provide alternative frontend layouts based on date, such as holiday shopping season, or device, such as smartphone or tablet.

Scheduling a theme variant

It would be painful if changes that affect your public site content had to be manually turned on at the exact date and time you wished. For products, you can schedule price changes to automatically take effect between any two dates and times (you could have a one-hour sale price!) simply by adding the date/time configuration in the product detail screen.

Likewise, you can schedule changes in your stores' themes to take effect while you sleep! To schedule a theme variant based on a date:

1. Go to **Content | Design | Schedule** in your Magento backend.

2. Click on **Add Design Change**.

3. Select the Store View you wish to change.

4. Choose from the **Custom Design** drop-down for the theme variant you want.

5. Enter the **Date From** and **Date To** dates and times for the period of time you want the change to take effect.

6. Click on **Save**.

Customizing themes

I've never met a person yet that installed a theme and was ready to launch their Magento store without wanting or even needing changes made to the store design. It's natural, as a store needs to have its own personality and its own brand. In this section, we hope to uncover many of the mysteries of how Magento controls a store's look and feel through layered components that, once you understand how they work together, will give you a tremendous ability to make your Magento store a unique, productive online retail destination.

Finding CSS

While you can view the source code of a webpage in any browser, there are better ways of identifying not only the HTML elements of a page, but the exact CSS style(s) that are controlling how that component appears.

 For Firefox browsers, you can install the Firebug plugin (http://getfirebug.com). For Safari and Chrome users, this functionality is included with the browser. Another great tool for Firefox users is the Web developer add-on (https://addons.mozilla.org/pt-br/firefox/addon/web-developer/). These tools allow you to select an element on the page and view in another window, what the styling rules are that apply to the element. Once you know that, you can easily find the CSS style statement in the theme's CSS stylesheets and make any changes you wish.

Customizing layouts

Page layouts in Magento are managed by XML files that control how the various components on a page are to be assembled. Think of layout files as the blueprints of your site, in that they contain the instructions that direct how various content blocks and template files are combined to produce the structural blocks that define the final output.

Blocks are elements in Magento that are responsible for rendering a discreet piece of content to the page. For example, a product display, category list, user login area, all would likely have their own blocks. These blocks in turn reference template files to generate the HTML for any given area.

Let's take a visual look at how structural blocks and content blocks are combined on a typical page, by analyzing a category page captured from our sample data default installation:

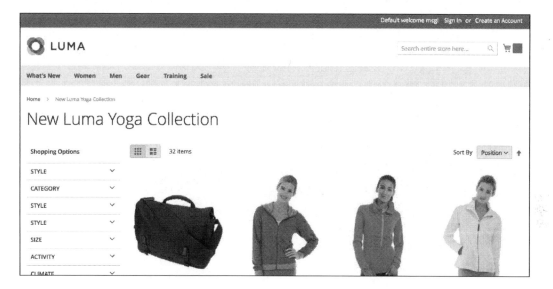

Now, let's look at this page with the structural blocks and content blocks shown inline:

To enable a view like this, that shows which blocks are being rendered on a page, you can visit **Stores | Configuration | Advanced | Developer** and enable template hints in the debug section:

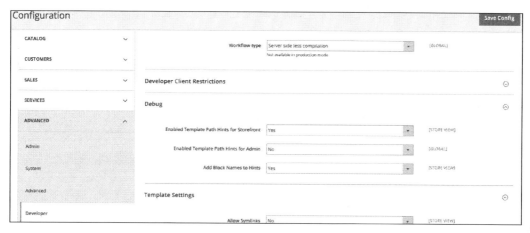

Enabling template path hints in Debug section

 Another less cluttered way to view which blocks and templates are included in any given page is to install the commerce bug extension for Magento 2.0. The extension was written by the exceptional Alan Storm, and can be found here: `http://store.pulsestorm.net/products/commerce-bug-3/`. As you can see in the following screenshot, the tabular section at the bottom of the page provides a much cleaner account of the blocks and templates being used on a page. If you plan to do any significant work with Magento 2 theming, this extension is well worth its cost.

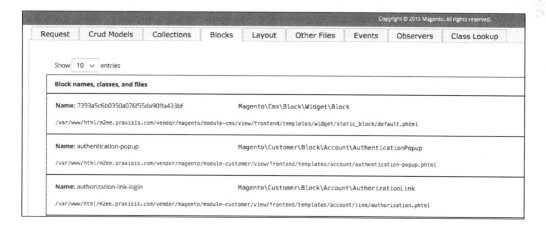

Expertly controlling layouts

Magento newcomers, particularly designers, feel a bit lost among the many layout and template files that comprise a Magento theme. However, with a bit of study (this book!) and adherence to a few best practices, anyone can become a Magento design aficionado.

First, keep in mind the concept of the Magento fallback method we previously covered. Layouts are dictated by the most forward layer. This means that if the chosen theme lacks a needed layout or template file, Magento will look into the default directory for the design package, then into the blank theme where, unless you've been naughty and changed anything, Magento will at last find any missing components.

As a designer, this means that you can change layout structures and blocks by creating or editing files within your theme directory, and focus on overriding any base theme behaviors. In short, a theme only has to have only those components that are different from the base design package.

I want to emphasize the enormity of this concept. When I wear my designer's hat, I don't have to replicate all the many layout and template files when creating a theme; I only have to include those most likely few files that will define the delta or difference between the base package and my new theme.

> This more robust fallback method (when compared to previous Magento versions) has not been completely absorbed by third-party theme producers. You may find some themes that have many files that really define no difference from the base package. This practice does not conform to Magento's best practices, as it can cause core Magento updates to not be properly reflected in the theme files. In general, we look for themes structures—whether third-party or home-grown—to add only those files necessary to provide the differences between the default layouts and the customized design.

When looking for a file to edit for your intended change, first look into your theme directory. If the file is not there, look to the parent or blank theme directories. If you find the file there, copy it into the same relative position within your theme directory.

Layout files control the various Magento modules, such as Sales, Customers, and Catalog, by using a layout XML file defining their structural blocks, content blocks, and functional components. Page layouts can be located in one of two spots:

- For module page layouts, you'll find them in the `<module_dir>/view/ frontend/page_layout` directory:

- In the case of layouts specific to a theme, you'll find them in the `<theme_ dir>/<Namespace>_<Module>/page_layout` directory:

Now, here's where it may get just a bit complex: each layout file contains **Layout Handles**, groups of block definitions that generally correspond with a type of page produced by Magento. Handles fall into three categories:

- The first is the **page type layout handle**, which corresponds to the controller actions. An example of this might be `catalog_product_view`.

- The second type of layout handle is the **page layout handle**. The page layout handle refers to identifiers of specific pages and corresponds to controller actions with arguments that specify particular pages, like `catalog_product_view_type_simple_id_128`.

- The third and most common type of handle is an arbitrary handle, which doesn't correspond to any page type but can be included by other blocks or containers.

To get a better understanding of handles, let's review an example handle. This is a handle from `/layout/catalog_category_view_type_default.xml`.

```
<page xmlns:xsi="http://www.w3.org/2001/XMLSchema-instance" xsi:noN
amespaceSchemaLocation="urn:magento:framework:View/Layout/etc/page_
configuration.xsd">
    <body>
        <referenceContainer name="sidebar.main">
            <block class="Magento\Catalog\Block\Navigation"
name="catalog.leftnav" before="-" template="navigation/left.phtml"/>
        </referenceContainer>
    </body>
</page>
```

From this code snippet, we can find out quite a bit about what it does to affect your layout:

`<referenceContainer>` tells us in what container the enclosed content is to be defined. For example, `<referenceContainer name="footer_links">` suggests that the output generated by the enclosed code will be placed within a block defined elsewhere as `footer_links`. We can use these references to modify where various elements may appear on a page, as we will explore a little later in this chapter.

As you look within each `<referenceContainer>` or `<referenceBlock>` tag, you'll typically find a `<block>` tag and corresponding `<argument>` tags. Here's the block reference from the preceding handle:

```
<block class="Magento\Catalog\Block\Navigation" name="catalog.leftnav"
before="-" template="navigation/left.phtml"/>
```

While it may appear to be a bit "inside-out", it is the `<block>` tag we are most interested in. The `<block>` defines the content. The `<referenceBlock>` tag merely designates where the content block is to be placed. We can change the `<referenceBlock>` tag without affecting the output of the content block.

The `<block>` tag also specifies a template file, in this case `left.phtml` that contains the HTML and PHP code defining the visual output for this block (not all blocks have related `.phtml` files, though).

The attributes for the `<block>` tag include:

- `type`: Defines the functional purpose of the block. Do not modify this.
- `name`: Used by other blocks as a reference to which the block is to be assigned.
- `before` and `after`: this attribute can be used to position the block before or after other referenced blocks that will be placed within the same referenced block. `before="-"` and `after="-"` position the block at the very top or very bottom of the referenced block.
- `template`: calls the template file that supplies the output functionality of the block.
- `action`: a subordinate tag that controls functionality, such as setting values, loading or unloading JavaScript, and more.
- `as`: the name which is used by templates to call the block. For example, `getChildHtml('left.permanent.callout')` would include the block within the template file.

 It's important to remember that like all XML tags, `<block>` tags must be closed. That is, the tag must either be matched with `</block>` or, where there are no child tags, closed with `/>`, such as in `<block name="call-out" />`

Using the reference tag to relocate blocks

In our previous example, the graphic callout defined by the `catalog.leftnav` block was designed to be placed within the left structural block, not by the name of the block, but rather by the `<referenceBlock name="left">` tag. The block could be named just about anything; it's the reference tag that dictates into which structural block on the page the block will be rendered.

If we wanted this block to be positioned within the right structural block, we simply change the reference tag to `<referenceBlock name="right">`. By using reference tags, we can position our content blocks into the general areas of the page. To refine the placement, we can use the block attributes of `before` and `after`, or call the block from within a template file using the `as` attribute.

Customizing the default layout file

Up to this point, we've discussed how, by copying and modifying a few files for your theme, you can change the appearance of various blocks within your layout file. This often-overlooked feature is perhaps one of the most powerful layout tools in your arsenal.

By creating a file called `default.xml` and placing it within the corresponding module directory of your theme, you can alter your layout by turning off any blocks defined by the base package `default.xml` file. In other words, if you don't need or want a specific block, you can simply tell Magento to ignore it or, in Magento-ese, remove it. You can also use the default layout file to reposition blocks (as we described previously) or re-define specific handles. In short, it's a great way to make changes to your layouts without having to get deep into the various layout files we discussed earlier.

The first step is to create a `default.xml` file, if one doesn't already exist, and place it within the `/app/design/frontend/[design package]/[design theme]/[module name]/view/frontend/layout/` directory. Add the following code to this text file:

```
<?xml version="1.0" ?>
<page>
  <!-- Put block overrides here -->
</page>
```

Within this small collection of code, you can add blocks and handles, as well as specialized statements. For example, to remove the callout block with which we have been working, add the following code between the `<page>` and `</page>` tags of your `default.xml` file:

```
<remove name="[block_name]" />
```

Just like that, the block is no longer appearing on your site.

The scope of possibilities for using the default layout file is quite extensive. As you begin exploring the use of this file, I would offer the following advice:

- Use the `<remove>` tag to completely disable blocks rather than removing them from layout files. If you don't have any other use for the layout file that contains the block, then you won't even have the need to copy it from the base package into your theme.

- Use `<action method="unsetChild">` to simply disable the block from the current layout, but allow it to be used in another position.

- If you want to modify a block or handle, copy it from the base package layout file and paste it into your `default.xml` file. Then make the changes you want to make. Again, this negates the need for replicating layout files, and it gives you a much quicker ability to make modifications and test them to see if they are behaving as you expected.

Summary

Creating the look and feel of a new Magento store is, for those designers among us, one of the most exciting aspects of creating a new website. However, as we have seen, to give store owners the level of power and functionality that Magento affords, designers can no longer build static HTML pages, slap in a bit of PHP, and upload to the server. With high levels of functionality come higher levels of architectural complexity.

Fortunately, the complexity of Magento is not nearly as daunting once you understand the methodologies of how pages are built, rendered, and styled. I struggled initially to fully understand this system. However, today I feel very comfortable navigating the design-related components of Magento, after taking the time to understand how it all pieces together. Today, you have the added advantage of a much improved architecture, as well as this book in your hands.

Hopefully, I've also shown you that in most cases, if you want an extensively customized theme, you really don't have to start from scratch. By using the existing default themes, or using a third-party theme, you can do some quite extensive customizations simply by modifying a few key files.

Experiment and have fun!

In this chapter, we explored the Magento theme architecture, learning how the Magento Fallback Method works to ensure our pages always have something to show. We also covered the installation and configuration of themes in the Magento 2 store structure and learned how to modify our themes by understanding the use of layouts, handles, and blocks. Finally, we were introduced to a very powerful tool—the default layout file.

You'll no doubt want to spend some time exploring the concepts of this chapter. I don't blame you. Just writing this chapter makes me want to dig into a new design!

When you're ready to move on, we will begin the process of configuring your store for what it is intended: to sell.

5
Configuring to Sell

If you've been following along, chapter by chapter, you've created a working, accessible online store front by now. Are you ready to take orders now?

Not just yet. There's still more to do before you can swing open the virtual doors to your new Magento store. Specifically, we need to:

- Understand the Magento sales process
- Configure the payment gateways to allow you to take online credit card payments
- Set up how your products will be shipped
- Configure sales tax rules
- Create customized outgoing e-mails

If you're the developer or designer of a Magento powered site, this is usually the time when you consult with your client – the store owner – to learn how they want to take payments, charge for shipping, and offer promotional discounts. Once you understand the concepts in this chapter, you'll be well prepared to ask the right questions.

For store owners and administrators, this chapter will give you insights into what can be managed with Magento. Fortunately, there are few limitations to Magento; however, we are consistently amazed at the various ways retailers price and vend their products. Hopefully, whatever unique selling programs you currently employ can be replicated online with your Magento store. We're betting they can.

The sales process

If you've shopped online before, you no doubt have some understanding of the usual online sales process:

1. You browse and find a product you want to purchase.
2. You "add" the product to your virtual shopping cart.
3. When you're finished shopping, you go to a checkout page.
4. In most online stores, you will first enter your billing and shipping addresses.
5. From this information, various shipping alternatives are presented, from which you choose the most appropriate for your needs and budget.
6. Next, you choose a payment method – usually a credit card – and enter your payment information.
7. After reviewing your order details, you commit to the purchase and moments later, you receive confirmation that your order has been processed. You usually receive an e-mail receipt of your purchase.
8. After a day or so, you receive another e-mail announcing that your order has been shipped. This e-mail may also include package tracking numbers so you can follow the progress of your package from distribution to doorstep.

The Magento sales process

Magento duplicates this sales process in pretty much the same way. For our purposes, though, we need to understand what happens after the customer commits to the order, for that is when the store administrator's participation is required.

The following chart illustrates both the frontend and backend steps of the Magento sales process:

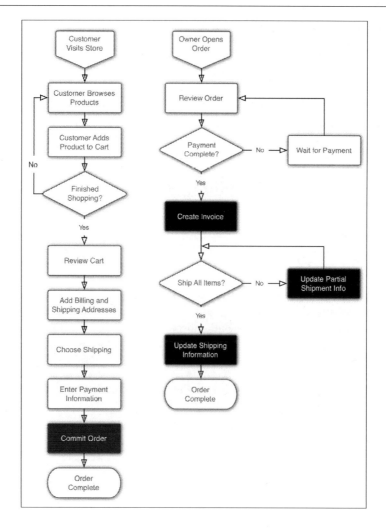

The black boxes with white type are steps that generally create an e-mail to the customer.

As we'll see in this chapter, there are occasional variations to this process, but in general, the Magento sales process is pretty straightforward. What you'll find impressive is the scope of Magento's ability to give you a wider latitude on adjusting the sales process to meet your particular needs. For instance, if you're selling downloadable products, such as e-books, music or software, you don't need the shipping process steps. Yet, if you sell proprietary digital media, you will need to manage the distribution of the products to your customers. For instance, to prevent unlimited downloads.

Managing backend orders

Before mapping out the business rules that you will use to configure Magento, it's helpful to see and understand how orders are processed in the Magento backend. Many times, developers and administrators new to Magento rush to configure the myriad of settings (which we will be covering in this chapter) without fully realizing how those choices might impact on the overall sales process. It's understandable because most will want to test the ordering system with all the settings in place. It's a bit of a catch-22: you have no orders to use to understand the configurations, yet without the configurations, you can't test the ordering process.

Fortunately, a basic Magento 2 install with the sample data (again with the sample data? Yes!) gives you the basic configurations to allow you to place some sample orders and review the order process.

Give it a whirl!

If you've installed the sample data, or you have a store already configured to accept some type of test payments, you should spend time placing and processing orders. Try any number of different combinations. Ask your colleagues to place dummy orders, imagining that they are actual shoppers. You'll soon get a real handle on the process, and if you're a developer, your client will certainly appreciate the added insight you have to the Magento ordering process. This is incredibly important to your client, so it should be important to you!

Logging into the Magento backend, we can see our latest orders listed in the left sidebar of the dashboard:

Last Orders		
Customer	Items	Total
Veronica Costello	1	$53.71
Veronica Costello	1	$37.00
Veronica Costello	1	$34.00

From here we can click on the **order** we wish to process, or we can go to **Sales | Orders** in the top navigation bar and then select the **order** from the list of all orders. Either way, we end up with a detailed view of the **order**.

Let's take each section of this screen separately and explain what each contributes to the ordering process.

Order & Account Information

Order # 000000003 (The order confirmation email was sent)

Order Date	Dec 6, 2015, 10:46:11 PM
Order Status	Complete
Purchased From	Sportswear Website / Sportswear Store / Sportswear English View

Account Information

Customer Name	Veronica Costello
Email	roni_cost@example.com
Customer Group	General

The first section, shown in the preceding image on the left, summarizes key order information, including the timestamp of the order (date and time), the current status (which by default is pending), and from which Magento store the purchase was made.

New orders, by default, are marked as **pending**. This means the **order** is awaiting your attention. The customer has already been charged and has received an e-mail confirmation of their order, but it's now up to you to complete the **order**, eventually taking it to a stage of complete.

The box on the right tells us the name of the customer, their e-mail address, and the fact that they checked out without registering (more on customer groups later in this chapter).

Address Information

Billing Address Edit

Veronica Costello
6146 Honey Bluff Parkway
Calder, Michigan, 49628-7978
United States
T: (555) 229-3326

Shipping Address Edit

Veronica Costello
6146 Honey Bluff Parkway
Calder, Michigan, 49628-7978
United States
T: (555) 229-3326

The next row of boxes shows the billing and shipping addresses for the purchaser. Notice that these are *editable*. Sometimes a customer, upon receiving their e-mail receipt, will see that they made an error in either or both of these. If the customer contacts you with corrected information, you can easily make the changes here.

Payment & Shipping Method

Payment Information

Check / Money order

The order was placed using USD.

Shipping & Handling Information

Flat Rate - Fixed $5.00

The third row of boxes give you information about the payment method and the buyer's choice of shipping for the order.

Items Ordered

Product	Item Status	Original Price	Price	Qty	Subtotal	Tax Amount	Tax Percent	Discount Amount	Row Total
Erika Running Short-32-Red SKU: WSH12-32-Red	Shipped	$45.00	$45.00	Ordered 1 Invoiced 1 Shipped 1	$45.00	$3.71	8.25%	$0.00	$48.71

On row four, you'll find the list of products ordered by the customer, the amount charged and the amount of sales tax applicable for each line item.

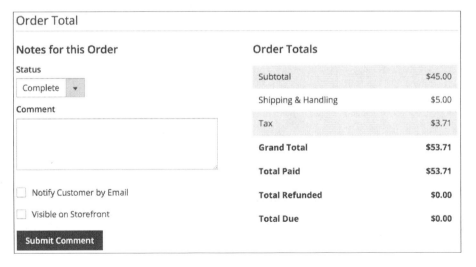

Order Total

Notes for this Order

Status

[Complete ▾]

Comment

[   ]

☐ Notify Customer by Email

☐ Visible on Storefront

[Submit Comment]

Order Totals

Subtotal	$45.00
Shipping & Handling	$5.00
Tax	$3.71
Grand Total	**$53.71**
Total Paid	**$53.71**
Total Refunded	**$0.00**
Total Due	**$0.00**

The final row of boxes are quite interesting and important. First, on the left in the preceding image, is how you can keep notes on an order and update the customer. Let's say, as in this case, that you have discovered that you only have one remaining chair and that more chairs won't arrive for another two weeks. By filling in this information here, and checking the **Notify Customer by Email** box, you can update the customer ("**Would you like us to hold your order, or cancel it?**") and have the update sent automatically to the buyer. Furthermore, by checking the **Visible on Storefront** box, the customer – if they are registered – can view the update in the **Account Information** section of your store.

All comments entered will be appended to the list at the bottom of the box.

The box to the right is the transaction summary of the order.

Convert orders to invoices

The next step for you, as the person who is processing orders, is to invoice this order. In Magento, this means that you are confirming the **order**, and proceeding with processing.

 You can go straight to shipping for an order without having to generate an invoice. However, it is good practice to go from **Order** to **Invoice** to **Shipping**. In this manner, you are tracking not only the products, but the payments, as well.

To convert an **order** into an invoice, click the button at the top of the page labeled **Invoice**. The resulting page is similar to the order page, except that it allows you to perform certain additional functions:

- **Create Shipment**: In the box titled **Shipping Information**, you can check the box labeled **Create Shipment** and add any tracking numbers to the invoice.

- **Change the Quantity of Products to Invoice**: As in our first example, if you have less products in stock than actually on hand, you may want to alter the number of products you are invoicing. Any remaining products will cause the order to remain open for future invoicing.

- **Add Comments**: As on the **Order** page, you can add a comment to the invoice and select whether the comment should be appended to the **Invoice**. Otherwise, the comment will be added to the order history.

Once you have made any of the preceding changes, you can click on **Submit Invoice**, which will convert the **order** to an invoice, and record the **order** as an actual **sale**. This is key, as your analysis of sales for your store rely on the analysis of invoices, not orders. If you have not shipped the items yet, the status of the order is now shown as **Processing**.

 Orders are not **Sales**. Invoices are **Sales**.

Now that we have converted an **order** into an **invoice**, the box on the **Dashboard** screen, titled **Lifetime Sales**, is now updated showing the total sales for the chosen period, less shipping and sales taxes, as shown in the following screenshot.

Lifetime Sales
$106.00

Average Order
$35.33

Creating shipments

Now that we have created our **invoice**, and once we have shipped the purchased products, we can create one or more **shipments**. To do this, open the **order** as before and click the **Ship** button near the top of the screen.

On this screen, you can add tracking numbers for your shipments, as well as indicate the quantity of each product shipped. In the following image, I have added a sample UPS tracking number. You can add as many as required (you may need to ship an order in more than one box, for instance).

Lower on the page, you will find each line item of the **order**, with a field allowing you to change the number of products shipped, as shown in the following screenshot:

Items to Ship		
Product	**Qty**	**Qty to Ship**
Olivia 1/4 Zip Light Jacket-L-Purple SKU: WJ12-L-Purple	Ordered 1 Invoiced 1	1
Erika Running Short-32-Red SKU: WSH12-32-Red	Ordered 1 Invoiced 1	1

Once you have made any changes, including adding any comments, you can click **Submit Shipment**. If you ship all ordered items, the status of the **order** will change to **Complete**; otherwise, the **order** will remain **Processing**.

Once you become familiar with the sales process, you'll have a much better understanding of how various system configurations affect how orders are moved through Magento.

Payment methods

In today's online retailing world, most purchasers use credit cards (or debit cards) as payment currency. Nothing new there. However, the process of taking someone's credit card online, verifying the card for available purchasing limit, and drawing the amount of the purchase from the buyer's account and into your bank account is one that remains a mystery to many. Of all the components that comprise online commerce, the process of moving money – in this case from the credit card account of the buyer to your bank account – remains one of the most complex of them all.

Without the ease of credit cards, online e-commerce might well be growing at a much slower pace. However, the use of credit cards – and the potential for misuse – concerns your shoppers, particularly when the press relates stories of hackers breaking into retailer databases. What is important is that online purchases have never been "hacked." That is, no one has been prosecuted for stealing credit card information used to buy online as long as the store is using SSL encryption. To ease consumers' fears, several payment systems have evolved over the past decade, each designed to help you process the financial transactions for your store, while providing the increased security and processes necessary to give both you and your buyer a safer, easier transaction process.

As a Magento administrator, you have within Magento, several default payment systems available based on your own needs. Each one requires that the store owner enrolls and qualifies, but, having done so, allows the store to provide buyers with a convenient, secure means of paying for their purchase.

In this section, we will cover the most common, popular payment systems and how they work with Magento. This is intended to familiarize you with how each system interacts with Magento, the buyer, and the store owner. Once you understand how they work, you will be able to decide on which system(s) you want to employ, which also makes configuring Magento easier.

PCI compliance

The protection of your customer's payment information is extremely important. Not only would a breach of security cause damage to your customer's credit and financial accounts, but the publicity of such a breach could be devastating to your business.

Merchant account providers will require that your store meet stringent guidelines for PCI compliance, a set of security requirements called **Payment Card Industry Data Security Standard (PCI DSS)**. Your ability to be PCI compliant is based on the integrity of your hosting environment and by which methods you allow customers to enter credit card information on your site.

Magento 2 no longer offers a "stored credit card" payment method. It is highly unlikely that you could — or would want to — provide a server configuration secure enough to meet PCI DSS requirements for storing credit card information. You probably don't want the liability exposure, either.

You can, however, provide SSL encryption that could satisfy PCI compliance as long as the credit card information is encrypted before being sent to your server, and then from your server to the credit card processor. As long as you're not storing the customer's credit card information on your server, you can meet PCI compliance as long as your hosting provider can assure compliance for server and database security.

 Even with SSL encryption, not all hosting environments will pass PCI DSS standards. It's vital that you work with a hosting company that has real Magento experience and can document proof of PCI compliance.

Therefore, you should decide whether to provide onsite or offsite credit card payments. In other words, do you want to take payment information within your Magento checkout page or redirect the user to a payment service, such as PayPal, to complete their transaction?

There are pros and cons of each method. Onsite transactions may be perceived as less secure and you do have to prove PCI compliance to your merchant account provider on an ongoing basis. However, onsite transactions mean that the customer can complete their transaction without leaving your website. This helps to preserve your brand experience for your customers.

Fortunately, Magento is versatile enough to allow you to provide both options to your customers. Personally, we feel that offering multiple payment methods means you're more likely to complete a sale, while also showing your customers that you want to provide the most convenience in purchasing.

Let's now review the various payment methods offered by default in Magento 2.

Magento 2 comes with a host of the most popular and common payment methods. However, you should review other possibilities, such as **Amazon Payments**, **Stripe**, and **Moneybookers**, depending on your target market. We anticipate that developers will be offering add-ons for these and other payment methods.

Note that as you change the **Merchant Location** at the top of the **Payment Methods** panel, the payment methods available to you may change.

Classes of payment systems

The determination of which payment system to utilize in your Magento store is driven by a comparison of pros and cons (isn't everything in life?). In terms of credit card sales, there are two basic classifications of payment systems: **off-site** and **on-site**.

Off-site payment systems

Off-site systems allow buyers to make purchase choices, but pay for their order on another website which offers the buyer a sense of greater security and fraud protection. The buyer is actually paying the off-site payment provider, who in turn pays the store owner once there is sufficient verification that the order has been processed and shipped. Each system has different degrees of verification based on the type of products sold, the history of the merchant (for example, has there been previous problems with the merchant's reliability?), and the amount of the purchase.

Pros

The pros of this type of payment method are as follows:

- Provides extra layer of protection to buyers against unscrupulous merchants.
- Quick merchant approval. No credit report is required.
- No PCI compliance requirements.
- Easy integration into almost any e-commerce platform.

Many buyers prefer these systems because of the added layer of protection against merchants who fail to deliver the expected results.

Additionally, the off-site system qualifies the merchant as opposed to a merchant account provider or bank. For first-time e-commerce merchants, this qualification is usually easier to obtain, as no credit report is required.

Cons

The cons of this type of payment method are as follows:

- Takes buyers off your e-commerce site
- May require the buyer to enroll in a third-party payment system
- Merchant has limited access to buyer information, including e-mail addresses

The dominant off-site systems are **PayPal Express, PayPal Standard,** and **Authorize. net Direct Post**.

On-site payment systems

Almost any well-developed e-commerce store will allow buyers to pay directly on the site without having to go off-site to another payment system. While most will also provide off-site payment alternatives, by providing an on-site payment process, the merchant eliminates any reluctance the buyer may have to enroll in a third-party payment system.

Pros

The pros of this type of payment method are as follows:

- Keeps the buyer on the site, surrounded by the merchant's branding design
- Eliminates the need for the buyer to register or enroll with an outside payment system
- Gives the merchant access to all buyer information for follow-up, processing, and future marketing

In order to succeed with on-site payment systems, merchants need to consider design elements and payment system brands that will help buyers have confidence in the security of the payment process. Most buyers have no history with new merchants; therefore, merchants, if they wish to offer on-site payments, should pay special attention to methods of communicating the security of the buyer's information.

Cons

The cons of this type of payment method are as follows:

- Requires a merchant banking account, which can be difficult to obtain for new businesses
- Site may be subject to PCI compliance
- Integration with e-commerce platforms is more complex

Off-site payments are processed through gateways. Gateways accept the customer payment information, as well as the order total, by means of a secure connection between your store server and the gateway's servers. The gateway validates the buyer's information and returns a result of success or error, which your store platform processes accordingly.

PayPal

Today, PayPal remains one of the most popular payment systems in the world because it does allow for global purchases. You can sell to buyers in other countries, as long as they have a PayPal account, knowing that you will receive payment. Most regular merchant accounts, such as those used by bricks and mortar retailers, restrict sales to only buyers with cards issued by US banks.

In the past, the downside to using PayPal was that buyers would have to sign up for PayPal if you, the merchant, offered it as a payment system. That changed some years ago: today your buyers don't have to sign up for PayPal. They can purchase using a credit card without enrolling.

PayPal all-in-one payment solutions

While PayPal is commonly known for their quick and easy PayPal Express, PayPal can provide you with credit and debit card solutions that allow customers to use their cards without needing a PayPal account. To the customer, the Magento checkout appears no different than if they were using a normal credit card checkout process.

The big difference is that you have to set up a business account with PayPal before you can begin accepting non-PayPal account payments. Proceeds will go almost immediately into your PayPal account (you have to have a PayPal account), but your customers can pay by using a credit/debit card or their own PayPal account.

With the all-in-one solution, PayPal approves your application for a merchant account and allows you to accept all popular cards, including American Express, at a flat 2.9% rate, plus $0.30/transaction. PayPal payments incur normal per transaction PayPal charges.

PayPal provide two ways to incorporate credit card payment capture on your website:

- **PayPal Payments Advanced** inserts a form on your site that is actually hosted from PayPal's highly secure servers. The form appears as part of your store, but you don't have any PCI compliance concerns.
- **PayPal Payments Pro** allows you to obtain payment information using the normal Magento form, then submits it to PayPal for approval.

The difference to your customer is that for Advanced, there is a slight delay while the credit card form is inserted into the checkout page. You may also have some limitations in terms of styling.

PayPal Standard, also a part of the all-in-one solution, takes your customer to a PayPal site for payment. Unlike PayPal Express, however, you can style this page to better reflect your brand image. Plus, customers do not have to have a PayPal account in order to use this checkout method.

PayPal payment gateways

If you already have a merchant account for collecting online payments, you can still utilize the integration of PayPal and Magento by setting up a PayPal business account that is linked to your merchant account. Instead of paying PayPal a percentage of each transaction — you would pay this to your merchant account provider — you simply pay a small per transaction fee.

PayPal Express

Offering PayPal Express is as easy as having a PayPal account. It does require some configurations of API credentials, but it does provide the simplest means of offering payment services without setting up a merchant account.

PayPal Express will add **Buy Now** buttons to your product pages and the cart page of your store, giving shoppers quick and immediate ability to checkout using their PayPal account.

Braintree

PayPal recently acquired Braintree, a payment services company that adds additional services to merchants. While many of their offerings appear to overlap PayPal's, Braintree brings additional features to the marketplace such as **Bitcoin**, **Venmo**, **Android Pay,** and **Apple Pay** payment methods, **recurring billing,** and **fraud protection**. Like PayPal Payments, Braintree charges 2.9% + $0.30/transaction.

Check/money order

If you have customers for whom you will accept payment by check and/or money order, you can enable this payment method. Be sure to enter all the information fields, especially **Make Check Payable to** and **Send Check to**. You will most likely want to keep the **New Order Status** as **Pending,** which means the order is not ready for fulfillment until you receive payment and update the order as **Paid**.

As with any payment method, be sure to edit the **Title** of the method to reflect how you wish to communicate it to your customers. If you only wish to accept money orders, for instance, you might change **Title** to **Money Orders (sorry, no checks)**.

Bank transfer payment

As with check/money order, you can allow customers to wire money to your account by providing information to your customers who choose this method.

Cash on delivery payment

Likewise, you can offer COD payments. We still see this method being made available on wholesale shipments, but very rarely on B2C (business-to-consumer) sales. COD shipments usually cost more, so you will need to accommodate this added fee in your pricing or shipping methods. At present, there is no ability to add a COD fee using this payment method panel.

Zero subtotal checkout

If your customer, by use of discounts or credits, or selecting free items, owes nothing at the checkout, enabling this method will cause Magento to hide payment methods during checkout. The content in the **Title** field will be displayed in these cases.

Purchase order

In B2B (business-to-business) sales, it's quite common to accept **purchase orders** (PO's) for customers with approved credit. If you enable this payment method, an additional field is presented to customers for entering their PO number when ordering.

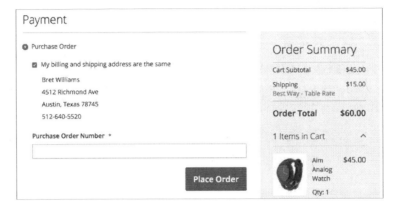

Authorize.net direct post

Authorize.net — perhaps the largest payment gateway provider in the USA — provides an integrated payment capture mechanism that gives your customers the convenience of entering credit/debit card information on your site, but the actual form submission bypasses your server and goes directly to Authorize.net. This mechanism, as with PayPal Payments Advanced, lessens your responsibility for PCI compliance as the data is communicated directly between your customer and Authorize.net instead of passing through the Magento programming.

Shipping methods

Once you get paid for a sale, you need to fulfill the order and that means you have to ship the items purchased. How you ship products is largely a function of what shipping methods you make available to your customers.

Shipping is one of the most complex aspects of e-commerce, and one where you can lose money if you're not careful. As you work through your shipping configurations, it's important to keep in mind the following:

- What you charge your customers for shipping does not have to be exactly what you're charged by your carriers. Just as you can offer free shipping, you can also charge flat rates based on weight or quantity, or add a surcharge to "live" rates.

- By default, Magento does not provide you with highly sophisticated shipping rate calculations, especially when it comes to "dimensional" shipping. Consider shipping rate calculations as *estimates* only. Consult with whomever is actually doing your shipping to determine if any rate adjustments should be made to accommodate dimensional shipping.

> **Dimensional shipping** refers to a recent change by UPS, FedEx, and others to charge you the greater of two rates: the cost based on weight or the cost based on a formula to determine the equivalent weight of a package based on its size: (Length x Width x Height) ÷ 166 (for US domestic shipments; other factors apply for other countries and exports). Therefore, if you have a large package that doesn't weigh much, the live rate quoted in Magento might not be reflective of your actual cost once the dimensional weight is calculated. If your packages may be large and lightweight, consult your carrier representative or shipping fulfillment partner for guidance.

- If your shipping calculations need more sophistication than provided natively in Magento 2, consider an add-on. However, remember that what you charge to your customers does *not* have to be what you pay. For that reason — and to keep it simple for your customers — consider offering table rates (as described later).

> WebShopApps (`http://webshopapps.com`) is perhaps the pre-eminent Magento shipping add-on provider. More recently, they have created a hosted shipping configuration system called ShipperHQ (`https://shipperhq.com`), which we have used to configure some rather complex shipping rules. If your shipping rules are more than Magento can natively accommodate, you may want to check these out.

- Each method you choose will be displayed to your customers if their cart and shipping destination matches the conditions of the method. Take care not to confuse your customers with too many choices: simpler is better.

Keeping these insights in mind, let's explore the various shipping methods available by default in Magento 2.

Before we go over the shipping methods, let's go over some basic concepts that will apply to most, if not all, shipping methods.

Origin

Where you ship your products from will determine shipping rates, especially for carrier rates (for example, UPS, FedEx). To set your origin, go to **Stores | Configuration | Sales | Shipping Settings** and expand the **Origin** panel. At the very least, enter the **Country**, **Region/State** and **ZIP/Postal Code** field. The others are optional for rate calculation purposes.

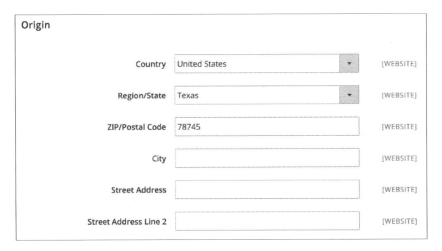

At the bottom of this panel is the choice to **Apply Custom Shipping Policy**. If enabled, a field will appear where you can enter text about your overall shipping policy. For instance, you may want to enter **Orders placed by 12:00 PM CT will be processed for shipping on the same day. Applies only to orders placed Monday-Friday, excluding shipping holidays.**

Handling fee

You can add an *invisible* handling fee to all shipping rate calculations. Invisible in that it does not appear as a separate line item charge to your customers. To add a handling fee to a shipping method:

- Choose whether you wish to add a fixed amount or a percentage of the shipping cost
- If you choose to add a percentage, enter the amount as a decimal number instead of a percentage (for example, 0.06 instead of 6%)

Allowed countries

As you configure your shipping methods, don't forget to designate to which countries you will ship. If you only ship to the US and Canada, for instance, be sure to have only those countries selected. Otherwise, you'll have customers from other countries placing orders you will have to cancel and refund.

Method not available

In some cases, the method you configured may not be applicable to a customer based on destination, type of product, weight, or any number of factors. For these instances, you can choose to:

- Show the method (for example, UPS, USPS, DHL, and so on), but with an error message that the method is not applicable
- Don't show the method at all

Depending on your shipping destinations and target customers, you may want to show an error message just so the customer knows why no shipping solution is being displayed. If you don't show any error message and the customer disqualifies for any shipping method, the customer will be confused.

Free shipping

There are several ways to offer free shipping to your customers. If you want to display a **Free Shipping** option to all customers whose carts meet a minimum order amount (not including taxes or shipping), enable this panel.

However, you may want to be more judicious in how and when you offer free shipping. Other alternatives include:

- Creating shopping cart promotions (see *Chapter 7, Marketing Tools*)
- Include a free shipping method in your table rates (see later in this section)
- Designate a specific free shipping method and minimum qualifying amount within a carrier configuration (such as UPS and FedEx).

If you choose to use this panel, note that it will apply to all orders. Therefore, if you want to be more selective, consider one of the above methods.

Flat rate

As with free shipping, above, the **Flat Rate** panel allows you to charge one, singular flat rate for all orders regardless of weight or destination. You can apply the rate on a per item or per order basis, as well.

Table rates

While using live carrier rates can provide more accurate shipping quotes for your customers, you may find it more convenient to offer a series of rates for your customers at certain break points.

For example, you might only need something as simple as follows, for any domestic destination:

- 0-5 lbs, $5.99
- 6-10 lbs, $8.99
- 11+ lbs, $10.99

Let's assume you're a US-based shipper. While these rates will work for you when shipping to any of the contiguous 48 states, you need to charge more for shipments to Alaska and Hawaii. For our example, let's assume tiered pricing of $7.99, $11.99, and $14.99 at the same weight breaks.

All of these conditions can be handled using the table rates shipping method. Based on our example, we would first start by creating a spreadsheet (in Excel or Numbers) similar to the following:

Country	Region/State	Zip/Postal code	Weight (and above)	Shipping price
USA	*	*	0	5.99
USA	*	*	6	8.99
USA	*	*	11	10.99
USA	AK	*	0	7.99
USA	AK	*	6	11.99
USA	AK	*	11	14.99
USA	HI	*	0	7.99
USA	HI	*	6	11.99
USA	HI	*	11	14.99

Let's review the columns in this chart:

- **Country**: Here, you would enter the three-character country code (for a list of valid codes, see `http://goo.gl/6A1woj`).

- **Region/State**: Enter the two-character code for any state or province.

- **Zip/Postal code**: Enter any specific postal codes for which you wish the rate to apply.

- **Weight (and above)**: Enter the minimum applicable weight for the range. The assigned rate will apply until the weight of the cart products combined equals a higher weight tier.

- **Shipping price**: Enter the shipping charge you wish to provide to the customer. Do not include the currency prefix (for example, "$" or "€").

Now, let's discuss the asterisk (*) and how to limit the scope of your rates. As you can see in the chart, we have only indicated rates for US destinations. That's because there are no rows for any other countries. We could easily add rates for *all other countries*, simply by adding rows with an asterisk in the first column. By adding those rows, we're telling Magento to use the US rates if the customer's ship-to address is in the US, and to use other rates for all other country destinations.

Likewise for the **Region/State** column, Magento will first look for matches for any state codes listed. If it can't find any, then it will look for any rates with an asterisk. If no asterisk is present for a qualifying weight, then no applicable rate will be provided to the customer.

The asterisk in the **Zip/Postal code** column means that the rates apply to all postal codes for all states.

> To get a sample file with which to configure your rates, you can set your configuration scope to one of your websites (furniture or sportswear in our examples) and click **Export CSV** in the **Table Rates** panel.

Quantity- and price-based rates

In the above example, we used the weight of the items in the cart to determine shipping rates. You can also configure table rates to use calculations based on the number of items in the cart or the total price of all items (less taxes and shipping).

To set up your chart, simply rename the fourth column **Quantity (and above)** or **Subtotal (and above)**.

Save your rate table

To upload your table rates, you'll need to save/export your spreadsheet as a CSV file. You can name it whatever you like. Save it to your computer where you can find it for the next steps.

Table rate settings

Before you upload your new rates, you should first set your table rates configurations. To do so, you can set your default settings at the default configuration scope. However, to upload your CSV file, you will need to switch your store view to the appropriate website scope.

When changing to a website scope, you will see the **Export CSV** button and the ability to upload your rate table file. You'll note that all other settings may have **Use Default** checked. You can, of course, uncheck this box beside any field and adjust the settings according to your preferences.

Let's review the unique fields in this panel:

- **Enabled**: Set to **Yes** to enable table rates
- **Title**: Enter the name you wish displayed to customers when they're presented with a table rate-based shipping charge in the checkout process
- **Method Name**: This name is presented to the customer in the shopping cart

You should probably change the default Table Rate to something more descriptive, as this term is likely irrelevant to customers. We have used terms Standard Ground, Economy, or Saver as names. The **Title** should probably be the same, as well, so that the customer, during checkout, has a visual confirmation of their shipping choice.

- **Condition**: This allows you to choose the calculation method you want to use. Your choices, as we described earlier, are Weight vs. Destination, Price vs. Destination, and # of items vs. Destination.

- **Include Virtual Products in Price Calculation**: Since virtual products (see *Chapter 3, Managing Products*) have no weight, this will have no effect on rate calculations for weight-based rates. However, it will affect rate calculations for price or quantity-based rates.

Once you have your settings, click on **Save Config**.

Upload rate table

Once you have saved your settings, you can now click the button next to **Import** and upload your rate table. Be sure to test your rates to see that you have properly constructed your rate table.

Carrier methods

The remaining shipping methods involve configuring UPS, USPS, FedEx, and/or DHL to provide "live" rate calculations. UPS is the only one that is set to query for live rates *without* the need for you to have an account with the carrier. This is both good and bad. It's good, as you only have to enable the shipping method to have it begin querying rates for your customers. On the flip side, the rates that are returned are not negotiated rates. Negotiated rates are those you may have been offered as discounted rates based on your shipping volume.

FedEx, USPS, and DHL require account-specific information in order to activate. This connection with your account should provide rates based on any discounts you have established with your carrier. If you wish to use negotiated rates for UPS, you may have to find a Magento add-on that will provide a modified rate query.

Managing taxes

The great unavoidable factor: taxes. If you're a retailer — and even as a wholesaler in some jurisdictions — you will need to master the management of tax rates and rules in your Magento store. We've had to deal with this issue on many other platforms, and while some do provide some cool features, none, in our opinion, offer as much flexibility for taxes as Magento; especially when it comes to VAT taxes.

You'll appreciate as you go through this section, that taxes can be quite complicated. Before configuring taxes in your online store, you should consult your tax professional. Making errors in taxes can not only present legal issues for your business, but also erode consumer confidence if the customers feel they're being inappropriately taxed on purchases.

How Magento manages taxes

Taxes are applied to products based on assigned **tax classes**. Tax classes are combined with **tax zones and rates** to create **tax rules**. Tax rules are what are applied to each product or shopping cart to determine the amount of tax charged in a transaction.

Here's a flow chart on how Magento calculates sales taxes based on a tax rule:

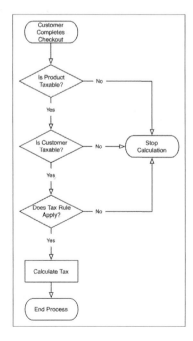

There are two types of tax classes in Magento:

- **Product tax class**: A product is usually considered taxable or non-taxable. If a product is not to be taxed, a value of None is selected for its tax class. You may find it necessary to have different product tax classes if you have different taxing rules for different products.
- **Customer tax class**: As we saw in creating customer groups, customers are assigned to a tax class, usually based on whether they are retail or wholesale customers.

Creating tax rules

Tax rules are created based on jurisdiction and rate: creating a zone for a country, state, and/or zip code, and a percentage used to calculate the tax.

To illustrate, let's review a tax rule included in the default installation for Magento 2:

1. Go to **Stores | Tax Rules** in your Magento backend.
2. Click on **Rule 1** listed in the tax rules table.

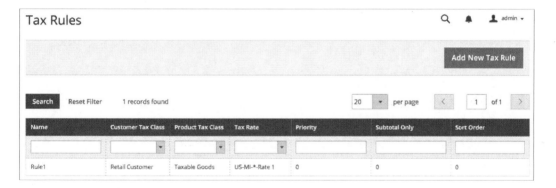

Let's now take a look at the layout of a tax rule:

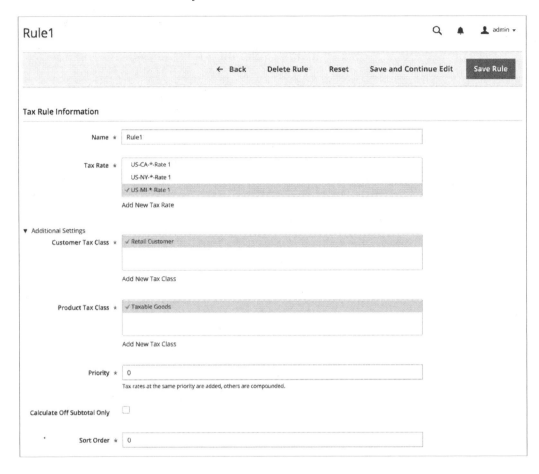

- **Name**: While Rule 1 is fine, it's not really descriptive, particularly in a list of rules. You can name the rule whatever you feel works best for you.

- **Tax Rate**: This field allows you to select one or more rates you want to apply to the rule. You might have to apply several tax rates if you have multiple distribution locations or nexuses. The rate is determined by the location of the buyer, usually their *Ship To* address.

> A **nexus** is generally considered if you have an active business in a particular state or locality. For instance, if your office is in Texas and you ship your products from a warehouse in Illinois, then, for taxing purposes, you're considered to have a nexus in Texas and Illinois. Therefore, as it stands at this moment, you are required to collect sales tax on any sales to buyers in Texas and Illinois. However, there are efforts in the United States Congress to radically change taxing laws on online sales transactions. Some state legislatures are also grappling with this issue. We know you're used to hearing this, but you do need to consult a tax professional to make sure you're correctly charging sales tax.
>
> A leader in e-commerce sale tax is TaxJar (`https://www.taxjar.com`), a company that can provide integration with your store to precisely calculate required sales taxes and help with reporting to the various taxing jurisdictions. Using a tool such as TaxJar could greatly reduce your tax configuration time, while providing greater sales tax accuracy.

You can add or edit tax rates here or under **Stores | Tax Zones and Rates**. Let's edit the California tax rate here to understand the process:

To the right of the **US-CA-*-Rate 1** item name, when you hover your mouse over the item, you will see a pencil icon. Click this to reveal the tax rate modal dialogue.

Let's have a look at the various fields here:

- **Tax Identifier**: You can enter whatever you wish in this space. The naming scheme shown was created by Magento in setting up this default rate.

- **Zip/Post is Range**: By checking this box, the **Zip/Post Code** field is replaced by range fields, into which you can enter a starting and ending code range. This is particularly useful if you need to apply a different rate to a range of zip codes within a larger region.

- **Zip/Post Code**: As indicated, an asterisk is considered a wild card. That is, any value will match. If you want to, for example, apply the rate to all zip codes beginning in 78 (for example, 78001, 78002, and so on), you could enter 78*.

- **State**: Select the state for which the rate applies. The selections will change based on your country selection. An asterisk in this selection will apply the rate to all states and regions within the country.

- **Country**: Select the country for which the rate applies.

- **Rate Percent**: Enter the rate to be applied as a percentage amount. In other words, if the rate is 8.25%, enter 8.25, not 0.0825.

- **Tax Titles**: As in so many places in Magento, you can specifically name this item as you would like it to appear in your various store views. You might, for instance, wish to call the rule CA Sales Tax for your English views, but CA La Taxe De Vente for your French store view. If you leave any of these blank, your customer will be shown the Tax Identifier value.

You can use the same field specifics for creating a new tax rate by clicking **Add New Tax Rate** at the bottom of the **Tax Rate list** field.

To view the remaining fields, expand the **Additional Settings** section.

- **Customer Tax Class**: As discussed earlier, **Customer Tax Classes** allow you to assign customer groups to different tax groups. For instance, you will probably have sales taxes only apply to retail customers.

Wholesale Customer Tax Class

In Magento 2, there is no one place to go to create **Customer Tax Classes**. Therefore, you should create a **Wholesale Customer** Tax class in any tax rule so that it will be available to you when managing customer groups.

- **Product Tax Class**: If you need additional **Product Tax Classes**, you can also add them here and they will be available for selection in product edit panels.

- **Priority**: If you have more than one tax rate that might apply to a customer's shopping cart, those with the same priority will be added. That is, each tax rule will be calculated separately, and then added together. If the priorities are different, then the rates will be compounded in order of priority. Let's take an example: you have two taxes that will apply to a product — a federal excise tax of 5% and a state sales tax of 8%. If the priorities for both are the same, the shopper's purchase of $100 will be taxed a total of $13: $5 for 5% and $8 for 8%. If you put a priority of 1 for the excise tax and a priority of 2, for instance, for the state sales tax, then the customer is taxed $13.40: $5 for the excise tax and $8.40 for the 8% of $105 ($100 plus the $5 excise tax). The latter is an example of compounded sales tax. Taxes with different priorities will also be listed as separate tax line items to your customers.

- **Calculated Off Subtotal Only**: Now, take what we just said about priority and consider this: if you want each applicable tax — such as GST and PST taxes in Canada — to display separately to the customer, each tax must have a different priority. However, you don't want these taxes compounding, as explained above. Therefore, to prevent compounding, yet have the tax shown as a separate line item, check this box and the tax will only be applied to the order subtotal, not as a compounded tax calculation.

- **Sort Order**: If you have more than one applied tax, you can control the order in which they are listed to your customers. This will not change any compounding based on priority.

Importing tax rates

While you can't import tax rules, you can import **tax rates**, which may be a time saver, particularly where you have multiple taxing jurisdictions to whom you have to report tax collections.

As with many importing capabilities in Magento 2, the easiest way to begin is by exporting the current tax rules and expanding on the CSV file, then importing your changes. To import tax rates, view any tax rule. At the bottom of the screen are buttons to import and export tax rates. Export the current tax rate file, add or edit your rates, then re-import.

Value added tax configurations

In some countries, goods and services are taxed in a means similar to sales tax, but calculated and managed differently. These **Value-Added Taxes (VAT)** are made even more complex due to varying rates among countries, different rules for registration, and rules for taxation based on the type of product or service sold.

As usual, we can't begin to counsel you on taxes. VAT rules can be complicated, especially for non-EU countries selling into EU countries. We highly suggest you consult with your tax professionals. If you doubt the complexity of EU VAT taxes, see http://goo.gl/y07Pb.

The VAT process in Magento involves three basic components — the needs of them are based on your location:

- **VAT validation**: For customers who provide a VAT ID, Magento 2 is able to query the European Commission to verify their VAT ID

- **VAT tax rules**: As with sales taxes, the creation of tax rules based on certain conditions or considerations

- **System configuration**: Activate the rules that will manage VAT-eligible purchases

In Magento, VAT is charged if both the seller and customer are located in the same EU country. If both are EU-registered businesses, no VAT tax is collected if the seller and customer are in different countries.

When selling to consumers in EU countries, the amount of VAT collected is based on what country the seller is located (if the seller is an EU country). These are called **intra-EU sales**.

One exception (there's always one, yes?) is that when selling digital goods (for example, music, software), the VAT rate to be charged is that of the destination country, not the source country.

The key to effectively managing this complexity is the creation of multiple customer groups that can be automatically assigned during the checkout or registration process based on the VAT ID validation of the buyer.

Setup VAT taxes

It would be so easy for us to stop here, call it a day, and leave VAT tax configuration to your imagination. After all, we can play the "too complex for a book" card, correct?

The truth is that VAT taxes can be quite complex. If you're an EU business or exporting to the EU countries, you already understand the complexities. However, we do want you to get the most from Magento 2 and demonstrate its incredible ability to fulfill your tax calculation needs.

To that end — and perhaps the best way to demonstrate the process — we're going to set up VAT taxes as if we were a business based in France (we love Paris!).

Since we're considered, in this example, as an EU member country, we will need to provide for VAT ID validation of our customers and classify them accordingly.

Earlier in this chapter, we added four additional customer groups, specifically for VAT tax use. If we look under **Stores | Customer Groups**, based on our example Magento install, we should see the following:

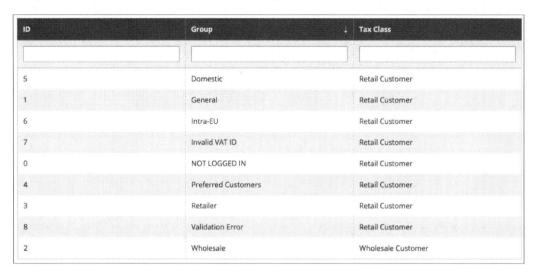

ID	Group	↓	Tax Class
5	Domestic		Retail Customer
1	General		Retail Customer
6	Intra-EU		Retail Customer
7	Invalid VAT ID		Retail Customer
0	NOT LOGGED IN		Retail Customer
4	Preferred Customers		Retail Customer
3	Retailer		Retail Customer
8	Validation Error		Retail Customer
2	Wholesale		Wholesale Customer

Next, we want to create the product classes that we will need for applying the appropriate French VAT tax rates. France groups products into four rate categories, each of which should have a different product class added for taxing purposes:

> All tax rates and information shown here are for illustrative purposes only and should not be used without validation.

- **Standard VAT**: These will be taxed at 20%.
- **Reduced VAT 1**: Applies to books, transportation, entertainment events and hotels. Taxed at 10%.
- **Reduced VAT 2**: Applies to medical, food and book products. Taxed at 5.5%.
- **Reduced VAT 3**: Applies to newspaper and pharmaceuticals. Taxed at 2.1%.

We now have to consider that for customers living in other EU countries, we will charge our VAT tax rate on purchases of physical products, but charge the buyer's VAT tax rate for digital or virtual purchases.

That means that if we are selling digital products (for example, music, software, and so on) to other EU customers, we have to charge VAT tax at the rate in *their* country, not France. In order to do that, we have to add tax rates in Magento for every other EU country. As you can imagine, setting up all those tax rates and rules can be quite time consuming.

We have created a CSV file of all EU countries with their standard VAT tax rates (as of the time of writing). You can use this to upload the tax rates to your Magento 2 install.

For France, we need to create the four tax rates described above. After adding these under **Stores | Tax Zones and Rates** in our Magento 2 backend, the list of tax rates looks like this:

France Reduced VAT 1	France	*	*	10.00
France Reduced VAT 2	France	*	*	5.5
France Reduced VAT 3	France	*	*	2.1
France Standard	France	*	*	20.00

Our next chore is to create the product tax classes that are needed to separate our products according to the taxes we have to apply. For our France-based example, we will need five product tax classes:

- **Standard**: These are physical products and services that don't fall into the other product classes
- **Reduced Tax Class 1**: In France, these include passenger transportation, events (sports and entertainment), hotels, and restaurants
- **Reduced Tax Class 2**: Medical, food, and books
- **Reduced Tax Class 3**: Newspapers and pharmaceuticals
- **Virtual Products**: Music, software, and other non-physical products

While you may not currently sell products that fall into all of these classes, you may want to go ahead and set them up so they're available to you.

Remember, to create additional product tax classes; just click to edit any tax rule, expand **Additional Settings**, and add your new classes. After adding the above classes, this section will look like the following screenshot:

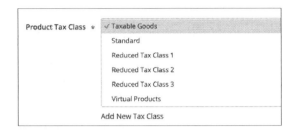

With the preceding preparation completed, we can now create the tax rules that will be used to calculate VAT taxes on purchases. We need to create the following tax rules to meet our needs as a French online business:

- Domestic customers purchasing standard products
- Domestic customers purchasing **Reduced Tax Class 1** products
- Domestic customers purchasing **Reduced Tax Class 2** products
- Domestic customers purchasing **Reduced Tax Class 3** products
- All customers purchasing virtual products
- Intra-EU customers purchasing non-virtual products

Once entered into our Magento 2 example, our **Tax Rules** screen would include the following:

Domestic Customer - Standard	Retail Customer	Standard	France Standard	0	0	0
Domestic Customer - Reduced 1	Retail Customer	Reduced Tax Class 1	France Reduced VAT 1	0	0	0
Domestic Customer - Reduced 2	Retail Customer	Reduced Tax Class 2	France Reduced VAT 2	0	0	0
Domestic Customer - Reduced 3	Retail Customer	Reduced Tax Class 3	France Reduced VAT 3	0	0	0
EU Customer - Virtual	Retail Customer	Virtual Products	Austria, Belgium, Bulgaria, Coratia, Cyprus, Czech Republic, Denmark, Estonia, Finland, France Standard, Germany, Greece, Hungary, Ireland, Italy, Latvia, Lithuania, Luxembourg, Malta, Netherlands, Poland, Portugal, Romania, Slovakia, Slovenia, Spain, Sweden, United Kingdom	0	0	0
Intra-EU Customer - Non-Virtual	Retail Customer	Standard, Reduced Tax Class 1, Reduced Tax Class 2, Reduced Tax Class 3	Austria, Belgium, Bulgaria, Coratia, Cyprus, Czech Republic, Denmark, Estonia, Finland, Germany, Greece, Hungary, Ireland, Italy, Latvia, Lithuania, Luxembourg, Malta, Netherlands, Poland, Portugal, Romania, Slovakia, Slovenia, Spain, Sweden, United Kingdom	0	0	0

Remember, we are NOT tax experts. Your tax rules may differ from the example shown. The purpose of this exercise is to demonstrate the various steps needed to add VAT tax calculations to a Magento 2 store.

The final piece is to configure your **Customer Configuration** so that customers are automatically assigned to the proper customer group based on their VAT ID validation. To do that, go to **Stores | Configuration | Customers | Customer Configuration** and expand the **Create New Account Options** panel. Some of these settings are done at the global, website, and store view levels, so pay close attention to your store view scope setting in the upper right-hand part of the screen. For our example, we only want to automatically assign customers who visit our French store. Therefore, we will only enable this feature at the **Sportswear French View**.

Once you have changed to the appropriate store view level, the key fields to configure are:

- **Enable Automatic Assignment to Customer Group**: Set to **Yes** and Magento will reveal additional configuration fields.

- **Tax Calculation Based On**: Usually, you will set this to **Shipping Address** so that taxes are based on the customer's taxing jurisdiction, although there are exceptions.

- **Default Group**: At the store view level, you may want to set this to **Domestic**.

- **Group for Valid VAT ID – Domestic**: Set to your domestic group, **Domestic**.

- **Group for Valid VAT ID – Intra-Union**: Set to **Intra-EU**.

- **Group of Invalid VAT ID**: Set to **Invalid VAT ID**.

- **Validation Error Group**. Set to **Validation Error** as the customer group.

- **Validate on Each Transaction**: If you're going to calculate VAT taxes, then you would most like set this to **Yes**.

- **Default Value for Disable Automatic Group Changes Based on VAT ID**: This feature allows Magento to re-assign customers if their VAT ID or address changes. If you do not want this feature, set this to **Yes**.

As with any store configuration, especially one as complex as VAT taxes, we highly recommend that you test your configurations thoroughly.

Transactional e-mails

As customers make purchases in your store, Magento sends — based on your configurations — a number of e-mails to notify customers about their purchases. There are also e-mails for recovering passwords, creating accounts and more.

Magento installs some basic templates for all these transactional e-mails. You can create new e-mail templates to use for your stores that reflect your branding and messaging. In Magento 2, this is quite easy to do.

 Many new Magento store owners will simply use the default e-mails that are installed with Magento. While these e-mails are not *bad*, you should invest the time to modify each to meet your specific brand and design.

When you first go to **Marketing | Email Templates**, you'll see an empty list. That's normal. The base templates installed with Magento will not appear in this list — but they are there, nonetheless. E-mail templates can also be included in Magento themes added to your installation. These will also not show in the list, but will be available for customization.

The process of customizing e-mail templates is:

1. Create a new template.
2. Apply an existing template to your new template.
3. Modify to accommodate your needs.

Once you create your new e-mail template, you can assign it for use as sales e-mails, customer account e-mails, and so on.

You can create new e-mail templates for the following purposes:

- Failed Payment*
- Contact Us Form
- Forgot Password
- New Account
- New Account Confirmation Key
- New Account Confirmed
- New Account Without Password
- Remind Password
- Reset Password
- Currency Update Warning*

- Subscription Confirmation
- Subscription Success
- Unsubscription Success
- Cron Error Warning*
- Price Alert
- Stock Alert
- Credit Memo Update
- Credit Memo Update for Guest (purchaser who does not log in)
- Invoice Update
- Invoice Update for Guest
- New Credit Memo
- New Credit Memo for Guest
- New Invoice
- New Invoice for Guest
- New Order
- New Order for Guest
- Order Update
- Order Update for Guest
- Shipment Update
- Shipment Update for Guest
- Send Product Link to Friend
- Sitemap Generation Warnings*
- Forgot Admin Password
- Reset Password
- Wish List Sharing

As you can see, Magento has quite a number of e-mails. The items in this list with an asterisk (*) are e-mails that are not sent to your customers, but, rather, sent to you or someone you designate. These e-mails are for alerting your team when something doesn't quite go right.

There are also two additional templates that are used to create the headers and footers for your e-mails. In other words, you can manage the top and bottom of your e-mails without having to modify every single e-mail if, for example, you want to change your logo or phone number.

To illustrate how to do this, let's create a new e-mail template for our sportswear store. We will begin by modifying the header and footer for our sportswear store, then create a new *New Order* e-mail template.

Create a new header template

On the **Email Templates** panel, click on **Add New Template**. At the top of the **New Template** panel, you'll see an area titled **Load default template**. Here, you can select the base template — or a template provided by a theme — and load it into the **New Template** panel for modification.

 You could, of course, create a template from scratch, but it can be a real time-saver to modify an existing template.

For our new header, select **Header** and click on **Load Template**. This will load the base header template into our **New Template** form.

Let's first review the fields shown on this screen:

- **Currently Used For**: Not actually an editable field, this shows where this e-mail is assigned for use. In this case, we can see that the header template we loaded is being used in the **Stores | Configuration | Design | Emails | Header Template** configuration at the *Default* configuration scope. That means that the header template is used as the default header for all e-mails in your installation. Once we build our sportswear header (and footer) templates, we will assign them at the sportswear website configuration scope so that they will be used for all sportswear e-mails.

- **Template Name**: Use a name that is useful when shown in the list of e-mail templates. In our example here, we might use **Header** (Sportswear).

- **Template Subject**: For e-mails, this is the subject that would appear in the e-mail sent. For the header and footer, leave as shown so they are properly included in generated e-mails.

- **Template Content**: It is into this field that you will make any changes to layout and content.

Once we have modified the header to our liking, we can save it by clicking **Save Template**. If we look at our list of e-mail templates, we now have the one template listed.

ID	Template	Added	Updated	Subject	Template Type	Action
		From	From			
		To	To			
1	Header (Sportswear)	Feb 28, 2016, 3:41:53 PM	Feb 28, 2016, 3:41:53 PM	Header	HTML	Preview

Assign e-mail header and footer

If we click on the template and view its detail, we can see that it has no **Currently Used For** field, as it has not been assigned to a particular website or store. Once we have created our sportswear footer (it is not necessarily required to create both to be able to create and assign only a header or footer), we can now assign these to our sportswear website so that they appear for each store view.

This capability gives you the ability to create multiple language e-mails, as well as translating your website for your international customers.

1. Go to **Stores | Configuration | General | Design** in your backend.
2. Change your **Store View** setting to **Sportswear Website**.

3. Expand the **Emails** panel.
4. Beside **Header Template** and **Footer Template**, uncheck the **Use Default** checkbox.
5. For **Header Template**, select **Header (Sportswear)** in the drop-down menu.
6. For **Footer Template**, select **Footer (Sportswear)**.
7. Click **Save Config**.

We have now assigned our new e-mail header and footer to all outgoing e-mails related to the sportswear stores. If you view the detail for your header and footer e-mail templates, they will now display a **Currently Used For** value.

Currently Used For	Stores -> Configuration -> Design -> Emails -> Header Template (Sportswear Website)

Create new e-mail template

Now that we have created our special header and footer, we can create our new order email for our sportswear customers.

1. Return to **Marketing | Email Templates**.
2. Click on **Add New Template**.
3. Load the **New Order** default template. Note that for the Magento Luma theme, there is an installed new order template specific to the Luma theme. Since we're using the Luma theme for our example stores, we will choose **New Order (Magento/luma)** as our default template.

4. Give your new e-mail template a suitable name. In our case, we'll use **new order** (sportswear).

5. For our template subject, we're going to adjust it a bit by replacing its default contents with `Thanks for Your {{var store.getFrontendName()}} Order!`

> As you can see, the subject contains a Magento variable that will dynamically include the name of the store. Since we name our sportswear stores Sportswear English View, Sportswear French View, and Sportswear German View, we may not want to use the dynamic store view name, as these don't sound particularly consumer-friendly.
>
> For our example, we would prefer to use **Thanks for Your Acmes Sportswear Order!**

6. Make any other changes you wish to the **Template Content** and **Template Styles**.

7. Click on **Save Template**.

As with the header and footer, we will now assign this e-mail to the appropriate sales e-mail:

1. Go to **Stores | Configuration | Sales | Sales Emails**.

2. Change **Store View** to **Sportswear Website**.

3. Open the **Order** panel.

4. For **New Order Confirmation Template**, uncheck **Use Default** and select **New Order (Sportswear)** in the dropdown.

5. Click on **Save Config**.

We have now created a modified new order template for our logged-in purchasers and assigned it for our sportswear stores.

> There are different e-mails for logged in and guest customers because logged-in customer e-mails can include links to the customer's account. Guest customers cannot log into your Magento store, as no account is set up when a customer checks out as a guest.

Summary

As we've seen in this chapter, before you can begin selling on a Magento store, there are considerable configurations that have to be addressed. We have covered managing orders, payment gateway settings, shipping configurations, sales and VAT taxes, and transactional e-mails.

Take your time with these settings and continually test to make sure you have the configurations correct. Mistakes could end up being costly.

In the next chapter, we will discuss how to manage the non-product content of your site: the static pages and text that helps define your brand and give greater confidence to your customers.

6
Managing Non-Product Content

As important as products and product information are to e-commerce, successful online stores need more in order to attract customers and fortify the store's brand. Even printed catalogs often contain information about the seller, including hours of operation, return policies, company history, and more. This **non-product content** is essential.

To gain an understanding of how to create and manipulate non-product content, we will cover the following topics:

- Review how Magento incorporates content
- Learn how to create content pages in your Magento store
- Create and use static blocks
- Utilize built-in content widgets

Once you know how to interweave non-product content throughout your online store, you will no doubt discover innovative ways to increase customer engagement.

The Magento content management system

As with most e-commerce platforms, Magento's management of non-product content lacks some of the more robust features of a dedicated **content management system** (**CMS**) – such as *WordPress*, *Business Catalyst*, or *Joomla*. However, to its credit, Magento does provide a versatile system that takes into account the possible need for unique content for each of your stores.

As you would expect, the area of the backend for managing the CMS functions of Magento is under the **Content** menu. This area includes sections for managing **Pages**, **Blocks**, and **Widgets**, as shown in the following screenshot:

Before we dig into each of these items, it's important to recall our discussion about blocks in *Chapter 4, Designs and Themes*. Whether configuring a page, or placing a static block or widget, Magento builds the final results by assembling blocks of information.

Pages

The pages we will use in the CMS are not actually complete pages, as they lack controls for the overall template items of header, navigation, and footer. These pages actually refer to the central content of a page – that which lies within the overall page template. Within this page, we can add text, images, static blocks, and widgets to give the page its core content. As we will examine in this section, you can add some of the same code as you did in the `default.xml` file to even manipulate elements outside the core content area, including blocks within the header, navigation, and footer.

To begin, let's look at and alter a default page provided by the sample data installed into a new Magento store.

Go to **CMS | Pages** in the Magento backend. With the sample data installed, you should see a list of pages, much like those shown in the following screenshot:

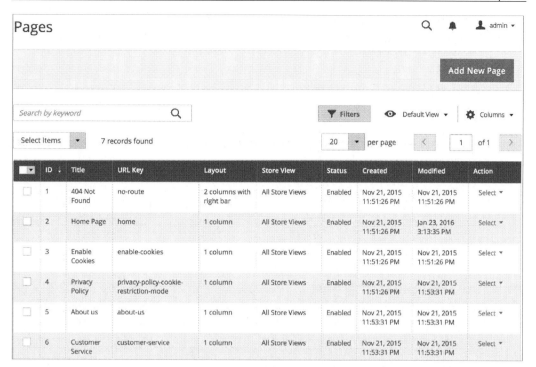

While it's not absolutely necessary that you keep these pages enabled, for e-commerce best practices, it's generally a good idea to retain these core pages.

- **404 Not Found**: This page is displayed to visitors who land on a non-existing page in your site. For example, you might have a product that is discontinued and you no longer wish to have it visible to your customers. However, a search engine, blog, or other websites may have a link to that product. If a customer clicks that link and comes to your site, since the item is no longer visible, they would be shown this page. A 404 error is *webspeak* for a missing page. You can provide branded content to visitors who try to access a missing page. Without this page, such a visitor would simply see a stark 404 error page provided by your web server, and it's neither appealing nor branded.

- **Home Page**: Obviously, this is the home page for your site. The content and design elements that appear in the core of your home page are managed on this page.

- **Enable Cookies**: In order for your store's shopping cart, login, and other features to work properly, a customer's web browser must allow cookies to be used. If Magento detects that cookies cannot be used on a customer's browser, they will see the content of this page. You can use this page to help customers understand cookies and how to activate them on their browser.

- **Privacy Policy**: Online privacy and the sharing of information is increasingly important to consumers. Furthermore, Google will favorably consider sites that have a comprehensive privacy policy on their site. It's just good business sense! The default Magento privacy policy content is a great boilerplate with which to construct your own policy.

- **About Us**: Would you hand over your hard-earned money to someone you didn't trust? There are lots of ways to demonstrate your good faith and reputation on your site, and the About Us page is one ideal place to start. Give your shoppers a sense of your mission, leadership team, and history.

- **Customer Service**: You can create other service-related pages (for example, **Returns Policy**, **FAQs**). In the least case, you should have a page that discusses your customer service policies. Magento provides this page with the initial installation because any reputable online store should make their service policies available to online shoppers.

No doubt, you will find other pages to insert in your Magento store. Creating and managing CMS pages is really quite straightforward.

Customizing a CMS page

The first place most designers want to begin modifying a store's design is with the **Home Page**.

Modifying the Home Page layout

First, we need to understand that pages created in the Magento CMS primarily dictate what appears in the **content section** of the page. This is the area, highlighted below, apart from the **header**, **top navigation,** and **footer** regions.

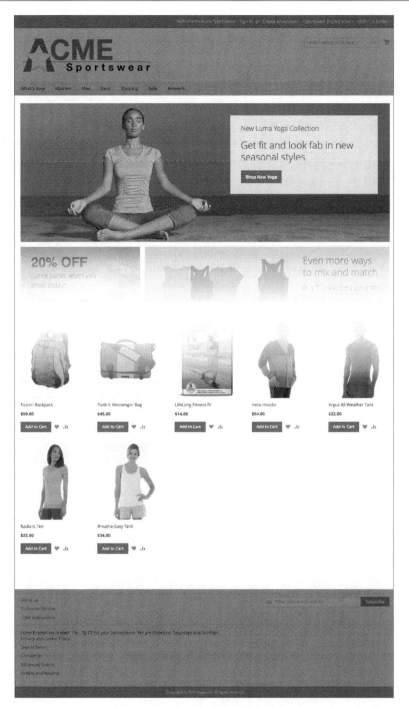

The content section of the Home Page

On the **Page Information** panel of the **Edit Page** screen, you should see the following:

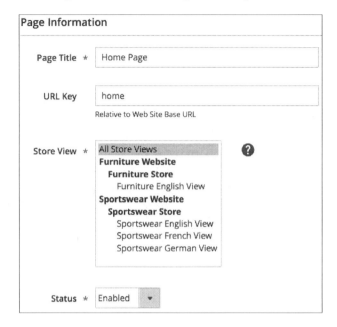

Let us go through the various fields:

- **Page Title**: This is the title that will appear in the top of your browser, as well as the default name of any link you create to this page.

- **URL Key**: This field shows how the page is accessed in a URL path. For example, this page is accessible by going to `http://www.storedomain.com/ home.html`. Magento assumes that your **Home Page** will have a **URL Key** of home. You should not change this unless you know what you're doing.

- **Store View**: This field allows you to select for which stores your page is applicable. When you save your page, Magento does check to make sure another page with the same **URL Key** has not already been assigned to the same stores.

- **Status**: Of course, means whether the page is active or not.

The Content screen

In the left tabs, click **Content**. This is the screen where you can add text, images, or dynamic content that will display in the center content area of your page.

Notice that in the following screenshot, this sample data home page contains a widget.

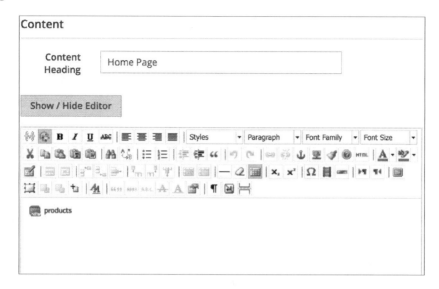

This widget displays products according to the parameters of the widget (we'll discuss widgets later in this chapter). What you don't see — and we're sure you've realized this — are the instructions that control the other graphics and "Hotsellers" shown on the home page.

The other parts of the home page are inserted by using blocks. We will explore the use of blocks a bit later in this chapter. What is important here is that you can create tremendous versatility in your CMS pages by using tools beyond hardcoding layout changes within the theme modules.

> When we create home page layouts, we use blocks and widgets wherever possible so that the store operator can immediately manage changes that they feel are important. We use the content area of the CMS page to allow the store operator to quickly edit text.

For our exercise, let's add some copy to our home page so that it precedes the featured product display.

In the editor field, enter the following before the widget:

Welcome to our store. We hope you enjoy shopping with us. Our goal is to provide you with the best products at the best value.

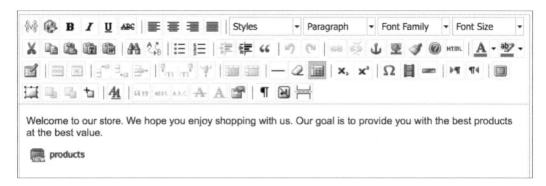

Click on **Save and Continue Edit** (this will let you remain on this screen) and open your home page in another browser window or tab. It should display your new content:

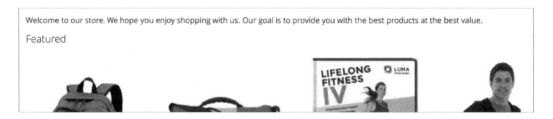

You've now added content to your default home page. As you go through the remainder of this chapter, you'll discover additional ways to add or affect the content of your home page. We will now create a new CMS page to use on our site. This exercise will also give you additional insights into how to use Magento's CMS feature.

Creating a CMS page

Let's add a new page to our site called **Care Instructions**. We want to provide information to our apparel site customers on proper techniques for washing the clothing items they purchase from Acme Sportwear:

1. Go to **Content | Pages** in the Magento 2 backend.
2. Click on **Add New Page**.

The first panel is titled **Page Information**, as shown in the following screenshot:

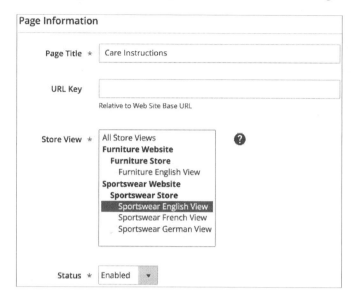

As shown, we have entered the initial information for our new page. Magento will create the URL Key once the new page is saved. However, you can enter a URL Key here. The URL Key will be the actual name used in the URL to access your page: `http://www.acmesportswear.com/care-instructions.html`. If you want another URL Key value, you can enter it here.

If you build different pages for different store views, they can each use the same URL Key. However, if you try to use the same URL Key for two pages which are both assigned to the same store view, you will get an error.

The next panel in the new product screen is **Content**. It is in this panel that you can create the words, images, and so on that will appear in the main content portion of your new page.

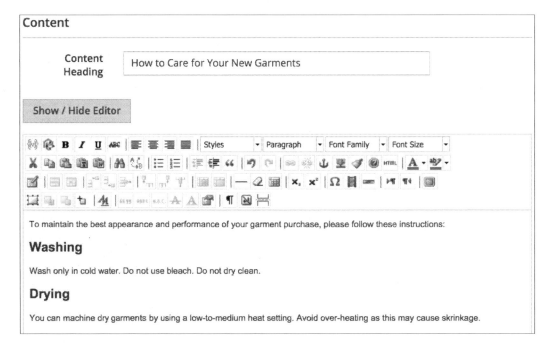

The **WYSIWYG editor** gives you a lot of great tools to help you build your page content. You can easily insert images, videos, tables, and other styled content.

The **Content Heading** will appear at the top of your page. It will be displayed within a <h1> tag.

If you're not familiar with HTML heading tags — or other HTML elements — you should consider enlisting the assistance of an experienced web content editor. The proper use of headings, styles, and other HTML elements can have an effect on how well your content is indexed by Google.

The third panel in the menu on the left side is labeled **Design**. Based on your theme, you can change the layout of the page to a one-, two-, or three-column display. You can also specify a special theme design. There are additional XML statements that can be inserted that will affect your display. See *Chapter 4, Designs and Themes*, for guidance on various XML statements that can be used to control layout.

The last panel is **Meta Data**. Keep this in mind for when we discuss meta information later in this chapter.

Once saved, we can view our new page by going to the URL path we created for this page.

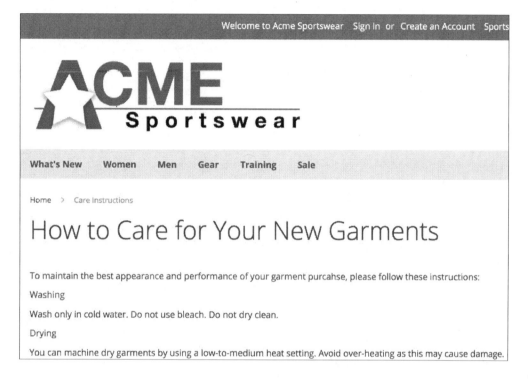

The next step is to add a link to your new page from your site navigation. One easy way is to edit a block that contains links to pages within your site.

Using blocks and widgets

Blocks are sections of content that are specified by your theme to appear in various places throughout your site. Blocks can be placed on all pages, some pages, product pages, category pages, or in special, designated spots.

In addition to block locations that are configured within your theme, blocks can be inserted into various areas and pages within your site by using widgets, which we will explore just a bit later in this section.

To view all the blocks in your site, go to **Content | Blocks**. If you have installed the Magento 2 sample data, you'll see as many as 18 blocks. By their names, you can probably figure out where they appear on your site.

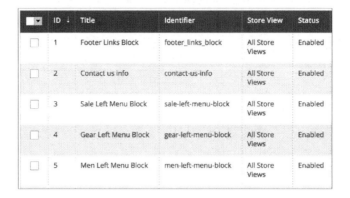

	ID ↓	Title	Identifier	Store View	Status
☐	1	Footer Links Block	footer_links_block	All Store Views	Enabled
☐	2	Contact us info	contact-us-info	All Store Views	Enabled
☐	3	Sale Left Menu Block	sale-left-menu-block	All Store Views	Enabled
☐	4	Gear Left Menu Block	gear-left-menu-block	All Store Views	Enabled
☐	5	Men Left Menu Block	men-left-menu-block	All Store Views	Enabled

Adding a page link

To understand how CMS blocks work — and to add our **Care Instructions** page link — click on the **Select** drop-down menu to the far right of the first block, **Footer Links Block**, and click on **Edit**.

This block contains the information that appears in the bottom footer of all our sites.

We want to add our **Care Instructions** link to this block. Now, this is where things get just a bit complex, so read through this process carefully, as it applies anytime you wish to add a link to a page in your site to a block. We are going to explain three different methods of accomplishing the same result.

Using WYSIWYG

We can add a link using the WYSIWIG editor, or we could change the view to HTML mode and edit the actual HTML code. Let's do it using the WYSIWYG editor, first.

In the editor space, add the link name as you wish for it to appear on the frontend by adding another bullet row below the **Customer Service** label. You can, of course, insert your new link anywhere in the list.

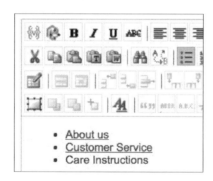

To create the link, select the title you just entered and click the link icon in the menu toolbar. A *modal* dialogue will appear for entering your link URL.

Magento provides a library of variables which can be used to dynamically insert values and content where appropriate. In this case, the use of a system variable for inserting the store URL is worth learning for our purposes.

The store URL variable is inserted when used in the following format: `{{store url=URL_Key}}`, where `URL_Key` is the URL Key for the page, category, or product you wish to access.

Therefore, for our new page, we will insert the following into **Link URL**: `{{store url=care-instructions}}`. Add a **Title** for your link so that it will appear when your customer mouses over the link, and to help describe the link to search engines.

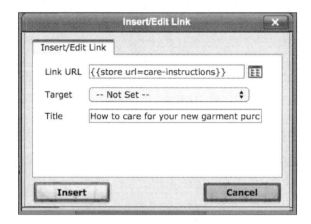

In most Magento help guides, the format for entering a store URL variable is `{{store url="URL_Key"}}`, with quotes (") around the URL Key. However, we must leave out the quotes when using this variable within the link dialogue box. It's quite possible to use the store URL variable without quotes elsewhere, too. This behavior does not apply when adding links using HTML (see the next section).

Once you click on **Import**, the text will be linked. If you look on the frontend of your website, you will now see a new link in the footer.

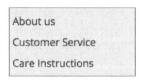

If you select a link in WYSIWYG and click the link icon, the URL that shows in the dialogue field is a very long, encrypted string. This is due to the way Magento stores link references. You can edit the link by replacing it with what you prefer as the link, but you may find building and managing links much easier using HTML rather than the WYSIWYG view.

Using HTML

The method of adding a link using the store URL variable is the same if you work in the HTML view. The key, of course, knows how to properly code an HTML link.

In the block screen, click on **Show/Hide Editor** to reveal the underlying HTML for this block.

```
<ul class="footer links">
<li class="nav item"><a href="{{store url="about-us"}}">About us</a></li>
<li class="nav item"><a href="{{store url="customer-service"}}">Customer Service</a></li>
<li class="nav item"><a title="How to care for your new garment purchases." href="{{store%20url=care-instructions}}">Care Instructions</a></li>
</ul>
```

You'll notice that the link you created for the **Care Instructions** page is slightly different from the other links in the block. This is due to the manner in which the link dialogue saves your entry.

You could also use `{{store url="care-instructions"}}` for the link code — in HTML view only — and achieve the same results.

Using a widget

If you're hesitant about using the store URL variable or coding HTML, you can use one additional technique for inserting a link: the CMS widget. In fact, as you explore this method, you'll find it can be used to insert the following:

* A CMS page link
* A CMS block
* A link to a category listing
* A link to a product page
* A list of new products
* A list of products belonging to a specific category
* A form for customers to use to look up orders and/or request a return
* A list of recently compared products
* A list of recently viewed products

For our example, we want to insert a link to a CMS page. In the WYSIWYG view (you can also use the HTML view), click the widget icon in the top menu bar.

A panel will open from the right side of your screen. For **Widget Type**, select **CMS Page Link**. Additional fields will appear:

- **Anchor Custom Text**: Enter how you wish the link to show to your customer. In our case, we would enter **Care Instructions**.

- **Anchor Custom Title**: Enter the hidden title that you wish to use to describe the link to search engines and have displayed to customers if they hover over the link with their mouse.

- **Template**: If you wish to insert the link on a line by itself, select **CMS Page Link Block Template**. If the link is to appear within a paragraph of text, choose **CMS Page Link Inline Template**.

- **CMS Page**: Click **Select Page...** to choose the page that you want to link.

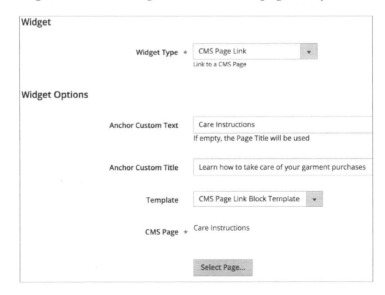

After you insert the widget, it will appear in your WYSIWYG editor as an icon labeled **page link**. If you want to edit the link, simply double-click on the icon to open the **Widget** panel.

You may find that using a widget will add additional HTML to the actual code. In our example case, the link title is enclosed by a <span> tag. Your site's CSS styling may add additional styling to this added HTML code that may affect your site appearance.

Using variables

The store URL variable is only one of many available for use in Magento 2. Within the CMS page and block editors, you do have access to a list of standard variables that will *dynamically* insert information into your content.

- **Base Unsecure URL**
- **Base Secure URL**
- **General Contact Name**
- **General Contact Email**
- **Sales Representative Contact Name**
- **Sales Representative Contact Email**
- **Custom1 Contact Name**
- **Custom1 Contact Email**
- **Custom2 Contact Name**
- **Custom2 Contact Email**
- **Store Name**
- **Store Phone Number**
- **Store Hours**
- **Country**
- **Region/State**
- **Zip/Postal Code**

- **City**
- **Street Address 1**
- **Street Address 2**

Let's say we wanted to include the name and store hours of our business in the same footer block we have been editing:

1. Click in the WYSIWYG where you wish to insert your new text and variables.

2. Insert any text you wish.

3. Place your cursor where you wish to insert a variable.

4. Click the variable icon in the WYSIWYG editor menu.

5. Click on the variable you wish to insert. In our case, we will be clicking on **Store Name** and **Store Hours**. Magento will insert the proper variable code into your text.

After saving the block, you will see on your site that the actual saved information for store name and store hours (see *Chapter 2, Installing Magento 2*) is inserted into its proper places.

About us

Customer Service

Care Instructions

Acme Enterprises is open 10a - 7p CT for your convenience.

Creating your own variables

This is one of the least known features of Magento, and yet it can be powerful for reducing the need to edit changes in multiple places in your site. In fact, custom variables can be used not only in pages and blocks, but also in e-mail templates.

As an example, let's say you'd like to add the days on which you are closed to your footer message, but you'd like to use a variable just in case you decide later to change the days on which you are not open:

1. Go to **System | Custom Variables** in your store backend.
2. Click on **Add New Variable**.

Let's go through the various fields you will encounter here:

- **Variable Code**: Enter a code for your variable, using only lowercase letters, numbers and underscore (_). This code is used by Magento's programming to reference your variable.
- **Variable Name**: Enter a name that will appear in the list of variables.
- **Variable HTML Value**: If you wish to insert HTML code as part of the variable value, enter it in this space.
- **Variable Plain Value**: If you do not need any HTML code, enter the value of the variable in this field.

The various fields are shown in the following screenshot:

Variable Code *	closed_days
Variable Name *	Closed Days
Variable HTML Value	
Variable Plain Value	Saturdays and Sundays

Now, you can return to your footer block and insert your new variable just as you inserted the variables for **Store Name** and **Store Hours**.

```
{{config path="general/store_information/name"}} is open {{config
path="general/store_information/hours"}} for your convenience. We are
closed on {{customVar code=closed_days}}.
```

With these variables inserted, your site footer now shows the added variable value.

About us

Customer Service

Care Instructions

Acme Enterprises is open 10a - 7p CT for your convenience. We are closed on Saturdays and Sundays.

Custom variables could be handy for managing content that you may wish to edit from time to time, yet needs to be displayed in multiple places such as the following:

- Estimated shipping time
- Credit cards and payment methods accepted
- Store pick-up hours
- Alternate phone numbers
- Customer service hours and/or phone number

If any of these need updating on your site, you simply have to change the value of the custom variable.

Using widgets to insert content onto site pages

The widgets we used in editing blocks allowed us to insert dynamic links to blocks and pages. However, widgets can also be used to insert dynamic content into multiple pages and theme locations, such as products, categories, footers, and so on. In fact, the footer links block we have been editing is inserted into the theme's footer content area using a widget.

Let's take a look at this particular widget to see how that is configured. Go to **Content | Widgets**. Click on the **Footer Links** widget shown in the list.

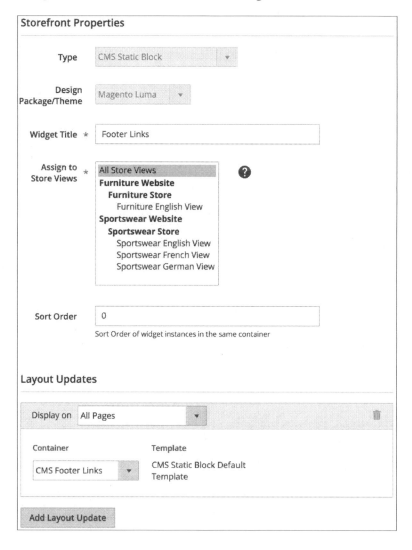

The first panel, **Storefront Properties,** configures where the widget will display its contents. The **Type** and **Design Package/Theme** are set when the widget is created and cannot be changed later (although the widget can be deleted and re-created).

You can assign the widget to appear in only certain store views, as well, and control the order in which it may appear if other widgets are also assigned to the same layout section.

The **Layout Updates** section is where so much of the magic of widgets comes in. You can assign a widget to appear on all pages, certain pages, or certain types of page (or any combination thereof!).

For categories and products, you can also specify specific categories and products. For instance, you could create a widget that would insert a block of content to appear only on the **Furniture** category page.

In this particular example, this widget inserts a CMS block (our footer links) into a container called **CMS Footer Links**. Depending on your theme, you can have many different containers to choose from, such as in the Luma theme used in our demo store.

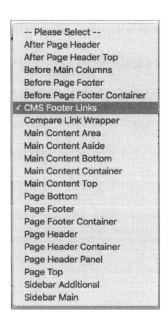

By clicking **Add Layout Update**, you can also insert the widget content into other containers in your site.

Finally, the **Widget Options** panel allows you to select the block, link, and so on. Your widget will be inserted. This depends on the type of widget you are creating.

 Widgets can be very powerful tools, especially when combined with blocks. We've seen many situations where even experienced developers have programmed block insertions instead of using the simple widget tools in Magento. Get to know blocks and widgets, and we're certain you'll come up with some very creative ways of adding true value to your brand and customer experience.

Summary

The Magento CMS provides you with the capability to customize your store without directly altering the XML and HTML files of your theme. You can build productive pages, blocks, and widgets, adding increased functionality and buyer conveniences.

That said, we should never shy away from rolling up our sleeves and diving into the actual theme files. By combining both disciplines, you have greatly elevated the potential of Magento to meet your retailing needs.

In this chapter, we learned about the Magento CMS functionality, viewed how to create and customize pages, explored the creation of blocks, and reviewed the many widgets available for your use.

Now that our store has products and content, it's time to let the world know your store exists as a premiere online shopping destination.

7
Marketing Tools

The online marketplace is crowded. Thousands of new stores are coming online each day. With Magento 2, you have one of the most powerful open source platforms for presenting and selling your products and services. But to be noticed — and to create valuable repeat business — you have to do more than just point a domain name to your store.

The key is marketing: presenting a selling proposition to potential customers that will entice them to at least visit your online showroom.

In this chapter, we will explore some of Magento's key marketing tools, including:

- Customer groups
- Promotions
- Newsletters
- Sitemaps
- Search engine optimization

As you prepare your store for launch, you need to spend some time becoming familiar with how these tools can help you attract and close more sales.

Customer groups

If you're new to e-commerce, you may not quite have a handle on how to group your potential customers outside of retail and wholesale. Most of you will build retail stores, fewer will build wholesale businesses, and even fewer will do both.

Yet, if you give some careful thought to how you intend to market to your customers, you may find that there are more **customers segments** you need to identify. Here are examples of some other possible customer groups:

- Distributors who will re-sell your product to retailers
- Tax-exempt organizations, such as charities or government agencies
- Groups or teams, such as associations or athletic leagues
- Professionals, as opposed to hobbyists or amateurs
- Certified or approved buyers meeting a licensing or other qualification

 Customer groups in Magento are not to be confused with customer profiles, such as age, sex, or preferences. A customer can only belong to one Magento group, so profile attributes cannot really be accommodated.

As you contemplate your groups, consider the following:

- Groups should be segments of your customer base that might have different pricing, benefits, or product focus
- Groups can be used (as we'll see later in this chapter) for specific marketing promotions using newsletters and promotional codes
- Groups can be assigned different tax classes for the purpose of charging (or not charging) sales tax

By default, Magento creates three customer groups: **General**, **Retailer**, and **Wholesale**. When a customer registers in your store, they are automatically put into the General group. You can manually assign a customer to another group, either after they have registered or if you create the customer yourself in the administrative backend to your store.

Creating a customer group

Creating a new customer group is perhaps the simplest operation in Magento!

1. Go to **Stores | Customer Groups** in your Administration menu.
2. Click on **Add New Customer Group**.
3. Enter a **Group Name**.
4. Assign a **Tax Class**.
5. Click on **Save Customer Group**.

And that's all there is to it. Now that you understand how customer groups are created in Magento, let's see how we can use these for marketing.

Promotions

Every retailer with whom we work finds it beneficial to offer promotions from time to time. From free shipping to coupons, promotions can help consumers choose your products over competitors, particularly if they feel they're getting a great bargain in the process.

As with sales tax, promotions are rule-based, meaning that the application and calculation of a promotion are based on rules you create. In Magento, there are two types of promotion rules:

- **Catalog price rules** apply to any product that meets certain criteria. The discount is applied automatically.

- **Cart price rules**, on the other hand, can be set to be only applied when a valid coupon is entered by the customer during checkout. **Shopping cart rules** can also be applied automatically. Furthermore, shopping cart rules — or coupons — can be publicized by adding them to an RSS feed for your site.

Creating a catalog price rule

As described, a catalog price rule is a discount that is applied to selected products automatically. For example, let's assume you wish to provide a 5% discount on all women's apparel priced over $50 sold between November 24, 2016 through November 26, 2016, as a special *Black Friday* promotion.

Black Friday and Cyber Monday

For years in the United States, the day after Thanksgiving — the last Friday of November, *Black Friday* — has been one of the busiest shopping days of the Christmas season. Retailers offer huge discounts and shoppers begin lining up well before dawn just to be the first one in the door. To counter the brick and mortar retailers, online retailers created *Cyber Monday*, the Monday following *Black Friday*, likewise offering huge discounts and special offers. Personally, we like the sound of *Cyber Monday* over the morbid moniker of *Black Friday*. We also like e-commerce!

To create a catalog price rule, you need to perform the following steps:

1. Go to **Marketing | Catalog Price Rules**.
2. Click on **Add New Rule**.
3. Enter the following in the **Rule Information** screen:

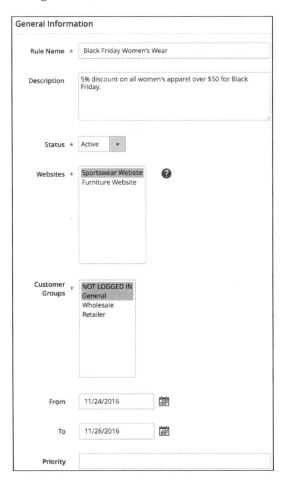

4. Click on **Conditions** in the left tab menu. Now, here's where it gets interesting!
5. Click the green plus sign to add a condition to your rule.

Any underlined items in these screens can be clicked to reveal additional choices. Don't hesitate to click and discover!

6. In the drop-down menu that appears, choose **Category**.

7. Click on **is** and select **is one of**.

8. Click the ellipsis (**...**).

9. Click the small, square icon to the right to reveal a hierarchy of categories. Select the categories you wish to apply the discount to. Your selections will add the category IDs into the empty field.

10. Click on the green checkmark icon to save your category selections.

11. Click on the green plus sign again and choose **Price** from the drop-down menu.

 If you don't see **Price** in the drop down of choices, you may need to change the **Price** product attribute. Find **Price** under **Stores | Product**. In the **Storefront Properties** panel, change **User for Promo Rule Conditions** to Yes and click on **Save Attribute**.

12. Click on **is**. Select **greater than** from the drop-down menu.

13. Click the following ellipsis. Enter **50.00** in the field and click outside the field.

Conditions (don't add conditions if rule is applied to all products)

If **ALL** of these conditions are **TRUE** :

Category **is one of** 21, 23, 24, 25, 26

Price **greater than** 50 ⊛

⊛

> The amount of the discount is based on the default currency for the website. If your site's default currency is Euros, then the discount would be 500 Euros.

Now, we need to create the discount calculation:

1. Click on the **Actions** menu tab.

2. Since we're going to apply a percentage discount to the price of the product, we can leave **Apply** as is.

> The four choices for **Apply** give you tremendous flexibility but may not be clearly understood.

3. **By Percentage of the Original Price** reduces the price of the product by the percentage specified, such as 15%off the price.

4. **By Fixed Amount** will reduce the product's price by a specified amount, such as 50 dollars off.

5. To **Percentage of the Original Price**, by contrast to **By Percentage of the Original Price**, sets the price at the percentage you enter. For example, if you enter 75, the price of the product would be 75% of its original price.

6. Likewise, **To Fixed Amount**, sets the price of the product at the price you enter instead of reducing the price by a fixed amount.

7. In **Discount Amount**, enter **5**.

8. If you want the discounts to apply to not only a complex product type (for example, configurable, bundle, or group) but to their associated products as well, set **Subproduct discounts** to **Yes** and configure the amount of discount to apply to any subproducts.

9. If we do not want to apply any other promotion rules to these applicable products, choose **Yes** for **Discard subsequent rules**. For example, you may not want a customer to receive multiple discounts on the same product.

10. Click on **Save Rule**.

You now have a new rule that will automatically take effect at 12:01 AM on Friday, November 24th and run until 11:59 PM on Sunday, November 26th. However, there is one final action to take!

Before your new rule can take effect, click on **Apply Rules** at the top of the **Catalog Price Rules** page. Magento needs to set itself to apply the rules to the applicable products.

> Please note that immediate price changes (promotions without a set start date) will be visible when Magento re-indexes its prices, usually within a few minutes.

Creating cart price rules

Magento has some very powerful and flexible tools for creating discounts that can be applied once the customer has reached the shopping cart part of their visit. In fact, we have found it difficult to identify a single discount scenario we could not accommodate in Magento.

The key features of cart price rules for which you should be aware are:

- You can create rules for any or all of your websites. Rules apply to all store views within a website.

- You can allow discounts for only selected customer groups. You could offer coupons to wholesalers, for instance, that could not be used for retail customers.

- You do not have to use a coupon code. Your rules can be applied automatically as long as the shopping cart meets the required criteria.

- You can limit the number of times a coupon is used. Or you can allow a coupon code to be used multiple times by a given customer.

- Product attributes can be used as criteria. As noted in *Chapter 3, Managing Products*, a product attribute can be configured so that you can apply a discount based on the value of that attribute within one or more products in the customer's shopping cart.

- You can apply the discount to the entire cart or to only select products in the cart. For instance, if you are giving a 20% discount to shirts only, but customers put other types of products in their cart, you can configure the discount so that it deducts 20% from the price of the shirts in the cart and not from any other product.

- Magento can generate coupon codes. Some e-commerce systems require that you contrive the coupon codes you wish to use. In Magento, you have the ability to generate and manage as many codes as you need.

 We have worked with clients that have had millions of generated coupon codes. While this many codes may require more horsepower for your server, Magento has no problem storing and using a very large number of codes.

Let's use a specific example to learn how to create a cart price rule:

- Retail customers only. We'll assume we have 100 customers on our newsletter list.
- Unique coupon codes for each user (we'll email them to existing customers).
- Customer must buy $100 or more of women's tops or three or more of any women's apparel items.
- Discount gives 20% off on women's apparel.
- Discount also provides free ground shipping.
- Coupon can only be used once per customer.
- Coupon is only active starting on April 1, 2016 and expiring on August 31, 2016.
- Coupon cannot be combined with any other discounts.

The process of building our rule will follow these steps:

1. Adding the new rule.
2. Defining the rule's conditions.
3. Defining the rule's actions.
4. Modifying the rule's labels.
5. Generating coupon codes (if needed).
6. Testing the rule.

Adding the new rule

To begin building our cart price rule, go to **Marketing | Cart Price Rules** in your Magento 2 backend. Click on **Add New Rule**.

The **Rule Information** panel for our new rule has several fields to use to set up the rule:

- **Rule Name**: Enter **Free Shipping & 20% off Women's Apparel** as the name of your rule. This will be shown in your list of rules.

Rule Name ∗	Free Shipping & 20% off Women's Apparel

- **Description**: You can use this field to fully describe the rule. In our example, we will enter the coupon specifics we outlined for this example.

Description	• Retail customers only. We'll assume we have 100 customers on our newsletter list. • Unique coupon codes for each user (we'll be email them to existing customers). • Customer must be $100 or more of women's tops or 3 or more of any women's apparel items. • Discount gives 20% off any women's apparel products. • Discount also provides free ground shipping. • Coupon can only be used once per customer. • Coupon is only active starting on April 1, 2016 and expiring on August 31, 2016. • Coupon cannot be combined with any other discounts.

- **Status**: Select **Active** when you wish for the coupon to be available for use.

- **Websites**: Select **Sportswear Website**, since our example rule only applies to products purchased in that store. You can select any number (or all) of the websites shown. Our selection also means that visitors to all three sportswear store views (English, French, and German) can use the code.

- **Customer Groups**: Since we only want our coupon to be used for retail customers, we would select **NOT LOGGED IN** and **General**. If we only want logged in retail customers, we would only select **General**.

- **Coupon**: We will be using a coupon code; therefore, select **Specific Coupon**.

- **Coupon Code**: Our goal is to create 100 unique codes to distribute. This may help us track code usage by customer, and it will allow us to restrict the usage of the code to only one use, since we will be distributing to customers that are not logged in. Instead of entering a specific coupon code, check the box labeled **Use Auto Generation**. (We will be managing the generation of codes in a moment.)

- **Uses per Coupon**: Enter **1**, as we want to only allow a customer to use it once before expiring.

- **Uses per Customer**: This value only applies to logged in customers. We will also enter **1** in this field.

 Entering zero (0) in either of the **Uses** fields allows unlimited use of a coupon.

- **From/To**: These are the first and last dates the coupon can be used. If you leave **FROM** blank, the coupon will be immediately available (if "**Active**"); if **TO** is blank, the coupon code will never expire. Using the calendar pop-up (click the small icon to the right), choose April 1, 2016 for **From** and August 31, 2016 for **To**.

- **Priority**: If you have more than one active rule, they will be applied in an order based on this field. The order is numeric, descending, with 1 being the highest priority.

- **Public In RSS Feed**: If you want to publicize your discount in your store's RSS field, set this option to **Yes**. Since ours requires a specific coupon code and we wish to limit to known newsletter subscribers, we will select **No** for this field.

 As with all multi-panel screens in Magento, it's probably a good idea to click **Save and Continue Edit** after you complete each panel. Just in case!

Defining the rule's conditions

A rule's conditions can be considered as minimum requirements. In other words, what is necessary about a customer's shopping cart for the rule to be valid?

In our example, a coupon code can only be used if the shopping cart contains $100 or more of women's tops or 3 or more women's apparel items. To create this condition, go to the **Conditions** panel.

 If we leave this panel blank (for example, do not add any conditions), then the coupon code will be valid for any products present in the shopping cart and for any amount.

Since we have two conditions, both of which are valid, click the **ALL** in **In ALL of these conditions are TRUE**. It will allow you to select **ANY**. These creates an "or" condition.

 Pay attention if you use nested conditions, as the ALL/ANY applies to only the top level conditions. You can use condition combinations to create nested and/or conditions.

Our first condition will test whether the customer has $100 or more of women's tops in their shopping cart:

1. Click the green **+** icon to create your first condition.
2. In the dropdown, choose **Products subselection**. We are creating a rule that will apply to only a particular selection of qualifying products.
3. Click on the words **total quantity is** and select **total amount**.
4. Click the word **is** and select **equals or greater than**.
5. Click the following ellipsis (**...**) and enter **100**. Hit your *Enter* key.
6. Change **ALL** to **ANY** in the condition description.
7. Click the green **+** icon nested within this condition.
8. Select **Category** from the dropdown menu.
9. Click **is** and select **is one of** from the dropdown menu.
10. Click the following ellipsis (**...**), and by either using the list icon or by typing the category IDs of the categories you wish to use, choose the **Tops** category and all sub-categories within, as shown in the following screenshot:

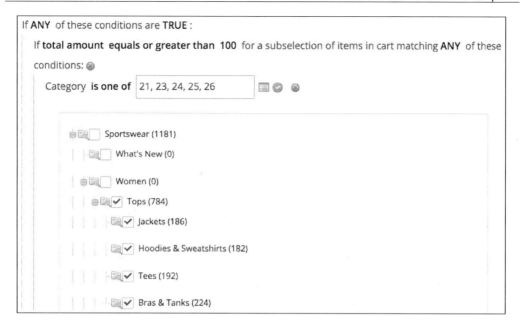

> It's a good idea to select all subcategories as well, since you may have items that are only assigned to a sub-category and not to the top level category.

11. Once you have selected your categories, click the green checkmark icon to save your choices.

Next, we need to add the or condition that tests whether the customer has three or more women's apparel items into their cart:

1. Click the left-most green + icon.
2. Select **Products subselection** in the resulting dropdown.
3. Select **equals or greater than** for the comparison value.
4. Enter **3** for the amount.
5. Change **ALL** to **ANY** in the condition description.
6. Click the nested green + icon.
7. Select **Category** from the dropdown.
8. Click **is** and select **is one of** from the dropdown choices.

9. Click the ellipsis (...) and select all categories within the women's apparel section, as you can see in the following image.

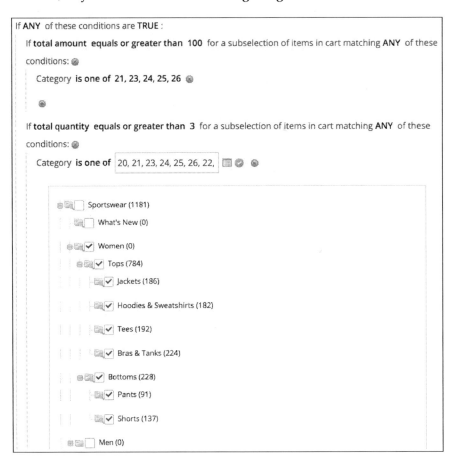

10. Click **Save and Continue Edit** to save your work to this point.

Once your conditions are set, your **Conditions** panel should look like the following image.

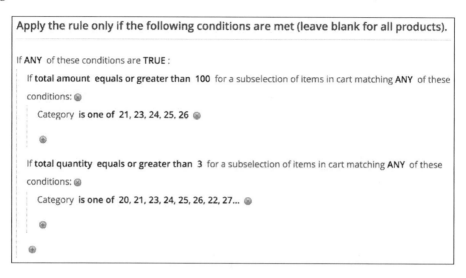

Now we can move on to specifying the actions that will take place for shopping carts that match our conditions.

Defining the rule's actions

There are two parts to a rule's actions:

- The amount discounted
- For which products the discount is to be applied

This is important to understand, as many are confused by the fact that action conditions appear very similar to the rule conditions that we created before. The conditions in this panel dictate which products qualify for the discounts.

In other words — as in our case — we're using one set of conditions to qualify the shopping cart and another set, within the **Actions** panel, to identify to which products the discount will be applied. These conditions are different. If they were the same — for example, you're discounting a shopping cart containing $100 or more in products — then you do not have to add any conditions to the **Actions** panel.

Let's now configure our **Actions** panel for our needs:

1. For **Apply,** select the default: **Percent of product price discount**.

   Let's go over the various choices here, so you have an idea as to which discount will work best with your purposes. Any value that is required will be entered into the **Discount Amount** field.

   - **Percent of product price discount**: Subtracts a percentage discount from the price of the applicable products.
   - **Fixed amount discount**: Subtracts a fixed amount from the price of the products.
   - **Fixed amount discount for whole cart**: The fixed amount entered here will be discounted from the entire cart total (you can specify whether the discount applies to shipping elsewhere on this panel).
   - **Buy X Get Y Free (discount amount is Y)**: You can specify that if a customer buys X quantity of a product (entered into the **Discount Qty Step (Buy X) field**), they will receive Y quantity of the same product for free.

2. Enter **20** into the **Discount Amount field**. You do not need to enter % for percentage discounts.

3. Since we are not limiting the number of the same item to which the discount may be applied, we will set **Maximum Qty Discount is Applied To** as **0**.

4. The **Discount Qty Step (Buy X)** does not apply for our case (see above regarding the Buy X Get Y Free discount choice).

5. Set **Leave Apply to Shipping Amount** as **No**.

6. Set **Discard subsequent rules** to **Yes**. We do not want other offers to apply if this discount is used.

 If the priority of your rule is lower than another rule, the higher priority rule will still be applied. This setting only applies to lower priority rules.

7. Set **Free Shipping** to **For shipment with matching items,** as our example discount also gives the customer free shipping for the entire qualifying order.

 For free shipping to work, you have to have at least one free shipping method configured. See *Chapter 5, Configuring to Sell,* for more information on shipping.

8. Click on **Save and Continue Edit** to save your settings so far.

The fields mentioned above can be visualized in the following screenshot:

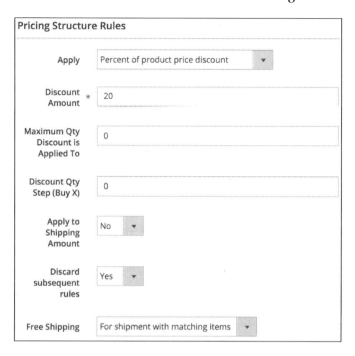

The next part of our actions configuration is to designate to which products the discount will be applied. In our case, any women's apparel (up to the three we set in the top part of the panel).

Using the same methodology we use in the **Conditions** panel, our **Actions** panel rules, when completed, will look like the following:

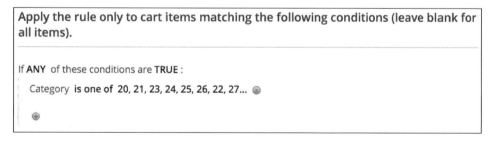

Modifying the rule's labels

While you could use the name of the rule as what displays to customers, it's probably more prudent to compose a discount label that more succinctly describes the discount. Furthermore, as in our example, we need different labels for each of the foreign language sites on which we sell sportswear.

For our example, we're going to label our discount for our customers as **Save 20% & Free Shipping!**

1. In the **Labels** panel, enter **Save 20% & Free Shipping!** in **Default Rule Label for All Store Views**.

2. Since we can use this same label for our English store view, we can leave **Sportswear English View** blank.

3. For **Sportswear French View**, we might enter (and, again, our French and German are not polished at all!) **Économisez 20% et livraison gratuite!**

4. In the **Sportswear German View**, we might use **Sie sparen 20% & Kostenloser Versand!**

And, of course, we click on **Save and Continue Edit**. Our **Labels** panel now looks like the following screenshot:

Generating coupon codes

In our example, we want to create 100 unique coupon codes that we can send to our selected customers. Magento does an amazing job of helping you generate codes and also keeps track of how many times specific codes have been used.

To begin, go to the **Manage Coupon Codes** panel. Let's assume we want to create codes that are alphanumeric (both letters and numbers), 12 characters long, and have a prefix of ASW and a suffix of F20. Our coupon pattern would be ASW-XXX-XXX-F20, where "XXX" is a unique alphanumeric code. To configure this, we set up the parameters for the codes and then click on **Generate** to allow Magento to create the 100 unique codes we need:

1. In **Coupon Qty**, enter **100**.

> For testing purposes — and particularly if these are single-use coupon codes — you should generate a few more than you need. In this case, we might want to generate 110 or 120 codes, just so we can thoroughly test. See the next section about testing for more information.

2. Our **Code Length** is **6** (we do not count the hyphens or the prefix and suffix, as we specify those a bit later).

3. For **Code Format**, select **Alphanumeric**.

4. In **Code Prefix**, enter **ASW-** (we're using this for Acme Sportswear).

5. In **Code Suffix**, enter **-F20** (for Free and 20% off).

> The use of a prefix and/or suffix is purely optional. If you're using unique coupon codes, you may want to use some designators that will help you identify that the code is a valid code for the order. When an order is viewed in your backend, it will show what codes, if any, were applied to the order. If you only use randomly generated codes without other designators, you might not be able to easily determine what actual discount rule was applied. If you want hyphens before or after a prefix/suffix, you need to include it in the appropriate fields.

6. Since we want a hyphen inserted into our codes, we can enter **3** in **Dash Every X Characters**.

The fields mentioned above can be visualized in the following screenshot:

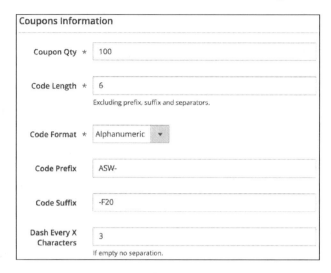

Now, we can click on **Generate** to create our 100 unique codes. Once generated, you should see 100 records created in the lower portion of the panel. Although your codes will be different (they are randomly generated, after all), your list should look similar to ours.

 Customers may enter codes using either lower or upper case. asw-xqu-u7i-f20 will work just as well as ASW-XQU-U7I-F20 or AsW-xQu-U7I-f20.

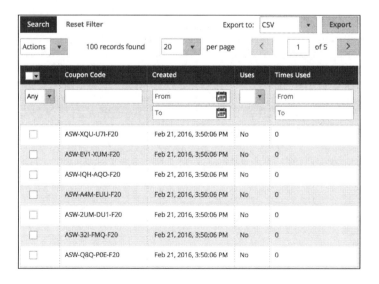

Using the export tool at the top of your list, you can now export your codes and use them with your email program to send these codes to your customers.

> Unfortunately, Magento 2 does not have a native means of sending your unique codes to your customers. You will have to use a third-party email solution or extension if you wish to send these codes to your customers.

Testing the rule

As with any configuration you make in Magento, you should test and re-test to make sure your settings are correct. Try various tests, too. In developer-ese, these are called use cases.

> If your coupon code is only valid at a future date, you should change the start date to TODAY, then change to the future date once you have completed testing.

The more you test, the more confident you'll feel that your rule is valid.

Newsletters

When you acquire a new customer, it makes great sense to keep them interested in your offerings so that they will return again to make a purchase from your online store. The *Cost of Acquisition* for a sale is far less with a repeat transaction.

Magento 2 is able to help you keep your brand in front of your customers with basic email newsletter tools. With these tools you can:

- Allow customers to subscribe
- Create newsletter templates
- Schedule the sending of your newsletter
- Manage your subscribers

Magento will be the first to admit that their newsletter tools are pretty basic. If you want to be more sophisticated in how you construct your newsletters, segment your customers, and more, you should consider a more robust third-party tool. We use **MailChimp** (http://www.mailchimp.com), a leading email system that makes it easy to manage campaigns. It's fun to use, as well.

For connecting your Magento 2 store to MailChimp, we recommend the *MageMonkey for Magento 2* extension (http://store.ebizmarts.com/magemonkey-magento2.html). Ebizmarts, the creator of this extension, worked closely with MailChimp. The extension also adds emails for abandoned carts, supports multiple MailChimp lists, and creates autoresponders — emails for customer birthdays, related products, and product reviews. And, best of all, at the time of this writing, the extension was offered for free!

Subscribing customers

The newsletter function is enabled by default in Magento 2. As long as you have a newsletter subscription form on your site, your customers can subscribe and be added to your newsletter list.

Settings for newsletters are configured under **Stores | Configuration | Customers** in the Magento 2 backend.

By default, a subscription form is placed in the footer of the base theme. If you use a third-party theme, the subscription form may be placed in another location.

Creating newsletter templates

Before you can send a newsletter, you have to create a newsletter template. The template contains your marketing message but can also contain dynamic content.

To begin, go to **Marketing | Newsletter** templates in your Magento backend. Click on **Add New Template**. On the **Template Information** panel, you will see the following fields:

- **Template Name**: Enter a name for the newsletter that is meaningful to you, as shown in your list of templates. You might use something like Marketing Newsletter, Feb 2016 or Spring Sale Announcement, 2016.

- **Template Subject**: This is the subject that will appear in the email subject received by your customers. Use something that is both enticing without sounding spammy.

- **Sender Name**: The From email shown in the email header will contain a name and an email address, something like: Acme Support `<support@ acmefurniture.com>`. This field is the name part (for example, Acme Support).

- **Sender Email**: This is the email address part of the From address. It is also the email address to which replies to your newsletter will be sent.

> Some people use `noreply@` as a sending email address. Some spam filters will object to this, and if you're intent on customer service, this is considered poor form.

- **Template Content**: As with other complex text fields in Magento, this one has a WYSIWYG editor to give you several tools for building an attractive and meaningful email newsletter. As with the blocks and CMS pages we discussed in *Chapter 6, Managing Non-Product Content*, you can insert variables and widgets, as well. This gives you the ability to insert products, category links, and more!

> When creating a new template, you'll see default content for inserting a variable for an unsubscribe link. This is key if you want to avoid violating anti-spam standards. However, there are more guidelines you should follow if you want your newsletters to be considered valid emails to subscribed customers. A good resource for compliance guidance can be found at `http://kb.mailchimp.com/ accounts#Compliance_Tips`.

- **Template Styles**: If you wish to add CSS styles to your newsletter content, you can add the CSS styling in this field.

The fields mentioned above can be visualized in the following screenshot:

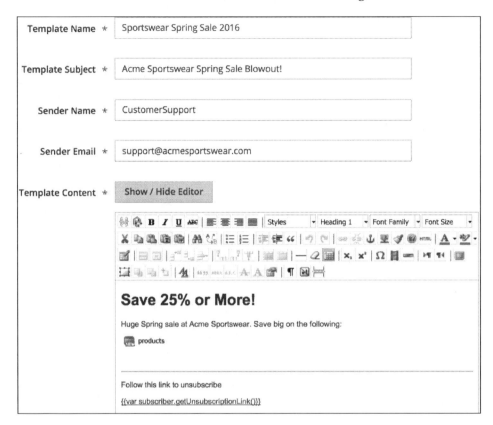

Once you've completed your template, you can click on **Preview Template** to view your newsletter as it will appear to your customers.

Scheduling your newsletter

When you're ready to schedule your newsletter to be sent, go to **Marketing | Newsletter Templates**. In the **Action** column to the right of the newsletter you wish to send, select **Queue Newsletter** in the dropdown menu. The screen will redirect to the **Queue Information** panel.

Here, you can select the date on which you wish to send your newsletter, select the store views for whose subscribers you wish to receive your newsletter, and review the contents of your newsletter.

Queue Date Start	Feb 29, 2016 9:26:4...

Subscribers From	**Furniture Website**
	   Furniture Store
	     Furniture English View
	Sportswear Website
	   Sportswear Store
	     Sportswear English View
	     Sportswear French View
	     Sportswear German View

Subject *	Acme Sportswear Spring Sale Blowout!
Sender Name *	CustomerSupport

Once you have made your selection, click on **Save Newsletter** to add it to the internal queue. Magento will send your newsletters to your chosen subscribers on the date you have selected.

To view your newsletter queue and the status of your queued newsletters, go to **Marketing | Newsletter Queue**.

> As of writing this, there is no means of cancelling a queued newsletter. You can, however, set the **Queue Date Start** to **blank**, which will prevent it from being sent.

Checking for problems

Once your newsletter is sent, you can see how well it is sent — and check for any problems — by going to **Reports | Newsletter Problems Report**. If any problems are found, a report identifying each error will appear in this list.

Managing your subscribers

Under **Marketing | Newsletter Subscribers**, you can view all or a filtered sub-set of your newsletter subscribers. This can be helpful if you wish to see how many have come from various stores in your installation. You can also unsubscribe customers from this screen.

As with most other grid listings in Magento, you can export your subscriber list to use for other purposes.

Using sitemaps

Many websites have pages that show sitemaps — a hierarchal list of pages within a site. For our purposes, a sitemap is an XML file that resides on your server and is read by Google and other search engines to learn about your site.

If you've ever worked with Google Webmaster Tools (`https://www.google.com/webmasters/`), you're familiar with the concept of providing a sitemap URL to Google. By doing so, Google can become fully aware of the pages and products within your Magento store without having to figure it out themselves. Sitemaps are an important component of your **Search Engine Optimization (SEO)** efforts.

Magento 2 has a built-in sitemap functionality that you can configure to generate sitemaps for each store view within your installation.

Adding a sitemap

To create a sitemap for a store view, go to **Marketing | Site Map** in the Magento 2 backend. Click on **Add Sitemap**.

> Magento spells it "Site Map" as two words in many places. We use the one word, sitemap as it is used by Google and others. We're not sure why Magento prefers the two-word version. Given that Magento uses the single word version in some places, it appears they're not entirely consistent.

For our first sitemap, we'll create one for our furniture store view. We only have the one English language view for that website.

1. Enter **furniture_sitemap.xml** for **Filename**. If you only have one store view, you can simply use `sitemap.xml`. However, if you use the same file name for each store, you would not have unique sitemaps for each store view.

2. We'll enter **/** for **Path**. This places the sitemap file at the root folder of our installation. You could create a subdirectory on your installation for storing your sitemap files as well, but any directory must be writeable.

> You could also create sub-folders for each of your store views and use `sitemap.xml` as the file name, such as `/furniture/sitemap.xml`, `/sportswear_en/sitemap.xml`, `/sportswear_de/sitemap.xml`.

3. Choose the applicable **Store View**.

4. Click on **Save & Generate**.

The fields mentioned above can be visualized in the following screenshot:

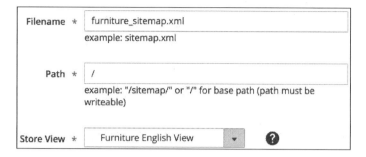

When Magento returns you to your list of sitemaps, you can click on the listed URL to view the actual XML file. The first part of your sitemap file may look like this:

```
<urlset xmlns="http://www.sitemaps.org/schemas/sitemap/0.9"
xmlns:content="http://www.google.com/schemas/sitemap-
content/1.0"xmlns:image="http://www.google.com/schemas/sitemap-
image/1.1">
<url>
<loc>http://acmefurniture.novusweb.com/sofas.html</loc>
<lastmod>2015-12-06T17:24:17+00:00</lastmod>
<changefreq>daily</changefreq>
<priority>0.5</priority>
</url>
<url>
<loc>http://acmefurniture.novusweb.com/sofas/couch.html</loc>
<lastmod>2015-12-30T23:09:56+00:00</lastmod>
<changefreq>daily</changefreq>
<priority>1.0</priority>
<image:image>
<image:loc>
http://acmefurniture.novusweb.com/pub/media/catalog/product/s/a/
sample-couch-red_2.jpg
</image:loc>
<image:title>Couch</image:title>
</image:image>
<PageMap xmlns="http://www.google.com/schemas/sitemap-pagemap/1.0">
<DataObject type="thumbnail">
<Attribute name="name" value="Couch"/>
<Attribute name="src" value="http://acmefurniture.novusweb.com/pub/
media/catalog/product/s/a/sample-couch-red_2.jpg"/>
</DataObject>
</PageMap>
</url>
```

This XML code is parsed by search engines to determine all the products and content of your site. You can control the frequency and importance of various sitemap elements under **Stores | Configuration | Catalog | XML Sitemap**.

 The discussion of these elements is beyond the scope of this book. For a good explanation of indexing sitemaps, go to https://support.google.com/webmasters/answer/156184.

Optimizing for search engines

Search Engine Optimization, or SEO, is both important and often misunderstood. There's probably as much misinformation on the Internet about SEO as there is good, solid advice.

While we don't have the opportunity or space to go into great detail about SEO in this book, we can help you establish good practices that can reap great rewards in terms of increasing your search engine visibility and helping online shoppers know what you're offering.

Meta fields are data that are stored in the HTML code of a web page. Customers can't see this code, as it's not displayed by the browser, but search engines can see this data (in fact, they can see everything under the hood). Google, Bing, and others use this meta data in conjunction with many other analyzed items on your page to determine how to present your site to search users, including rank and content.

Using meta fields for search engine visibility

It begins with a basic understanding of how search engines use meta fields, particularly Google, since Google will provide you with most of your search engine referred traffic.

Take a look at this Google search result:

Magento CSS Manager Extension | Mage Revolution™
www.magerevolution.com/mr/custom-**css-manager** ▾
$39.00 - In stock
Stop uploading custom.**css** files! Manage your custom **CSS** in your **Magento** backend. Instantly view your changes. Includes LESS preprocessor. From Mage ...

The title, **Magento CSS Manager Extension | Mage Revolution™** is taken from the **Title** field of the product page, unless a value is used in the **Meta Title** field of the product in Magento. If so, Google would use the **Meta Title** value instead.

The URL of the page is, of course, the actual link to the product page. As we described in *Chapter 2, Installing Magento 2*, the use of canonical URLs is important, as it gives Google one link to the product, even though, as in this case, the product is also accessible by going to `http://www.magerevolution.com/mr/magento-content-management-extensions/custom-css-manager`. Without the use of canonical URLs, Google would see this as two different pages, each with the exact same content. Google is known to penalize sites that contain duplicate content by decreasing their rank position.

Finally, the description part of the listing comes first from any existing **Meta Description** field. If none exists, Google attempts to construct a meaningful description from the content of the page. By using a **Meta Description** field, you can control how the product is described in search engines.

Meta fields in Magento

In *Chapter 2, Installing Magento 2*, we talked about the use of **Product Fields Auto-Generation**: the use of variables to automatically construct meta values for your products. While that is certainly a fast way of populating meta fields in products, it's also important to attend to meta fields for CMS pages and categories. There may also be certain products for which you want to insert special titles and descriptions to enhance their search engine presentation.

Do not under-value the efforts you take to improve your site SEO. So much of your traffic will come from search engines. But also be aware of SEO scams and bogus offers from so-called SEO experts. If anyone says they can guarantee you first page position, they are scammers. No one can guarantee first page search results. That position comes from careful attention to your meta information, product and page content, and really knowing your customers and your products. There are no shortcuts, but there are best practices. If you do need help in managing your SEO, shop around for reputable firms. Visit SEO-related forums and groups and ask others who are successful with SEO for recommendations. Never pay anyone who simply contacts you by unsolicited email. You'll just end up wasting your money with no credible result. And finally, use someone familiar with Magento's SEO features. We've seen several sites compromised by so-called SEO "experts" who tried hard-coding SEO features.

SEO checklist

As you prepare your site for launch — and beyond launch — take time to address each important SEO feature in Magento:

- **Meta title fields**: Enter a title no longer than 50-60 characters. Any more will be truncated when displayed in search results. Including your company name is nice but not critical; the customer is looking for a specific product. Use your company name on the home page meta title and they'll find you if searching for your brand. If customers shop by SKU, include the SKU or part number in the title.

- **Meta description fields**: Describe your product in 150 characters or less. Use action verbs and strong adjectives: "Save 20% on Yoga gear today! Top quality, 100% guarantee and free shipping" or "Premium 48 inch Yoga ball. Great durability, hypoallergenic material. Guaranteed. Free shipping."

> Note that descriptions may not show up in Google for some time. Therefore, avoid using time-sensitive descriptions — such as for temporary discounts and the like — or you may have upset customers expecting a discount well after it has expired!

- **Meta keywords**: Meta keywords are no longer given any ranking weight by search engines. However, it doesn't hurt to include at least the name of the product as a clue to search engines.

- **Canonical URLs**: Make sure to activate **Canonical Link Meta Tags** under **Stores | Configuration | Catalog | Catalog | Search Engine Optimization**. This will reduce any potential duplicate content penalties.

- **XML Sitemap**: Configure and activate your XML sitemap in **Stores | Configuration | Catalog | XML Sitemap**. Search engines use this to learn the hierarchy of your site and to make sure they visit all pages in your store. Don't forget to change **Enable Submission to Robots.txt** to **Yes**.

- **Category and product descriptions**: Don't be shy about describing your products. Use 300 words or more to really sell your product. Category descriptions can also help by informing the search engines about your categories, noting brands offered, and generally inspiring customers to carefully consider your product offerings.

Magento 2 also includes a number of SEO features, such as rich snippets. These are hidden data that provides Google et al with specific information about your products in a format that they understand. Price, availability, SKU, and more are easily read by search engines regardless of how this information is or is not presented to your customers.

Summary

As you prepare your Magento store for launch — or even if you're up and running — there's always more you can do to increase the sales productivity of your operation. It's important to continue working on your store.

In this chapter, we dove into customer groups, pricing rule promotions, newsletters, sitemaps, and Search Engine Optimization.

By mastering these features, you'll find new customers and new opportunities to sell more.

In the next chapter, we begin exploring the more technical aspects of Magento 2, by learning how to leverage its new architecture and features to customize functionality to meet your e-commerce objectives.

8

Extending Magento

One of Magento's strengths is the fact that the platform can be extended to provide additional features and functions. These **extensions**—or **add-ons**—number in the thousands. They include themes, payment gateway integrations, site management enhancements, utilities and many, many more features.

In this chapter, we will discuss the two primary ways of extending Magento:

- Extending existing Magento functionality to meet your own needs
- A quick overview of the current iteration of Magento Connect
- Creating your own Magento extensions

By learning how Magento can be enhanced, you will find that the power of Magento can be broadened to meet almost any specific e-commerce need you might imagine.

Magento Connect

Third-party extensions that are offered to the Magento community are, for the most part, listed in a special section of the Magento website called Magento Connect (http://www.Magentocommerce.com/Magento-connect/):

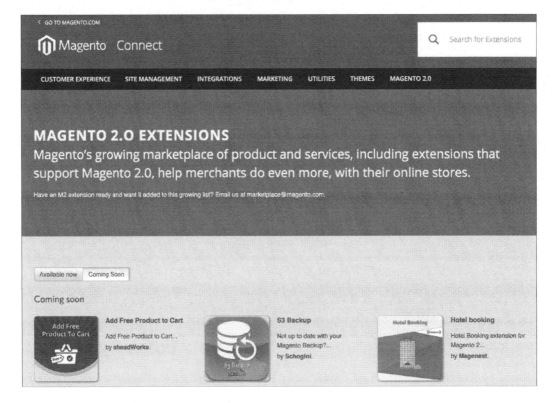

Let's now review some of the features of Magento Connect, as they relate to researching possible add-ons for your Magento installation.

Searching Magento Connect

At the center-right of the Magento Connect home page is a search field. As with any intuitive search, simply enter in one or more keywords. You can also select the specific version – which Magento calls a platform—in the drop-down menu to the right of the keyword entry field. As shown in the following screenshot, we are searching for any extensions relating to sales:

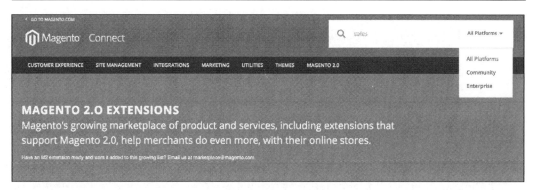

Search field in Magento Connect

Furthermore, we can narrow our search to the specific Magento platform, such as the one on which this book is focused: Community.

The results of our search can be further refined by identifying extensions that are free versus paid, or, if paid, fall within a certain price range.

You can also browse the extensions using the categories in the top navigation bar, or the groupings listed below the search form on the main **Magento Connect** page.

Why developers create free extensions

Magento extensions take time to create, test, package and distribute. Additionally, responsible developers provide support to those who install their extensions. Considering this investment of time and effort, why would any developer offer a free extension?

- In some case, the free extension is a light, or less-featured, version of a paid extension. If you like how the light version works in your Magento installation, you might pay to get additional functionality.

- Some extension developers provide other paid extensions as well. Again, if you like how the free extension works, you might be more trusting of the developer's paid extensions. This is particularly popular among theme developers who create one or more free themes with modest features, but sell much more feature-laden themes.

- I downloaded an extension once that did exactly what it promised, but I needed it to do something slightly different. Rather than change the code myself, I hired the extension developer to create a modified version to meet my needs. I ended up paying a lot less than if I had hired a developer to create the entire extension from scratch.

- Finally, there are developers who simply like to share. Amazing as it may seem, some people actually like to contribute to the overall success of Magento. Of course, I'm being cheeky here, but in many cases a developer has created a solution for their own needs that they realize could benefit others in the world of Magento. By providing a free extension, or theme, the developer is also validating their expertise. If I need to hire a developer for a specific Magento need, I would first look to developers who have solved similar issues. For example, if I need a payment gateway extension that doesn't already exist, I would first look to those developers who have demonstrated their ability to successfully create payment gateway integrations for Magento. A free extension, therefore, becomes a portfolio piece for a developer.

> At the time of writing this, the Magento Connect site for 2.0 was still evolving, and there were no protocols available for uploading extensions to the Connect marketplace. In its current iteration, the Connect site is a module catalog that directs the user to different developer websites. For the latest information on submitting extensions, go to `http://www.magentocommerce.com/magento-connect/create_your_extension`. The packaging process here is still specific to 1.0 extensions, but will be updated with information when Magento Connect for 2.0 comes online.

The new Magento module architecture

Much like Magento 1.0, Magento 2 is divided into modules. These modules are meant to encapsulate functionality related to a certain business feature. The framework provides organization for these modules, which can be found in the `app/code` directory with the following convention: `app/code/(vendor)/(modulename)`.

Under the `(modulename)` directory, there are a series of nested directories that contain the blocks, helpers, controllers, and models that make up a module. The hierarchy looks like this:

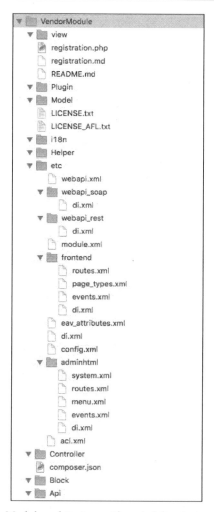

Module architecture with nested directories

The following is a brief description of these directories and the programmatic roles of the files they contain:

- `Block/`: This directory has PHP classes that contain logic to manage the view template. Blocks, therefore, are fundamentally related to display logic and are key to managing this logic.

- `Controller/`: This directory contains controllers for the module. A controller is responsible for routing requests in Magento, and handles requests by defining actions in controller class methods. These methods collect relevant data, and prepare and render the view.

- etc/: The etc/ directory contains files related to Magento configuration. For example, the module.xml file, a required file, contains information about the module version number and name.

- Model/: This directory has files that provide logic related to the model. The model provides abstraction for managing data from the relational database underlying Magento. Class methods here will allow you to perform **CRUD** (create read update, and delete) operations without the use of SQL (Structured Query Language), by providing an interstitial layer that generates SQL as a result of method invocation.

- Setup/: This directory contains classes for the setup of a new database structure and the data it needs to contain. This code is invoked when the module is installed.

- Api/: The Api/ directory contains module classes that are exposed to the Magento API, making them available to API calls.

- I18n/: This directory contains module language files used for localization.

- Plugin/: This directory contains plugins that can be used to extend the functionality of any public method in a Magento class. We'll discuss this directory in greater detail in the section immediately following this one.

- view/: This directory contains view files, including static templates, design templates, and layout files. We have discussed the contents of this directory and theming in general in greater detail in *Chapter 4*, *Designs and Themes*.

Extending Magento functionality with Magento plugins

We'll review a simple example of extending Magento functionality to give you an idea of what's involved and get you on your way. Magento 2.0 has introduced the concept of plugins that rely on dependency injection. While it's tempting to think of a plugin as interchangeable with extension or module, a plugin actually plays a significantly different role. It listens to any public method call on another object. As long as the class or method doesn't use the final keyword, any class and any public method is fair game, including methods in your classes, third-party classes and Magento classes. That's pretty impressive!

Start by declaring the plugin in the di.xml file, in the app/code/(vendor)/ (modulename)/Plugins/ path, with the following XML code:

```xml
<config>
    <type name="ObservedType">
        <plugin name="pluginName" type="PluginClassName" sortOrder="1"
```

```
disabled="false"/>
    </type>
</config>
```

In this example, the `type name` is the class being observed. This is the class with methods we're trying to extend. The `plugin name` is an arbitrary name you provide to the plugin, and the type is the name of the plugin's class in the `\Vendor\Module\Model\class\Plugin` format.

This is the class where we'll be defining the custom functionality that extends the method established in the type node.

The sort order attribute in the preceding XML allows for even greater flexibility. Multiple plugins can call the same method, and this field determines the order in which they are run.

The disabled attribute is pretty straightforward. It simply determines whether or not the plugin is active.

Once we've got the `di.xml` file in place, our next step is to create the class that's going to extend the original method in the `\Vendor\Module\Model\class\Plugin.php` file. Once it's there, we can choose to extend functionality before, after, and around the original method. So, say you wanted to execute some code, such as logging some data or firing off a call to a third-party API before the result of another public method; the following code would do this before the method was called:

```php
<?php

namespace My\Module\{class};

class classPlugin
{
    public function beforeGetName(\Magento\Catalog\Model\Product
$subject, $variable)
    {
        //execute code here
    }
}
?>
```

Now, say you wanted to insert some arbitrary code after the original public method. It would simply look like the following code snippet. Note that `before` has been replaced with `after`. So the naming convention involves the original method name with `before`, `after`, or `around` as a prefix:

```php
<?php

namespace My\Module\class;

class classPlugin
{
    public function afterGetName(\Magento\Catalog\Model\Product
$subject,$variable)
    {
        //execute code here
    }
}
?>
```

In the final example, code can be executed before and after the target method, as follows:

```php
namespace My\Module\class;

class classPlugin
{
    public function afterGetName(\Magento\Catalog\Model\Product
$subject,$proceed)
    {
        //execute code before original method here.
     $result = $proceed();
     //execute code after original method here.
     return true;
    }
}
?>
```

The special sauce here is in the `$proceed` parameter passed in, which allows delineation between code to be executed before and after a target method.

Building your own extensions

If you're a strong PHP developer, you may find it beneficial to create your own Magento enhancements. In fact, if you've been working with Magento for any length of time, you've no doubt had cause to tweak the code, even perhaps adding new functionality. For those with experience in MVC object-oriented programming, building new functionality for Magento can be quite rewarding.

If you do plan to create an extension you would like to share with other Magento developers, whether for free or profit, you should know about certain guidelines and resources that can help you create an extension which will be well-received by the Magento community.

Whether others have gone before

If you can't find an extension for Magento to meet your needs, and you think you want to do your own enhancements, take a moment to do some online searching first. One of the first places I look is the Magento documentation (`https://magento.com/help/documentation`). At the time of writing this, the Magento documentation has been rewritten for Magento 2.0 and is a fantastic source for understanding how extensions work in Magento. Additionally, for a deep dive into Magento functionality, the writings of Alan Storm are without parallel. You can find his articles on Magento 2 here: `http://alanstorm.com/category/magento-2`. The articles there are quite technical, but remarkably readable and laced with humorous nuggets.

You can also search on Google for possible solutions for your issue. There are numerous blogs where developers freely share some significant solutions. One of my favorites is the Inchoo blog (`http://inchoo.net/blog/`). These Magento experts have tackled some very interesting challenges with some quite elegant solutions. I also post solutions and tweaks on our website (`http://www.novusweb.com`).

Therefore, before you dive into your own modifications, check around. Why start from scratch if others have already done most of the work for you?

Your extension files

For your new extension to work, it must be placed correctly within the Magento file hierarchy. We've reviewed the entire hierarchy at the top of the chapter, but for the purposes of this example, we'll only be touching on the subset of those files and directories necessary to stub out a basic module. We've broken this into a series of steps, grouped functionally, to make it a bit more digestible.

Step one

The first thing we'll need to do is create a `module.xml` and register the module. This is actually pretty straightforward in comparison to a lot of what we've been reviewing. You'll place the `module.xml` file in the `app\code\{vendor}\{module_name}\etc\` folder and edit it, adding the following content:

```
<?xml version="1.0"?>
<config xmlns:xsi="http://www.w3.org/2001/XMLSchema-instance" xsi:noNa
mespaceSchemaLocation="../../../../../lib/internal/Magento/Framework/
Module/etc/module.xsd">
    <module name="{module_name}" setup_version="1.0.0">
    </module>
</config>
```

Next, in the root directory of the module `{vendor}\{module_name}\`, create a file named `register.php` with the following content:

```
<?php
\Magento\Framework\Component\ComponentRegistrar::register(
    \Magento\Framework\Component\ComponentRegistrar::MODULE,
    '{vendor}_{module}',
    __DIR__
);
```

The inclusion of `register.php` is a new step in Magento 2.0, and it's required. I was surprised when reviewing a series of themes and modules to find it frequently left out. If you're having problems with a theme or module, this is a good first place to check. If you leave it out, you won't be able to activate the module.

Step two

The second thing we'll need to do is create a frontend router. Add the following text to `etc/frontend/routes.xml` in your module:

```
<?xml version="1.0"?>
<config xmlns:xsi="http://www.w3.org/2001/XMLSchema-instance" xsi:
noNamespaceSchemaLocation="../../../../../lib/internal/Magento/
Framework/App/etc/routes.xsd">
    <router id="standard">
        <route id="{module}" frontName="{module_name}">
            <module name="{vendor}_{module_name}" />
        </route>
    </router>
</config>
```

It's beyond the scope of this book to pick apart and discuss the constituent parts of this XML, but if you're curious about the details, the resources alluded to earlier in this chapter (especially Alan Storm's series of articles) are an excellent place to go for detail.

Step three

The third thing we'll need to do is create a controller action. Start by creating an `index.php` file in `app\code\{vendor}\{module_name}\Controller\Index\` with the following content:

```php
<?php
namespace {vendor}\{module}\Controller\Index;

class Index extends \Magento\Framework\App\Action\Action {
protected $resultPageFactory;
public function __construct(\Magento\Framework\App\Action\Context $context,
        \Magento\Framework\View\Result\PageFactory $resultPageFactory)
{
        $this->resultPageFactory = $resultPageFactory;
        parent::__construct($context);
    }

public function execute()
    {
        $resultPage = $this->resultPageFactory->create();
        $resultPage->getConfig()->getTitle()->prepend(__('vendor
examplemodule'));
        return $resultPage;
    }
}
```

Every action extends the core Magento action class, and always has an `execute()` method, which is executed when the action is invoked. It's also important to note how this impacts the URL. The `frontname` specified in the router is the first part of the URL, the `controller` folder the second part, and the name of the file containing the controller code, the third part.

Again, there's more fun detail here, but for the purposes of this rudimentary example, we don't want to get bogged down breaking this down into too much detail.

Step four

The fourth thing we'll need to do is create a layout file. You'll add this file in the `app\code\{vendor}\{module}\View\frontend\layout\` directory using the name `default.xml`.

The contents should look like this:

```
<?xml version="1.0"?>
<page xmlns:xsi="http://www.w3.org/2001/XMLSchema-instance"
layout="1column" xsi:noNamespaceSchemaLocation="urn:magento:framework:
View/Layout/etc/page_configuration.xsd">
  <body>
    <referenceContainer name="content">
      <block class="{vendor}\{module}\Block\{module}.php"
name="{vendor}_{module}" template="arbitrary_template_name.phtml">
      </block>
    </referenceContainer>
  </body>
</page>
```

Step five

The fifth thing we'll need to do is create a block for our module. Once this is done, we can create a template file and activate the module. The block will be intuitively added to `app\code\{vendor}\{module}\Block\{module}.php` and contain the following content:

```
<?php
namespace {vendor}\{module_name}\Block;
class {module_name} extends \Magento\Framework\View\Element\Template
{
  public function _prepareLayout()
  {
    return parent::_prepareLayout();
  }
}
```

For the template, we'll just add valid HTML content to the `app\code\{vendor}\ {module}\View\frontend\layout\ arbitrary_template_name.phtml` file, as follows:

```
<h1> This is text from the arbitrary_template_name.phtml template
file. Maybe add some CSS? </h1>
```

Step six

Activate the module. This is most easily done by editing the `app\etc\config.php` file and adding an entry for your module here:

```
143        'Magento_Sitemap' => 1,
144        'Magento_Solr' => 1,
145        'Magento_WishlistSampleData' => 1,
146        'Magento_Support' => 1,
147        'Magento_Swagger' => 1,
148        'Magento_Swatches' => 1,
149        'Magento_SwatchesSampleData' => 1,
150        'Magento_GoogleTagManager' => 1,
151        'Magento_TargetRuleSampleData' => 1,
152        'Magento_ProductLinksSampleData' => 1,
153        'Magento_TaxImportExport' => 1,
154        'Magento_TaxSampleData' => 1,
155        'Magento_ReviewSampleData' => 1,
156        'Magento_CmsSampleData' => 1,
157        'Magento_Translation' => 1,
158        'Magento_Shipping' => 1,
159        'Magento_Ups' => 1,
160        'Magento_UrlRewrite' => 1,
161        'Magento_SalesRuleSampleData' => 1,
162        'Magento_Usps' => 1,
163        'Magento_Variable' => 1,
164        'Magento_Version' => 1,
165        'Magento_BannerCustomerSegment' => 1,
166        'Magento_VisualMerchandiser' => 1,
167        'Magento_Webapi' => 1,
168        'Magento_CatalogPermissions' => 1,
169        'Magento_SalesSampleData' => 1,
170        'Magento_CatalogWidget' => 1,
171        'Magento_WidgetSampleData' => 1,
172        'Magento_GiftRegistrySampleData' => 1,
173        'Magento_MultipleWishlistSampleData' => 1,
174        'Magento_Worldpay' => 1,
175        'Vendor_ExampleModule' => 1,
176    ),
177 );
```

There's another way to activate the module as well. If you have access to the command line, and are comfortable with its use, you can simply invoke the Magento binary to activate the module, by running the following command from the document root of your website:

```
bin/magento setup:upgrade
```

You should see output similar, but not identical, to the following screenshot:

```
[ec2-user@ip-172-30-0-146 m2ee.praxisis.com]$ bin/magento setup:upgrade
Cache cleared successfully
File system cleanup:
/var/www/html/m2ee.praxisis.com/var/generation/Composer
/var/www/html/m2ee.praxisis.com/var/generation/Jonathanbownds
/var/www/html/m2ee.praxisis.com/var/generation/Magento
/var/www/html/m2ee.praxisis.com/var/generation/Pulsestorm
/var/www/html/m2ee.praxisis.com/var/generation/Symfony
/var/www/html/m2ee.praxisis.com/var/generation/Vendor
The directory '/var/www/html/m2ee.praxisis.com/var/di/' doesn't exist - skipping cleanup
Updating modules:
```

Once the module is active, clear the system cache using the following command:

```
bin/magento cache:clean
```

The cleared cache types will be displayed:

```
[ec2-user@ip-172-30-0-146 m2ee.praxisis.com]$ bin/magento cache:clean
Cleaned cache types:
config
layout
block_html
collections
reflection
db_ddl
eav
full_page
config_integration
config_integration_api
target_rule
translate
config_webservice
```

After the cache has been cleared, you can view the result of your labor. Remember, the `frontname` defined in the `route.xml` defines the first part of the URL, and the second and third are defined by the `controller` folder and the PHP file. In the example reviewed above, this URL would be `http://magentostore/{module_name}/index/index/`. Depending on what HTML you've put in your sample template, you should see a result that looks something like the following screenshot:

Summary

Almost every week, I search Magento Connect just to see what new features and themes are being added. The creativity of the Magento developer community can be quite impressive.

One of the great joys of working with Magento is knowing that it is fully extendable in many ways, from simple theme enhancements, to full-fledged functionality changes. Depending on your own skills and talents, you may want to take solutions you've created and let others benefit, either as free contributions or money-making add-ons.

In this chapter, we have covered searching, evaluating, and installing Magento Connect extensions, the process of extending existing Magento functionality using plugins, and creating and registering your own extension from scratch.

Of course, we have a couple more interesting areas to cover in *Chapters 9, Optimizing Magento,* and *Chapter 10, Advanced Techniques,* which will further help you extend the power of Magento.

9
Optimizing Magento

As you've no doubt realized by now, Magento 2 is a very powerful e-commerce platform. From its robust product management suite to its virtually unlimited extendability, Magento packs a lot into one open source platform.

From our work within its files, we have learned that Magento combines a great number of separate files and data tables to present any page to online visitors. By its very nature, the MVC architecture of Magento puts a good deal of overhead on any web server. In the beginning, the complexity of Magento discouraged some developers because of the demands the platform placed on hosting servers.

However, over time Magento's developers have worked hard to improve overall performance, and Magento 2 represents a milestone in that regard. Magento 2 is indeed faster than before, even when taking faster servers into account.

That said, for Magento to perform at the highest levels of performance, there are areas with which you should become familiar. Specifically:

- The Magento EAV methodology
- Indexing and caching
- Server tuning configurations

After all, a faster website improves the customer's experience and helps improve your rankings with search engines.

Exploring the EAV

Most databases for open source platforms are quite simple in comparison to Magento's. For instance, in the past, when one designed e-commerce systems from scratch, it was likely that a simple relational model would suffice: one table for products that would contain all the key information relating to that product, such as price, available quantity, description, weight, and so on. The challenge with this traditional approach was that if we needed to add a new product attribute, such as height, that field would have to be added to the product table, thereby making previous versions incompatible and complicating any upgrade path.

In order for Magento to be a truly scalable platform, its developers utilize an **Entity, Attribute and Value (EAV)**, or **Sparse Matrix,** architecture. This database structure adds a great deal of complexity to the Magento data model to be sure, but its advantage is its ability to allow an unlimited number of attributes to be added to any core item, such as products, categories, customers, addresses, and more. Today's Magento installs an initial 296 data tables, many of which are related to EAV.

EAV allows developers (and you) the ability to extend any entity's attributes without changing any of the data tables. Let's break down EAV to understand how this works.

> As you go through this chapter, you may want to take an actual look at the tables of your Magento installation. With most hosting providers, you are provided **phpAdmin** as a tool for exploring and manipulating your database. If not, you can use any number of available tools, including the free *MySQL Workbench* (http://www.mysql.com/products/workbench/). See your hosting provider for information on how to directly access your database.

Entity

Products, categories, customers, customer addresses, ratings, and reviews are all entities in the Magento data scheme. Each entity has its own entity record in one of the following tables:

- `catalog_product_entity`
- `catalog_category_entity`
- `customer_entity`

- customer_address_entity
- rating_entity
- review_entity
- eav_entity (stores product attribute entities)

Each of these entity tables stores very basic information about the entity. For instance, let's take a look at the columns of the catalog_product_entity table:

- entity_id
- entity_type_id
- attribute_set_id
- type_id
- sku
- has_options
- required_options
- created_at
- updated_at

These are the only columns required to define any product in the database. Notice that the name, description, and price of the product are not included in this table.

Attribute

Attributes are the names of various items that belong to an entity. For instance, a product has attributes of price, description, and quantity. Attribute tables don't store the actual value of the item, only its name and its relationship to the entity. That's where value comes in.

Value

If you're following the bouncing ball so far, you now can surmise that value is the actual data of the attribute. So, if we use a simple graphic such as shown in the following figure, we can visualize the entire EAV relationship.

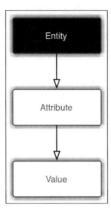

Putting it all together

Let's look at how this works in practice for a product. The product entity is stored in the `catalog_product_entity` table, as described before. To bring together all the information related to a product, we have to pull in all the various attributes (and their values) connected to the product.

To do that, we look into the `eav_attribute` table. This table connects all attributes to their respective entities. One column in this table is called `entity_type_id`. This column relates to the `entity_type_id` column in the `catalog_product_entity` table, as shown in the following figure:

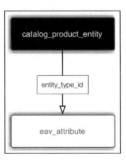

Once the associated attribute for an entity (in this example, a product) is determined, Magento next works to associate the actual value for the attribute. Here's where it gets a bit complicated, but fun!

For each attribute, Magento stores a type for the associated value. In other words, is the value a decimal value (such as price), a text value (for example, description), and so on. These are stored in the `eav_attribute` table in a column named `backend_type`. For each type, Magento has a corresponding table whose name ends in the particular type. The following are the value tables for product entities:

- `catalog_product_entity_datetime`
- `catalog_product_entity_decimal`
- `catalog_product_entity_int`
- `catalog_product_entity_text`
- `catalog_product_entity_varchar`

If a lookup of a product's attribute shows a type of decimal, then the associated value would be found in the `catalog_product_entity_decimal` table. The following figure illustrates this basic relationship:

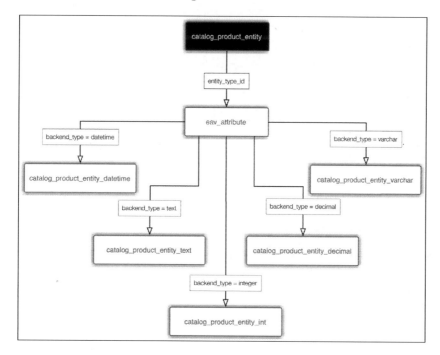

If you take a look at the Magento data tables, you'll now begin to understand the relationship between various entities, attributes, and values.

The good and bad of EAV

EAV is a key feature of Magento that allows developers to extend the platform without changing its core data structure. Imagine that you want to add new functionality that depends on a new product attribute - you could simply add that attribute into the system without adding a single new column to any table!

Unfortunately, there is a trade-off: performance. As you can see, in order to pull in all the information for a product — such as for a product detail page — Magento has to do a lot of calls to a lot of tables within the database. These lookups take time and server resources.

Fortunately, Magento's developers are still a step ahead of us.

Making it flat

Long ago, developers realized that while EAV was a cool way to build extendability into Magento, it added a major hit in performance. All the lookups, particularly for busy sites, can really slow down response times. MySQL, the database used for Magento, is a single-threaded database, meaning it can only handle one operation at a time.

The solution was to take all the various relationships and pre-compile them into other tables. In essence, Magento could do its lookups using fewer tables (and therefore fewer SQL statements) in order to get the same data.

If you look again at the data tables, you'll see a number of tables with index or flat in the name. These tables combine the EAV relationships into one table.

In order to take advantage of this feature for categories and products (sales orders are automatically flattened):

1. Log into your Magento backend.
2. Go to **Stores | Configuration | Catalog**.
3. Click to expand **Storefront**.
4. Select **Yes** for both **Use Flat Catalog Category** and **Use Flat Catalog Product**.
5. Click on **Save Config**.

After saving, you should get a notice at the top of your Admin page, like the following screenshot:

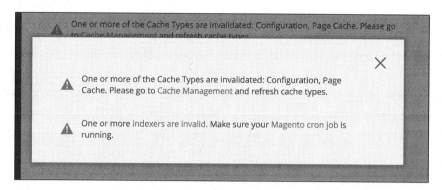

One of the things you will have to do as you add or update products and categories is to reindex your site. We'll discuss indexing in more depth in the next section.

Indexing and caching

Today's search engines have started measuring rendering times — the time it takes for a web page to download, including graphics and other files — as part of their ranking algorithms. In the past, we used to concentrate on download speed because so many users were connected to the Internet with slow, dial-up connections. With the proliferation of broadband speeds, most developers eased up on this goal, opting to include more flash animations, larger graphics, and complex JavaScripts. Now, we're moving back to the beginning in order to satisfy Google, Yahoo!, and Bing.

With Magento's complex MVC architecture and database structure, you can have the most efficient front-end design possible, yet still experience very slow download speeds as Magento works to build the pages and query the database. Therefore, to create a site with the lowest download speed, we need to take advantage of two important tools: indexing and caching. Each contributes its own benefit to your goal of speeding up the page generation process.

Indexing

As your Magento installation grows with products, customers, and orders, database lookups can become slower as the MySQL database has to look among a greater number of records to find the ones it needs. Magento uses a number of indexing tables which provide faster lookups by pre-organizing the data records. However, as your site grows, so do these index tables.

In our discussion on EAV, we talked about flattening the categories and products. In essence, when Magento is asked to index categories and products, it pulls in all the various related EAV data for each and creates records in special tables that contain all the related data in one record. In other words, instead of doing lookups among as many as 50 tables to display all the information on a product, Magento looks to only a handful of tables, thereby gathering the necessary information more quickly.

Flat or no flat

The speed difference when using a flat catalog versus a non-flat catalog is unnoticeable for low-traffic sites, as MySQL can adequately handle requests very, very well. However, as your site grows in traffic, you will notice a wider speed differential. Additionally, if your store hosts thousands of products, you'll certainly appreciate the added speed a flat catalog will give your site.

The trade-off is that reindexing a site with lots of products and/or categories can take a long time if you choose to use a flat catalog. For that reason, we generally keep the flattening feature turned off when we populate a new site with products. However, once we go live, we almost always turn on the flat feature to give our sites the fastest possible rendering possible, even if the initial site traffic is low.

Reindexing

As we saw in the previous figure, if you make changes to your site, Magento will notify you that you need to reindex your site. To do this, you need to perform the following steps:

1. Go to **System | Index Management** in your Magento backend.
2. Select the indexes that say **REINDEX REQUIRED**.
3. Select **Reindex Data** in the dropdown menu at the top right of the screen.
4. Click on **Submit**.

Once completed, you will see these indexes with a status of **READY**.

Caching

While indexing can help speed up database lookups by pre-organizing the data for faster lookups, caching does virtually the same thing for the HTML page components that make up the front-end experience. Caching stores completed pages or parts of pages so that website visitors will be provided with faster downloads.

In a nutshell, caching works like this (see the following chart, also):

1. Site visitor requests a page from your site.
2. Magento first checks to see if the request can already be fulfilled from a cached file.
3. If no cached file exists, or if the cached data is deemed to be old, Magento rebuilds the actual file.
4. Magento stores a new copy of the file in the cache.
5. Then, the file is sent to the visitor's browser.

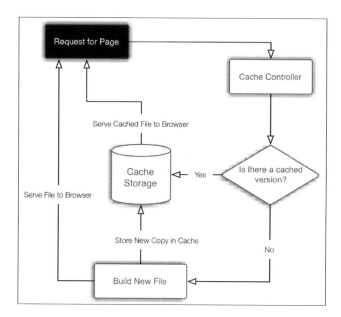

Caching in Magento is accomplished in a couple of ways: with core components, such as modules and layouts, and through whole page caching, which stores entire page outputs.

Core caching

Every time a page is accessed by a visitor, various modules, layouts, product images, and more are cached or stored for easy retrieval within the /var/cache directory of your Magento installation. If you explore this directory on your server, you'll see thousands of files with strange names. These are the actual pieces of cached data that are delivered to visitors to your site.

Full page cache

Whole page caching is just as the name implies: the caching of an entire web page. Imagine the speed boost if Magento did not have to build a new page by assembling dozens of layout and module components, cached or otherwise!

The impact of caching

I've run some tests of sites with and without caching turned on. In almost all of our tests, caching improved download speeds by approximately 25%-40%, depending on the overall load on the server. The heavier the load, the more the benefit since the server is naturally slower in building new pages versus serving cached pages.

This increase in speed, while perhaps not as noticeable to your site visitors, can have a huge impact on how search engines rank your site.

Managing caching

While caching does help speed up page delivery, it does take a bit of management on your part. Caching is controllable in two areas of your backend:

1. Go to **Store | Configuration | System**.
2. Expand the **External Full Page Cache Settings**.
3. Select **Yes** for **Enable External Cache**.
4. Click on **Save Config**.

Then, you need to set your core cache settings:

1. Go to **System | Cache Management**.
2. Click **Select All** over the first column.
3. Select **Enable** in the upper right menu.
4. Click on **Submit**.

Unfortunately, some extensions are not properly designed to participate in Magento's caching system. If you experience problems in how certain content blocks are rendered, you may want to leave the **Blocks HTML output** cache disabled. While this prevents content blocks from being cached, it may be your best remedy if you have a third-party extension which you're really fond of.

Caching in Magento 2 – not just FPC

Magento 2 has included a variety of new areas to the caching engine, as can be seen from the following screenshot:

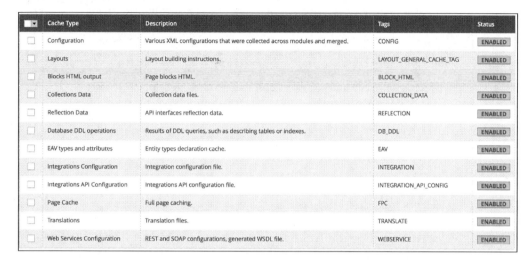

	Cache Type	Description	Tags	Status
☐	Configuration	Various XML configurations that were collected across modules and merged.	CONFIG	ENABLED
☐	Layouts	Layout building instructions.	LAYOUT_GENERAL_CACHE_TAG	ENABLED
☐	Blocks HTML output	Page blocks HTML.	BLOCK_HTML	ENABLED
☐	Collections Data	Collection data files.	COLLECTION_DATA	ENABLED
☐	Reflection Data	API interfaces reflection data.	REFLECTION	ENABLED
☐	Database DDL operations	Results of DDL queries, such as describing tables or indexes.	DB_DDL	ENABLED
☐	EAV types and attributes	Entity types declaration cache.	EAV	ENABLED
☐	Integrations Configuration	Integration configuration file.	INTEGRATION	ENABLED
☐	Integrations API Configuration	Integrations API configuration file.	INTEGRATION_API_CONFIG	ENABLED
☐	Page Cache	Full page caching.	FPC	ENABLED
☐	Translations	Translation files.	TRANSLATE	ENABLED
☐	Web Services Configuration	REST and SOAP configurations, generated WSDL file.	WEBSERVICE	ENABLED

This is great for performance but also good to keep in mind when making changes to the site. Translation changes not showing up? You probably need to clear the cached translation files to fix this. As a rule of thumb, clearing the cache is a good first step when troubleshooting Magento.

Tuning your server for speed

Everyone we talk to who works with Magento is concerned about speed. As we've noted earlier, Magento's complex architecture is simultaneously good and bad. The level of functionality and extendability is practically unparalled in the world of open source platforms, yet even with proper use of indexing and caching, substantial site traffic can make your Magento site feel like a tortoise on sedatives.

The problem lies, in part, in the fact that developers assume that open source is analogous to quick and easy. The fault is not Magento's: it is what is it — a powerful, yet complex, e-commerce platform.

Therefore, if you want to use Magento to its fullest, it's your responsibility to make sure you have the resources and tools to capitalize on its power. In *Chapter 1, Planning for Magento*, we discussed technical requirements for running a Magento installation. Now, let's discuss some ways of increasing its speed and performance.

Travel with Caution

You'll find an almost endless supply of online blogs, wikis, and postings relating to the optimization of Magento. Some offer quick tweaks; others go into elaborate schemas. The challenge when looking for any type of fix is knowing what is sound practice and what may be out-dated, or simply wrong. The following suggestions are based on what I have found are both within the reach of most developers and that work for the sites we develop and manage. That said, any time you find something you want to try, try it on a test server or your local computer first. Never apply these modifications to a live, production Magento installation.

Deflation

Apache web servers have a module called `mod_deflate`. This module, when called by a website, serves to compress files sent by the server. To engage this module, insert the following code into the `.htaccess` file located in the root directory of your Magento installation, replacing what is currently there for the `mod_deflate` directive:

```
<IfModule mod_deflate.c>
############################################
## enable apache served files compression
## http://developer.yahoo.com/performance/rules.html#gzip

# Insert filter
SetOutputFilter DEFLATE
# Netscape 4.x has some problems...
BrowserMatch ^Mozilla/4 gzip-only-text/html
# Netscape 4.06-4.08 have some more problems
BrowserMatch ^Mozilla/4\.0[678] no-gzip
# MSIE masquerades as Netscape, but it is fine
BrowserMatch \bMSIE !no-gzip !gzip-only-text/html
# Don't compress images
SetEnvIfNoCase Request_URI \.(?:gif|jpe?g|png)$ no-gzip dont-vary
# Make sure proxies don't deliver the wrong content
Header append Vary User-Agent env=!dont-vary

</IfModule >
```

Using BrowserMob (http://www.browsermob.com) as our testing source, a configurable product page on our test site (the one we built to use for writing this book) was reduced in size from 452 KB to 124KB, a 73% reduction in the amount of data delivered!

Enabling expires

Another Apache module, mod_expires, controls how browser caches should treat files they store on users' computers. When you visit a website, your browser caches the results. For files that have not changed since a previous visit, the browser will use the file in the cache on the local computer rather than pull it again from the web server.

The expiration of these cached files can be controlled by your web server. If your server provides no expiration instructions, then your site visitor's browser may assume that the cached information is not good (or is still good long after it is) and fail to pull the best information from your site.

Insert the following within the <IfModule mod_expires.c> directive in your root .htaccess file:

```
ExpiresActive On
ExpiresDefault "access plus 1 month"
```

You can also use a shorter period of time, but generally, you want to allow browsers to use unchanged, cached files for quite a while, thereby lessening the load on your server.

Increasing PHP memory

This is one of the more difficult items to change if you're hosting on a shared account, as many hosting providers will not allow you to increase the amount of memory allocated to PHP. The normal default of 64 MB may be sufficient, but if you're expecting a high volume of users, increasing this to 256 MB has produced noticeable improvements for us.

To increase this in your .htaccess file, simply place a hash mark (#) before php_value memory_limit 64M and remove the hash mark before php_value memory_limit 256M.

Increasing the MySQL cache

This is one configuration you may have trouble implementing as it involves changing a couple of core variables for MySQL. When we started looking more closely at ways of speeding up database lookups, we found that with our hosting provider, MySQL was configured to do lookups without a cache: the `query cache` and `query cache limit` were both set to zero.

By doing some research, we found that MySQL queries could be made faster by increasing the total size of the `query cache` and the `query cache limit` allowed for any one query. Other developers who had experimented with this suggested at least a limit of 1 MB for the individual query and a total limit of 64 MB would handle most initial, growing Magento stores. As your store grows, you may want to increase these limits to allow MySQL to take advantage of its own internal caching mechanism.

If you do have the ability to modify your MySQL database — or if you can request a modification with your hosting provider — you should set the `query_cache_limit` and the `query_cache_size` to amounts such as the ones given above.

 For specific information on how to set these in MySQL, see http://dev.mysql.com/doc/refman/5.0/en/query-cache-configuration.html.

Using the Nginx server

Nginx is an alternative to Apache when running Magento. Significant performance improvement out of the box is driving quite a bit of this adoption, and a large number of vendors have made the switch from Apache to Nginx. In recognition of this, Magento 2 has been built with full support for Nginx. It's beyond the scope of this chapter to discuss Nginx configuration, but a vast majority of hosting providers will install Nginx for you to use. Magento 2 also has a suggested Nginx configuration file in the root folder, which can be seen via GitHub as well, here: https://github.com/magento/magento2/blob/develop/nginx.conf.sample.

Using Varnish cache

Magento 2 supports Varnish and allows for general parameter and **VCL (Varnish Configuration Language)** management. It's beyond the scope of this book to dive into configuring a Varnish proxy on your server, but again, this is something that many Magento specific hosting providers will support and configure on your behalf. Once this is in place, you can manage Varnish through Magento 2 in the **Store | Configuration | Advanced | System | Full page cache**, as shown in the following screenshot:

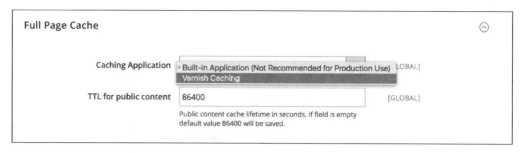

Using a CDN

CDNs (**Content Delivery Networks**), are servers which host your static or non-dynamic content on very fast servers and networks. For instance, if your images and JavaScript files are hosted on CDN servers, such as the ones provided by Amazon or Rackspace, your Magento server doesn't have to spend time processing and delivering those files to your visitors. Since web servers have limits in terms of the number of active connections they can support for delivering files, allowing other servers to carry part of the load means your server can accommodate more visitor requests.

Magento 2 has native CDN support, and if you navigate to **Store | Configuration | Web** you'll see an area called **Base URLs**. You can provide the CDN URL's here and Magento will automatically pull the resources from it.

Base URLs

Any of the fields allow fully qualified URLs that end with '/' (slash) e.g. http://example.com/magento/

Base URL

Specify URL or {{base_url}} placeholder. [STORE VIEW]

Base Link URL

{{unsecure_base_url}}

May start with {{unsecure_base_url}} placeholder. [STORE VIEW]

Base URL for Static View Files

May be empty or start with {{unsecure_base_url}} placeholder. [STORE VIEW]

Base URL for User Media Files

May be empty or start with {{unsecure_base_url}} placeholder. [STORE VIEW]

Summary

Magento continues to amaze me each day I spend building and managing e-commerce sites. There's little debate over the fact that it is both powerful and complicated; both configurably pleasant and frustratingly massive.

The marketing side of me enjoys the flexibility in design, presentation, and user interaction. The developer side finds satisfaction in learning new ways to squeeze additional performance and functionality from the world's most prolific open source platform.

Hopefully, this chapter has helped you gain a better understanding and appreciation of Magento's EAV data model; learn how to use the inherent indexing and caching capabilities of Magento, and dive into methods of fine-tuning your Magento installation for increased performance and shorter download times for store customers.

As we near the end of our journey toward Magento mastery, we have one final area to explore in the next chapter.

10
Advanced Techniques

By now, even if you're new to Magento, you should have a newfound appreciation for the power and extensibility of the industry's most active open source e-commerce platform. We've covered just about everything from installation to extending the platform. Your Magento store, if not already online, is most likely ready from a preparation viewpoint.

However, we're not quite finished yet. You may want to undertake a few more options that can make your installation act more like that of a Fortune 500 company — and less like a hobbyist's experiment in e-commerce.

In this chapter, I will take you through four advanced techniques that I feel any bona fide Magento *master* should have in their own personal knowledge base:

- Setting up a staging environment
- Versioning your site
- The Magento cron
- Backing up your database

You may not wish to undertake all of these now, or later, but at some point you will find these concepts helpful in turning Magento Community into an enterprise-level contender.

Setting up a staging environment

I know it is so very tempting to install Magento onto a production server account, do the initial configurations, and launch your new store. I also know that if you're only working with one Magento installation, there will undoubtedly come a time when — no matter how careful you are — a buggy extension, an errant piece of code, or a mistyped tag will cause your site to "go dark." You may even experience the dreaded Magento error screen (well known for offering little advice or remedy).

Therefore, if you take no other advice in this book to heart, take this one seriously: create a staging environment.

A simple approach

Some developers, particularly those working for large enterprise operations, may want to create an elaborate remote development, staging, and production setup with matching hardware for each environment, to decrease the number of variables present when deploying and testing code. If you're working with a large team and you have the funds available for the time and effort needed to create this type of setup, by all means do so. It's more likely, though, that if you do fall into this category, you're better suited for Magento's Enterprise solution, rather than the do-it-yourself Community edition discussed in this book.

For those of us on smaller budgets — who appreciate what Magento Community offers as a robust yet open source platform — I would suggest that you use a simpler, more rapidly deployable solution. Keep it simple and manageable.

The basic staging setup

There are actually two staging setups I maintain: one for testing and one for client development. The former is used to test new extensions, programming ideas, and design concepts, with no particular client use in mind. The latter is created for each client site and, except for the data, is an exact duplicate of the client site in terms of code, extensions, and design.

For client sites, this is my suggestion for a basic operation procedure:

1. Before installing the client Magento instance, install Magento into another server account (you can actually use one account with multiple sub-directories, one for each client staging site).

2. Install another copy of Magento onto the actual server account that will become the live (or production) store.

3. Complete your install design and configuration onto this first installation. As you complete each major task of your set-up, duplicate that task on the production server installation. By keeping the tasks in sync, it will be easier to make sure that every step taken is duplicated for the production installation.

At some point, you will feel you're ready to "go live." Guess what? You probably are. If your staging and production installations are in sync, going live is merely repointing the live domain name to your production account and setting payment gateways to "live" mode.

Don't be tempted to skip

One of the dubious benefits of writing a book like this one is that I get the pleasure of reliving some of my less brilliant moments as a student of Magento as I impart the wisdoms gained to you. This is one of those cases.

If you've followed the simple approach previously outlined, you should have a staging and a production environment that both work successfully. After all, you're not going to do anything to the production installation that you haven't already tried and tested on the staging installation. At least, that's the plan.

But once you launch the production store, there will come a time when you want to take a shortcut. Your client might be pressing to install a new extension they found at the Magento Connect website, or you might need to import some new product types the current store has not been using. Regardless, if you skip applying your changes to your staging installation and go directly to the production installation, you'll find that you will experience the moment when your heart drops out of your chest as your production store ceases to work as intended. It's another of Murphy's laws.

I only had to do that once — and suffer the client's anguished pleas to "get my store back online!" — to learn my lesson: staging first, then production. Never waiver from this dictum and you'll continue to successfully please your client, yourself, or whoever is the owner of the Magento store.

Version control

Version control is one of the most helpful and time-saving tools that can be used in support of software development. Even if you're only making small changes to the templates you're using, or adding modules without modifying the code inside of them, version control allows you to track changes that have been made and to evaluate code at any given point in time after the implementation. Even more importantly, it allows you to roll back the code to an earlier state, in cases where you're not quite sure what changes might have caused problems with the site.

At this point, the tool most widely used for version control by the development community is Git. Git is a system that was developed by Linus Torvalds (the originator of LINUX himself!) as a result of his frustration with existing tools. While it's beyond the scope of this book to go into much detail around what exactly it was that frustrated him, suffice to say that the changes he's made have positioned Git as the lingua franca for version control, and understanding its basics is a necessary endeavor if you want to do any development, or even just track changes to your system caused by upgrades.

Magento is a complicated system and even small changes can have a significant impact, causing errors that are obvious (site down) and some that are pernicious and creeping, such as the creation of bad data over time. Using a system to track all the changes that you and others have made to the system is a strongly recommended practice and will invariably, at some point, save you time, money, or both.

Let's start with a very basic prescription: installing the Git binary on your system and checking your current Magento site into a local repository. For the purposes of this example, we'll assume the use of OSX, although Git can be used for pretty much any modern operating system.

If you've installed the developer tools that come with OSX on your system, the Git binary will already be there. If you haven't and don't want to, you can download the Git binary from this link: `https://git-scm.com/download/mac`.

To make sure that Git has been installed on your system, open a terminal and type `git -version`. You should see the following output:

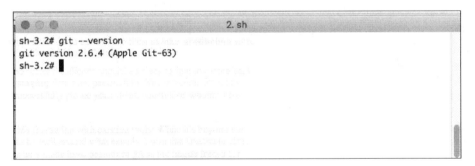

The next step you'll take will be to change to the document root of your Magento install. In this example, that's `/Users/jbownds/websites/magento2`. Once here, you can issue three simple commands to initialize the repository and check in the first version of your files. You'll start with `git init .`, followed by `git add .`, and finally `git commit . -m "first checkin of files"` (you can substitute another message here, if you like).

See the following screenshot for an example of what this will look like:

```
sh-3.2# git init .
Initialized empty Git repository in /Users/jbownds/websites/magento2/.git/
sh-3.2# git add .
sh-3.2# git commit . -m "First Checkin"

sh-3.2# █
```

Once you've checked in the files, you'll see a flurry of messages indicating which files have been added, which looks something like this:

```
                                    1. sh
create mode 100644 setup/view/magento/setup/home.phtml
create mode 100644 setup/view/magento/setup/index.phtml
create mode 100644 setup/view/magento/setup/install-extension-grid.phtml
create mode 100644 setup/view/magento/setup/install.phtml
create mode 100644 setup/view/magento/setup/landing.phtml
create mode 100644 setup/view/magento/setup/license.phtml
create mode 100644 setup/view/magento/setup/marketplace-credentials.phtml
create mode 100644 setup/view/magento/setup/navigation/header-bar.phtml
create mode 100644 setup/view/magento/setup/navigation/menu.phtml
create mode 100644 setup/view/magento/setup/navigation/side-menu.phtml
create mode 100644 setup/view/magento/setup/popupauth.phtml
create mode 100644 setup/view/magento/setup/readiness-check.phtml
create mode 100755 setup/view/magento/setup/readiness-check/progress.phtml
create mode 100644 setup/view/magento/setup/select-version.phtml
create mode 100644 setup/view/magento/setup/start-updater.phtml
create mode 100644 setup/view/magento/setup/success.phtml
create mode 100644 setup/view/magento/setup/system-config.phtml
create mode 100644 setup/view/magento/setup/updater-success.phtml
create mode 100644 setup/view/magento/setup/web-configuration.phtml
create mode 100644 setup/view/styles/lib/variables/_buttons.less
create mode 100644 setup/view/styles/lib/variables/_colors.less
create mode 100644 setup/view/styles/lib/variables/_typography.less
create mode 100644 var/.htaccess
create mode 100644 vendor/.htaccess
sh-3.2# █
```

This indicates that the Git repository has been initialized locally and you're ready for the next step. As mentioned before, Git is a distributed version control system. That means it's easy (and a good idea) to store copies of it in different locations. There are many services that allow for this, but the most popular is probably GitHub. For this reason, we'll walk through the steps necessary to take the repository you've created and push it out to GitHub. Start by creating an account here: `https://github.com/join`:

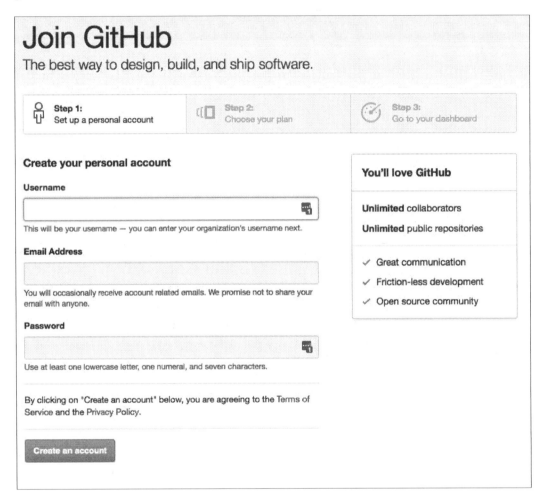

Once you've created an account (there are both free and paid options here), you can create a new repository by clicking the appropriate button on the right gutter:

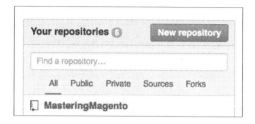

Click on the repository and there will be step-by-step instructions for pushing an existing repository from the command line:

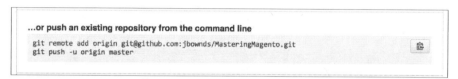

Go back to the document root for the repository you created and paste these commands into the terminal. The first one should run without a problem, but the second one will probably run into some authentication issues, as in the following example:

```
sh-3.2# git remote add origin git@github.com:jbownds/MasteringMagento.git
sh-3.2# git push -u origin master
The authenticity of host 'github.com (192.30.252.121)' can't be established.
RSA key fingerprint is SHA256:nThbg6kXUpJWGl7E1IGOCspRomTxdCARLviKw6E5SY8.
Are you sure you want to continue connecting (yes/no)? yes
Warning: Permanently added 'github.com,192.30.252.121' (RSA) to the list of known hosts.
Permission denied (publickey).
fatal: Could not read from remote repository.

Please make sure you have the correct access rights
and the repository exists.
sh-3.2# ssh-keygen
Generating public/private rsa key pair.
Enter file in which to save the key (/var/root/.ssh/id_rsa):
Enter passphrase (empty for no passphrase):
Enter same passphrase again:
Your identification has been saved in /var/root/.ssh/id_rsa.
Your public key has been saved in /var/root/.ssh/id_rsa.pub.
The key fingerprint is:
SHA256:dYJPashdm2caBFJwrcaiJfJRYTbAvLJAwLNNvFptzwE root@MacBook9ED9E205.attlocal.net
The key's randomart image is:
+---[RSA 2048]----+
|+ .o..B++.       |
| + ooE.+ o.      |
|. = oo....* .     |
|..o+++o++B =      |
| .o=.=oS = o     |
| .. o + =        |
|     .   .        |
|                 |
|                 |
+----[SHA256]-----+
sh-3.2#
```

As you can see in this example, the second command had issues. The specific error message is **Fatal: could not read remote repository. Please make sure you have the correct access rights**.

To address this, you'll need to add a public key for the user to GitHub, so GitHub recognizes the user trying to push this information into the remote repository. Don't worry - this sounds trickier than it is. All you need to do is type in `ssh-keygen`. You'll be prompted with several questions, all of which you can leave blank. At this point, you should have a generated public key for your user. You can view it by typing `vi ~/.ssh/id_rsa.pub`, and it'll look something like this (ignore the black arrow, this is just to blot out information in the private key).

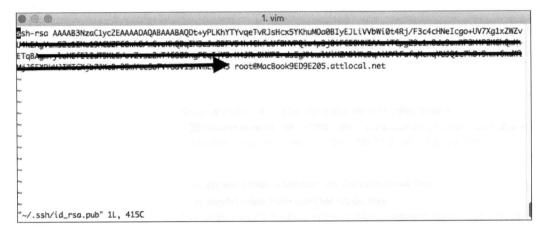

Copy this key and head back to GitHub. Once there, you can add this key in the **Settings** area of your account:

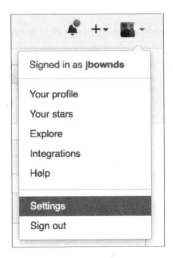

Click **New SSH key**, provide a title, and paste the value you copied into the text area. Save this value:

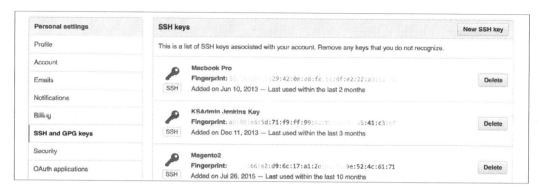

Now, when you go back to the command line and try `git push -u origin master` command again, you'll see results like this:

```
sh-3.2# git push -u origin master
Warning: Permanently added the RSA host key for IP address '192.30.252.129' to the list of known hosts.
Counting objects: 36044, done.
Delta compression using up to 4 threads.
Compressing objects: 100% (30064/30064), done.
Writing objects: 100% (36044/36044), 24.11 MiB | 2.71 MiB/s, done.
Total 36044 (delta 8312), reused 0 (delta 0)
To git@github.com:jbownds/MasteringMagento.git
 * [new branch]      master -> master
Branch master set up to track remote branch master from origin.
sh-3.2# █
```

Congratulations! You've created your first Git repository and pushed it out to GitHub.

Now, it's worth noting that there are a slew of very well-conceived visual tools that manage this process for you as well. It's beyond the scope of this text to evaluate these tools but it's worth mentioning a couple.

GitHub itself has a free desktop tool you can download and use, and it's quite handy for a visual representation of what's going on. The other tool we've seen used predominately is **Tower**. Tower can be obtained by visiting their website at `https://www.git-tower.com/`. While there is cost associated with the use of this tool (after a free trial), if you prefer a visual representation of what's happening with version control, this option may be more attractive to you.

Magento cron

If you're not up on Unix lingo, a **cron job** is a scheduled action that occurs at preset intervals on your server. For instance, Magento can create a new **sitemap** for your store according to the time interval you configure in the backend.

What is confounding to many new to Magento is that configuring cron intervals for various Magento functions doesn't actually cause anything to happen. The reason is that your server must still be told to run the configured tasks.

Cron jobs are configured by using what are called **crontabs**. These are expressions that dictate how often the server is to run the particular task.

Magento cron jobs

There are a few inherent functions included with Magento that can be run periodically, including:

- Catalog pricing rules
- Sending out scheduled newsletters
- Customer alerts for product price changes and availability

- Retrieval of currency exchange rates
- Creating sitemaps
- Log cleanup

Some third-party modules also include scheduled tasks, such as **Google Product feeds**. The frequency of most of these can be configured in your Magento backend. For those that aren't, you can find the crontab-style setting for each in the `config.xml` file of each module.

For example, the following is the cron schedule for the function that sends out scheduled newsletters, from `app/code/Mage/Newsletter/etc/config.xml`:

```
<crontab>
    <jobs>
        <newsletter_send_all>
            <schedule><cron_expr>*/5 * * * *</cron_expr></
schedule>
            <run><model>newsletter/observer::scheduledSend</
model></run>
        </newsletter_send_all>
    </jobs>
</crontab>
```

According to this crontab, Magento looks every 5 minutes to see if any newsletters need to be sent out.

Module	Cron job	Default frequency	Active?
Catalog	Reindex pricing	Every day at 2am	Yes
CatalogIndex	Reindex the entire catalog	Every day at 2am	No
CatalogIndex	Run queued indexing	Every minute	No
CatalogRule	Daily catalog update	Every day at 1am	Yes
Directory	Update currency rates	Controlled by **Currency Setup | Scheduled Import Settings**	Yes
Log	Clean logs	Every 10 minutes	No
Newsletter	Send scheduled newsletters	Every 5 minutes	Yes
PayPal	Fetch settlement reports	Controlled by **PayPal | Settlement Report Settings**	Yes
ProductAlert	Send product alerts to subscribing customers	Controlled by Catalog | **Product Alerts Run Settings**	Yes
Sales	Clean expired quotes	Every day at midnight	Yes

Module	Cron job	Default frequency	Active?
Sales	Generate aggregate reports (there are actually five configured)	Every day at midnight	Yes
SalesRule	Generate aggregate coupon data report	Every day at midnight	Yes
Sitemap	Generate sitemaps	Controlled by **Google Sitemap | Generation Settings**	Yes
Tax	Generate aggregate tax report	Every day at midnight	Yes

Many of Magentos core modules contain crontab scripts, although some are commented out. The following is a list of Magento Community 1.5 crontabs I have found within Magento, indicating for each whether the script is active or not. To make a script active, simply remove the comment tags surrounding the `<crontab>` code in the appropriate `config.xml` file.

> Note that some crontabs run according to values stored in your Magento database. The paths to these settings within **System \| Configuration** in your backend are included in this table. Even if these crontabs are active, your backend configuration may need to be enabled in order for these to run.

Triggering cron jobs

For your staging environment, you may want to keep cron jobs from running automatically. Rather, you may wish to have Magento run through its list of scheduled tasks at your command so you can watch for any problems or errors.

A wrinkle in Magento 2.0 is that there's no longer a `cron.php`, so Magento's cron can no longer be triggered from the command line (manually).

To manually run any scheduled jobs, access the `magento` file found in your site's root folder from the terminal and use the following command:

```
php <path to magento root>/bin/magento cron:run
```

For your production server, you'll want cron jobs to run as scheduled around the clock. To do this, you have to create a cronjob for your server, telling it how often to trigger Magento's cron tasks. For most servers — Unix and Linux — the cron program operates as a continuous daemon, waiting to take some action according to any programmed crontabs. In this case, we want to have the **magento** binary (also in our Magento root folder) run by the server every few minutes or so.

Generally, I set this to run every 15 minutes (we'll see in a moment how you can make sure that jobs set to run every 5 minutes by Magento are still completed).

The most straightforward way to schedule a cron job is to do so from the command line. Start by opening up a command prompt as the root user and typing in the following command:

```
crontab -e
```

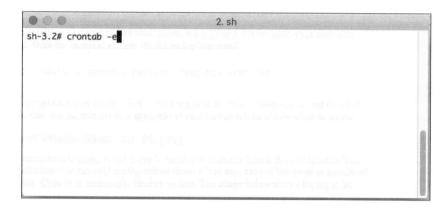

This command will take you to a screen where you can add entries to schedule the cron. To automate the Magento cron, you'll want to add entries that look like this:

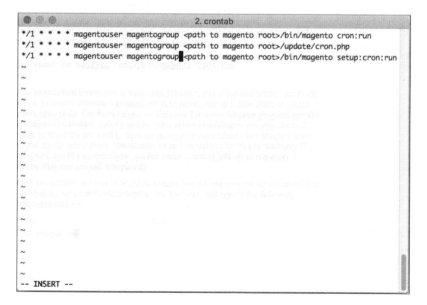

You can schedule crons to run every X number of minutes, hours, days, or months. You can schedule them to run only during certain times of the day, days of the week, or months of the year. Cron is an amazingly flexible system. The following screenshot shows the logic for scheduling crons:

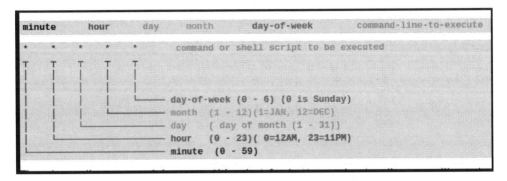

This can be a bit obtuse to understand, though; if you want a quick way to sort out timing for a cron job, you can visit one of the many crontab generating websites. One example is `http://crontab-generator.org/`. As you can see, this site provides assistance and makes it a bit easier to generate the desired schedule:

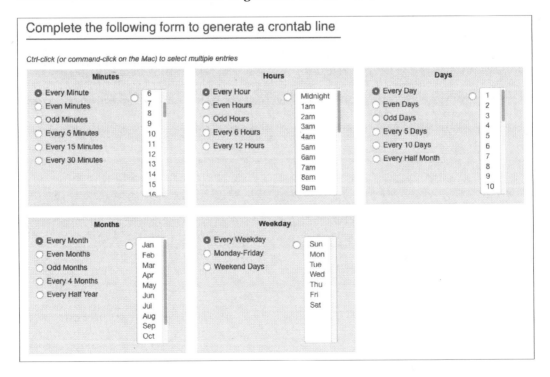

Tuning Magento's schedules

The Magento binary does a number of things when your server cron job runs:

- It executes any scheduled tasks
- The script generates schedules for any future tasks
- Finally, the script cleans up any history of scheduled tasks

The parameters that control this behavior are configured in your Magento backend:

1. Go to **Stores | Configuration | Advanced | System**.
2. Expand the **Cron (Scheduled Tasks)** panel.
3. For each item, fill in the number of minutes.
4. Click on **Save Config**.

Each field in this panel controls the timing actions of the `cron` script, as follows:

- **Generate Schedules Every** means that new schedules will not be created more frequently than the number of minutes configured.
- **Schedule Ahead for** is the number of minutes that will be generated in future schedules.
- **Missed if Not Run Within** tells the script to run any tasks that were scheduled within the indicated number of minutes before the script ran, but which haven't run already.
- **History Cleanup Every** deletes old history entries in the `cron_schedule` database table. This will help keep the table from growing too large.
- **Success History Lifetime** similarly purges successful entries from the `cron_schedule` table.
- **Failure History Lifetime** does just what you imagine: purges failure entries.

There remains considerable debate among bloggers on what values are ideal for this configuration. However, from my observations, there are some principles I follow when configuring Magento cron jobs.

Setting your frequency

Decide the frequency of your server cron job. If you configure your server cron to run every 15 minutes, then you do not need any Magento crontab or cron configuration to be set at anything less than 15 minutes. For example, the **Send Newsletter crontab**, as shown in the earlier table, is configured by default to run every 5 minutes.

If your system cron task runs every 15 minutes, then when `cron.php` is executed, the send newsletter task is actually run three times, since Magento schedules ahead and looks back to run any scheduled tasks. In order words, if your system cron runs at 10:00 am, it will run any tasks that were scheduled to run between 9:45 am (the last time it ran) and 10:00 am. Since the send newsletter task was scheduled to run every 5 minutes, at 9:45 am, Magento scheduled it to run at 9:50, 9:55, and 10:00. The task did not run at those times, but instead were all run at once at 10:00 when your system cron ran.

Therefore, you may want to go back through the various module `config.xml` files (such as the ones in the earlier table) and set the frequency of the jobs to match or be less frequent than your system cron.

Creating compatible settings

Once you have modified any crontabs to match your system cron job frequency, you should now configure the **Store | Configuration | Advanced | Cron (Scheduled Tasks)** panel:

- Use the same number of minutes as your system cron job frequency for **Generate Schedules Every**.

- Use the same value for **Schedule Ahead For**. In this way, you are capturing all the upcoming cron jobs Magento intends before your next system cron runs.

- Use the same value for **Missed If Not Run Within** to run any scheduled tasks that did not run during the last system cron.

- Use the same value for **History Cleanup Every**. You can use a larger interval if you wish, as this is not a critical function to running the necessary cron jobs for your store.

- For **Success History Lifetime** and **Failure History Lifetime**, you can use whatever settings you feel are most important. Generally, when launching a new Magento store, I set the **Failure History Lifetime** for a long time (as much as 3 days, or 4320 minutes) so that if something seems amiss, I can go into the `cron_schedule` database table and see if there are any failure messages that can help me diagnose the problem. In fact, even if your store is running smoothly, keeping this number large should not grow your database, as there will be no failure messages to record.

So, for example, if I set my system cron job to run every 15 minutes, my **Cron (Scheduled Tasks)** panel might look like this:

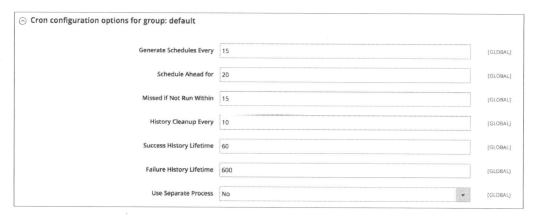

Backing up your database

While we're on the topic of cron jobs, one system cron job you should consider is backing up your Magento database. As usual, this advice is based on hard-earned experience. In the course of working with Magento, and especially if you have clients who have permissions to add extensions and change configuration, you may need to restore the Magento database to a previous working state.

While most server hosting providers provide backup services, restoring just the Magento database can take a long time as server backups restore all the files on the server, not just your database. Some providers do provide specific database back-ups, but to be safe, it doesn't hurt to schedule your server to do your own back-ups. Additionally, learning how to quickly and easily back-up and restore your database will come in handy, since you should always do a back-up of your database before installing new extensions or significantly changing configurations.

The built-in back-up

Magento does have a back-up function in the backend, under **Store | Tools | Backups**. While this is one way of backing up your Magento database, there is no built-in restore function. Furthermore, I have had problems in the past using the back-up file to restore, due to foreign-key conflicts. For extra, extra safety, it wouldn't hurt to use this function to create a back-up — especially if you do not have SSH access to your server account — but it is not as easy or quick as the following method.

Using MySQLDump

If you have SSH access to your server, using MySQL's built-in backup and restore functions are both quick and easy. You do need a username and password for your database (which you should have if you installed Magento):

1. To back up your database, access your server via SSH using a terminal program.

2. At the prompt, enter `mysqldump –u [username] –p[password] –h [hostname] [databasename] > [filename].sql`.

3. In very short order, MySQL will create a file containing a complete restoration script, including all of your database records.

To provide an example for the previous command, let's assume the following:

- **MySQL username**: `mageuser1`
- **MySQL password**: `magepassword1`
- **Host name**: `localhost`
- **Name of Magento database**: `magento_db`
- **File name for the dump**: `magento_db`

Using these example values, your command would look like this:

```
> mysqldump –u mageuser1 –pmagepassword1 –h localhost magento_db >
magento_db.sql
```

To restore your database, a slightly different format is used: `mysql –u [username] –p[password] –h [hostname] [databasename] < [filename].sql`, or the following to use our above examples:

```
> mysql –u mageuser1 –pmagepassword1 –h localhost magento_db < magento_
db.sql
```

It's as easy as that!

Setting a cron for back-up

Now that you know how MySQL can dump a back-up of your database, you can use your server cron to do a dump every night, every week, and/or every month, depending on how fervent you want to be about preserving backups.

Every developer will have their own back-up strategies; so, naturally, do I. While our hosting provider does a complete server back-up every night and preserves back-ups for 7 days, I like to augment that with my own database rolling back-up strategy:

- Daily backups for each day of the week. Monday's next backup will replace the current Monday backup. Therefore, we will have one backup for each day of the week, but not more than seven at any one time.

- Alternating weekly backups. In essence, we save a backup every other week, so that we have two weekly backups.

- One monthly backup. So far, after 15+ years of doing this, we've never had to revert to a monthly backup, but I certainly like having it there nonetheless.

One note here: if you can, you may want to consider dumping these to a computer other than your Magento server. Since our hosting provider does off-site backups, I feel quite comfortable backing up our Magento databases onto a local machine at our office. The chances of all three locations, our hosting provider's facility, the off-site back-up facility, and our office, all burning down at the same time (I'm sure)' is pretty darn remote, especially since all three facilities are spread across a continent.

To schedule your dumps as crontabs, invoke the crontab, as you did earlier in this chapter, and create as many jobs as you feel you need (if you're dumping to another server, you need to, of course, schedule these jobs on the machine to which the backup is to be dumped).

Create a new schedule according to your desired frequency (every day, week, month, and so on) and enter your MySQL dump command, as used previously. For the file name, though, use a name unique to the purpose of the dump. For example, for a dump on Monday, you might use `magento_db_Mon.sql`; for week 1, `magento_db_week_1.sql`. In this manner, the next dump for a given script will overwrite the previous dump without filling up your hard drive with dump files.

Upgrading Magento

From time to time, as Magento improves its platform features, or to address bugs and security issues, you will receive a notice that your system needs to be upgraded. With Magento 2, this upgrade process is made infinitely easier and better than in Magento 1.x.

If you are versioning your Magento installation, you should not upgrade your production installation using our instructions here. Rather, upgrade your development environment, test, and then promote your code to your production server.

In order to keep your Magento installation upgraded, you must take certain steps:

- Obtain Magento Marketplace keys
- Run the System Upgrade routine in your Magento 2 backend

Obtaining Magento Marketplace keys

In order for your store to communicate to Magento for upgrade verifications, you or a developer has to obtain developer keys. While this suggests that keys are only for developers, anyone can create an account at Magento and obtain keys.

If you don't already have an account at Magento, go to `https://www.magentocommerce.com/magento-connect/customer/account/create/` and create your free account. Once you are registered, log in to your account at `https://www.magentocommerce.com/magento-connect/customer/account/login/`.

After you log in:

1. Click on the **Connect** tab.
2. Click on the **Developers** side menu tab.
3. Click on **Secure Keys** in the sidebar menu.
4. Enter a **Name** for your keys. This is only a reference name (such as "Production Server"), so you can easily determine which keys are for which Magento installation.
5. Click on **Generate new**.
6. On the results screen, you will see two keys: **Public Key** and **Private Key**. You will use these for the next part of this process:

7. In your Magento 2 backend, go to **System | Web Setup Wizard**.
8. Click the large button labeled **System Configuration**.
9. On this page, paste the keys obtained previously into the appropriate spaces and click on **Save Config**.

Upgrading your Magento installation

Now that you're able to communicate with Magento Connect, you can begin the process of upgrading your installation.

After entering your keys, you should still be within the Wizard. Find the **System Upgrade** button or sidebar menu and click it to begin the upgrade process.

The **System Upgrade** screen shows the steps the process will undertake to complete:

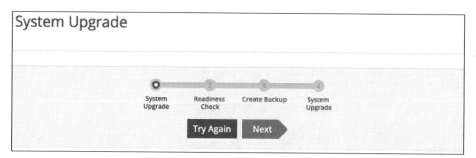

When this screen first loads, it goes through a series of checks to find out what needs to be upgraded. You can choose the version of Magento Core Components you wish to upgrade, as well as any other components that may have been added to your installation.

Once you make your choices, click on **Next**:

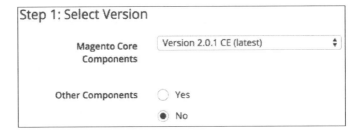

 There are many reasons why an upgrade might fail. We have certainly had our share of issues, although far less with Magento 2 than with earlier versions. If you are a developer, you can find that most upgrade errors can be fixed by going to `http://devdocs.magento.com/guides/v2.0/comp-mgr/trouble/cman/were-sorry.html` and reviewing the advice shown there.

On the next screen, you can determine whether your installation is truly ready for a system upgrade. Click on **Start Readiness Check** and wait for it to complete its analysis:

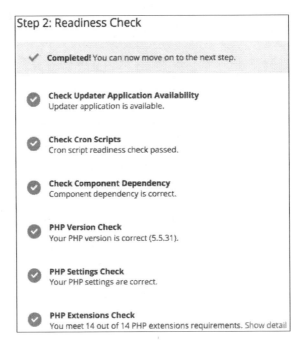

Click **Next** to create a backup of your installation.

If you're not using a hosting company that provides backups or you do not have a backup protocol, well, you're flirting with trouble. No matter how well a server is configured or you maintain your Magento installation, you should never fail to make regular backups. As in this process, you should also make a backup whenever you make any changes to your Magento code.

In most cases, you will want to include all items in your backup. However, if your server is regularly backed up and you have lots of product images (for example, thousands of product SKUs), you might consider not backing up site "media." Media can take a long time to back-up and consume considerable space. However, if you update your media often, don't hesitate to include it in your backup.

Click on **Create Backup** to trigger the backup process.

 Backups of even the most modest-sized Magento installations can take some time. Do not interrupt this process. If something goes awry, Magento will alert you with an error message. In other words, be patient!

When the backup is complete, click on **Next**. If all has gone well, the system will tell you it's ready for you to click on **Upgrade**.

Summary

After working your way through this book, you've now reached a level of familiarity and understanding that enables you to call yourself a Magento master. Of course, given the complexity and features of Magento, there's always more that you can learn. You should now have enough comfort with Magento that you can freely experiment. After all, one of the great features of open source software is that you have the access and freedom to augment the original system to meet your needs.

In this chapter on advanced techniques, we have learned a nifty way of integrating WordPress into a Magento installation, discussed a simple method of building and using a staging installation, provided a complete tutorial on scheduling Magento cron tasks, and covered strategies and techniques for backing up your Magento database.

With this book in hand, you most likely are close to completing a new Magento store. Launch date is just around the corner. If you've never launched a Magento store before, you're in for a treat now!

Just one task remaining now: go through the pre-launch checklist one final time before we are all set to go live. This is what we shall go through in the next chapter.

11
Pre-Launch Checklist

As you've no doubt realized — and one great reason for this book — Magento 2 delivers its power as an e-commerce platform by giving you a lot of versatility. This versatility comes at a price, though, most notably in terms of the vast number of configuration tasks and choices available.

Over the years, we have created our own Magento Pre-Launch Checklist to make sure we touch all the important configuration and design points within Magento 2 that are necessary for a live store to operate. If you've read through this entire book, you may have already addressed a number of these items, but having an itemized list to follow will save you a lot of time and give your store owner a great deal of immediate satisfaction.

We've broken down this checklist into the following areas:

- System
- Design and interface
- SEO
- Sales
- Products
- Maintenance

In this chapter, we will go over the configurations to review in order to have a successful Magento store launch.

 Since so many of the processes noted in this checklist have been discussed in previous chapters, many of the sections in this chapter will refer to previous chapters. Another very good reason to keep your *Mastering Magento 2* book close at hand!

A word about scope

In *Chapter 1, Planning for Magento*, we discussed the **Global-Website-Store** methodology. When planning your Magento installation, you set up whether your installation would have one or more websites, each with one or more store views. As you go through this checklist, you need to pay close attention to the scope in which you are updating configurations and designs. For instance, as we discuss base URLs, take care that your store view is set at the proper level for the configuration. In other words, if you're updating the base URL for the entire installation, your store view is **Default Config**. On the other hand, if the base URL applies only to your English language furniture store view, then set to that store view.

System configurations

The area of the Magento back-end that has the most configuration choices is within the **Stores | Configuration** menus and panels. So, let's begin there first.

SSL

Unless your store is using PayPal Express, PayPal Standard, PayPal Advanced, or another off-site payment processing method (for example, Authorize.Net Direct), your store may be taking credit card information on your server. Even though you're not storing the credit card information, you will need to get a **Secure Socket Layer (SSL) Encryption Certificate** installed on your server. Depending on the type of certificate you purchase, this process can take from 2 days to 2 weeks. It pays to plan ahead on this one: don't wait until the day before launch to try to get an **SSL Certificate**. Unless you're a master at web server configuration, consult with your hosting provider who can provide you with the necessary encryption keys and installation assistance. For most hosting providers, the installation of an SSL Certificate is outside the permissions of the client (you).

Base URLs

Using the procedures described in *Chapter 2, Installing Magento 2*, configure your base URLs for each store view level. You should also review the following panels:

- **General | Web | Url Options**: If you're using a shared shopping cart and/ or a shared SSL, set **Add Store Code to Urls** to **Yes**. To avoid duplication of content (which may hurt your search engine rankings), set **Auto-redirect to Base URL** to **Yes (301 Moved Permanently)**.

- **General | Web | Base URLs (Secure)**: If you have your SSL Certificate installed, and you have entered the secure URL as the base URL in this panel, set both **Use Secure URLs on Storefront** and **Use Secure URLs in Admin** to **Yes**.

Administrative base URL

Since anyone who has used Magento 2 knows that, by default, the administrative backend of your store is accessible by going to `http://www.storedomain.com/backend`, changing this URL may help keep out the bad guys. To set up a new admin domain:

1. Set up your new domain on your server to point to your Magento installation (see your hosting provider, if needed, for assistance).

2. Go to **Advanced | Admin | Admin Base URL**, set **Use Custom Admin URL** to **Yes** and enter the new domain into **Custom Admin URL**. Include any path that is necessary for your store front end, such as `http://www.newdomain.com/magento`.

3. Set **Use Custom Admin Path** to **Yes** and enter the new path for accessing the Magento backend into **Custom Admin Path**. For example, if you enter **mybackend**, you would then access the Magento 2 backend using `http://www.domain.com/mybackend`.

Now you should be able to access your Magento backend using the new domain name. If you have set a **Secure Base URL** and set **Use Secure URLs in Admin** to **Yes**, then the new domain should automatically change to the secure URL. However, this does provide a convenient and more secure means of isolating access to your Magento backend.

Reducing file download time

Today's search engines are monitoring the speed with which web pages download. The faster the download speed, the better your site is liked by Google et al. More importantly, it makes for a better user experience. Magento helps you by giving the backend administrator the means to combine CSS and JavaScript files, creating fewer files to download to render a page.

Merging JavaScript files

To combine your design's JavaScript files into one downloadable file:

1. Go to the **Advanced | Developer | JavaScript Settings** panel.
2. Select **Yes** for **Enable JavaScript Bundling** and **Merge JavaScript Files**.
3. Click on **Save Config**.

 You may find, when looking at your frontend source code, that not all JavaScript files have been combined. Some add-on modules add JavaScript links outside of Magento's JavaScript combine functionality. That said, combining most of them using this tool can help reduce overall download time.

Merging CSS files

The same process can be applied to your theme's CSS files:

1. Go to the **Advanced | Developer | CSS Settings** panel.
2. Select **Yes** for **Merge CSS Files**.
3. To further reduce the size of this combined file, you can set **Minify CSS Files** to **Yes**.
4. Click on **Save Config**.

Caching

We went into quite a bit of detail about caching in *Chapter 9, Optimizing Magento*. We mention it here because during development you may have turned off caching to help speed up design and code changes. Take the time now to set your optimum caching settings.

Cron jobs

If you haven't already, configure and turn on cron jobs on your installation. Refer to *Chapter 10, Advanced Techniques*, for information on how to configure cron jobs.

Users and roles

Before you launch, you may want to set up specific users for whoever will have access to your Magento backend. Certain users may only need access to orders and customers. Others may be responsible for product information and pricing.

Before setting up users, you need to set up various roles or groups of permissions to which you can assign users:

1. Go to **System | User Roles** in your Magento backend.
2. Click on **Add New Role**.
3. Give the new role an appropriate name in **Role Name**.
4. Click on **Role Resources** in the left sidebar.
5. Check the specific permissions you wish to give this role.
6. Click on **Save Role**.

Once you have your roles set up, you can set up your users:

1. Go to **System | All Users**.
2. Click on **Add New User**.
3. Enter the required fields for **User Info**.
4. Click on **User Role** in the sidebar menu.
5. Choose one of the roles you set up previously.
6. Click on **Save User**.

Once you save the user, an email will be sent to them with the login credentials.

Design configurations

Undoubtedly, you've invested a considerable amount of time creating a frontend design to meet your e-commerce needs. Before you launch, however, there are a few design-related tasks that need to be performed.

Transactional emails

Using the techniques described in *Chapter 5, Configuring to Sell*, build and assign the emails that will be sent to customers who purchase, register, and subscribe to newsletters.

Invoices and packing slips

The primary thing you need to do for invoice and packing slips is to upload an appropriate logo as a substitute for the default Magento logo. Upload the logo you wish to use for PDF print-outs and on-screen views in the **Sales | Sales | Invoice and Packing Slip Design** panel.

Favicon

Don't overlook this little item! You'd be surprised how many Magento-powered websites we visit that still show the Magento logo. To upload your own favicon, go to the **General | Design | HTML Head** panel under **Stores | Configuration**.

Placeholder images

For products that have no image, Magento inserts default placeholder images. You can create your own — perhaps with your own company's logo — to use instead of the default images with the Magento logo.

To upload your own versions, go to the **Stores | Configuration | Catalog | Catalog | Product Image Placeholders** panel. Use images similar in size to those that your theme design uses for regular product images.

404 and error pages

When you first install Magento, a CMS page is automatically created for use when a visitor tries to access a non-existent page. This default page, as shown in the following screenshot, is not bad, but you may want to update the banner images and, perhaps, provide even better information to visitors as to what they can do to find the correct page.

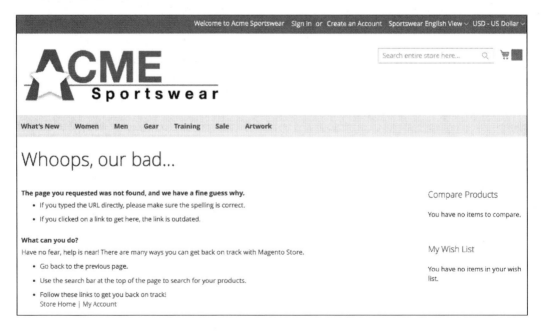

You may want to modify the layout to include a sidebar of categories. It might also be helpful to show your telephone number in large numbers if you want customers to call you for help.

Search engine optimization

Without exception, for an online store to prosper it has to have customers. Attracting customers comes from a variety of efforts, including search engine rankings. There are a number of SEO-related activities for increasing traffic, from blog postings and backlinks, to product descriptions and reviews. For pre-launch purposes, you want to make sure to do the initial tasks that will add to the SEO arsenal.

Meta tags

If you intend to use meta tags as part of your Search Engine Optimization, see *Chapter 7, Marketing Tools*, for specific procedural information.

Analytics

In your Magento backend, under **Stores | Configuration | Sales | Google API**, is a panel titled **Google Analytics**. To have Magento automatically include a Google tracking code on each page of your site, set **Enable** to **Yes** and enter your **Google Analytics ID** in the **Account Number** field.

Sitemap

If you did not already do it after reading *Chapter 7, Marketing Tools*, configure and activate your Magento store sitemap.

Sales configurations

Before you can begin taking orders on your new Magento website, you need to confirm that you have all the necessary configurations in place.

Company information

In your Magento backend, go to **Stores | Configuration | General | General**. Review your settings for the following panels:

- **Countries Options**: This panel allows you to restrict the countries to which you will sell products. Your store owner may have limitations where they can ship and/or receive payments. The **Default Country** sets the default for any country selection drop-down menu.

- **Locale Options**: Use these settings to accommodate the backend users of your Magento store.

- **Store Information**: The values entered here will be used throughout the Magento stores as defaults for name, telephone number, and address.

Store e-mail addresses

Even small online vendors may use different email addresses for different purposes. We often set up multiple email addresses for our client's stores, even if the same person may be receiving emails for sales and support. Having separate email addresses helps to segregate emails by purpose. Additionally, if the business grows and assigns different people to different purposes, you will have already established different email addresses with the store's customers.

A little known feature for those of you who use Google Apps — more specifically, Google Mail — you can create multiple email addresses for the same email account without having to add forwarding or alias configurations to Google Mail. For example, if you have an email address of info@domain.com, you could create the following emails and each one will go to the same email account: info+sales@domain.com, info+support@domain.com, and info+contact@domain.com. Google Mail will ignore the portion of the email address after and including the "+" in the address. We use this often to provide different email addresses without creating multiple email accounts.

Contacts

The panels on the **General | Contacts** screen allow you to enable the standard **Contact Us** form and set to whom these emails should be sent. You can also assign a customized transactional email.

Currency

Use the procedures in *Chapter 2, Installing Magento 2*, to confirm that any necessary currency conversion settings are ready to go.

General sales settings

Under **Stores | Configuration | Sales | Sales** are various panels that control a rather eclectic group of sales-related functions.

- **Checkout Totals Sort Order**: Using numbers of any value, you can control the order in which various order line items are displayed.
- **Reorder**: Select whether registered customers may use previous orders to generate new purchases.
- **Invoice and Packing Slip Design**: Earlier in this checklist, you uploaded any custom logo designs. You can also enter a company address that you wish to use as an alternative to the company address you entered before.
- **Minimum Order Amount**: In this panel, you can set any minimum order amount (if one is to be enforced), as well as set whether to validate multiple addresses submitted in a multi-address checkout.
- **Dashboard**: If you find that server processing power is low, you may want to set **Use Aggregated Data** to **No**.
- **Gift Options**: For sellers of gift items, such as flowers or jewelry, you may want to allow Magento to include a field for purchasers to use to include a gift message to the recipient. These messages will appear in your order detail page for processing.

Customers

If you plan on having more than one customer group (for example, wholesale, preferred, and so on), set up multiple customer groups according to the process described in *Chapter 7, Marketing Tools*.

In addition, there are a few settings you should review under **Stores | Configuration | Customers | Customer Configuration**:

- **Account Sharing Options**: Set whether you want customer accounts shared among all websites or not.

- **Online Customers Options**: The vaguely named **Online Minutes Interval** is used to calculate the number of current customers visiting your store, as displayed under **Customers | Online Customers**. For example, if you set this to 30 minutes, then any customer accessing a page of your site within the past 30 minutes will be considered a current online customer.

- **Create New Account Options**: Use these settings to control how new customer accounts are handled. Reference the transactional emails you created earlier for the email-related settings.

- **Password Options**: If you created a new transactional email for sending customers their forgotten password, select it for **Forgot Email Template**.

- **Name and Address Options**: In this panel, you can customize how you capture customer information.

- **Login Options**: Select if you want the customer to land on their **Dashboard** page or your site home page after logging in.

- **Address Templates**: This is an interesting panel and one often forgotten when customer address layout issues arise. If you find that any layout in your site is not displaying customer information properly, refer to this page.

Sales emails

The **Stores | Configuration | Sales | Sales Emails** screen provides panels to allow you to choose customized transactional emails and sender email addresses for orders, invoices, shipment notices, and credit memos.

Tax rates and rules

In *Chapter 5, Configuring to Sell*, we discussed at length how to configure sales tax rates and rules. Afterwards, you should go to **Stores | Configuration | Sales | Tax** in your Magento backend for additional sales tax configurations:

- **Tax Classes**: Select whether sales tax is to be calculated for shipping charges.

- **Calculation Settings**: Based on the expectations of your customers and your marketplace, you can configure how sales tax calculations are made and presented in online shopping carts and invoices.

- **Default Tax Destination Calculation**: Since sales tax is generally calculated for sales made to customers living in the taxing jurisdiction of the business, you can set the default sales tax rule for individual store views. Your actual taxing rules will override these default settings.

- **Price Display Settings**: These configurations affect whether products and shipping prices should be displayed with or without including any applicable sales tax calculation.

- **Shopping Cart Display Settings**: Generally, the default settings are appropriate, but this is especially useful if you should review how prices, totals, and taxes are to be displayed in shopping carts.

- **Orders, Invoices, Credit memos Display Settings**: This panel is the same as for the previous panel.

- **Fixed Product Taxes**: Where products are assigned fixed taxes, such as excise taxes, you can configure how those taxes are to be displayed on the site.

Shipping

Using *Chapter 5, Configuring to Sell*, for guidance, confirm that the shipping methods you want for your new store are configured and ready.

Payment methods

Likewise, you should confirm your desired payment methods. Most can be set in test mode during configuration.

Newsletters

Configure and test your newsletter configurations. Refer to *Chapter 7, Marketing Tools*, for detailed information on creating and sending customer newsletters.

Terms and conditions

Later in this checklist, you will set whether or not you want customers to confirm that they have read your site's terms and conditions before completing their purchase. To compose your terms, go to **Stores** | **Terms and conditions** in your Magento backend. Here, you can add the actual text that will be displayed during checkout.

Checkout

Now, let's turn our attention to the checkout process. Go to **Stores | Configuration | Sales | Checkout**, where you will find the following panels:

- **Checkout Options**: On this panel, you can decide whether or not to use the onepage checkout feature, allow guests (non-registered customers) to checkout, and require the customer to confirm they have read and will abide by your terms and conditions.

- **Shopping Cart**: This panel dictates settings for how long quotes should survive, to where shoppers are redirected after adding a product to their shopping cart, and what images should be displayed in the shopping cart for grouped or configurable products.

- **My Cart Link**: Set whether the **My Cart Link** shown on each page should display the total number of items in the cart (number of unique products) or the total item quantities (products X quantity of each). For example, if you choose **Display number of items in cart**, a shopping cart with two baseball bats will show 1 item in the **My Cart** link. **Display item quantities** would show 2 items.

Product configurations

Aside from the process of adding new products to your store, there are a number of configurations you should review that affect how products are managed and presented. The goal of any Magento store is to sell, and the ease with which customers can shop, as well as the presentation of the categories and products, greatly affects the success of any e-commerce venture.

Therefore, this section of the checklist may be a lengthy, yet necessary, process. There are no set recommendations, either, for most of these settings, as we find different intentions for each site we build. As with all Magento configurations, don't assume each setting's purpose is clear.

Some product categories lend themselves to long listings of products, each on its own line. Other products may be better suited to a grid layout of no more than six products to a page. Magento's immense flexibility means you not only have a variety of presentation options; it also means you have to be willing to experiment and test. And that, my friend, is one of the exciting aspects of configuring a Magento store.

Catalog

The **Stores** | **Configuration** | **Catalog** | **Catalog** configuration section has, perhaps, the most panels of any section in Magento. I'm going to break each panel down into its own subsection in order to address the many configuration choices.

Storefront panel

This is one panel with which we encourage you to experiment, as it dictates how products are to be displayed when a customer views a category in your store.

- **List Mode**: Set the default category view to **Grid Only**, **List Only**, **Grid by default**, or **List by default**.

- **Products per Page on Grid Allowed Values**: On grid view pages, there will be a drop-down menu to allow customers to select how many products should appear. The values you use here should be a multiple of how many products appear on each row. For the default of three products in each row, use values that are evenly divisible by three to avoid having an incomplete last row.

- **Products per Page on Grid Default Value**: Set the default number of products to display on a grid layout category page.

- **Products per Page on List Allowed Values**: This uses the same methodology as for the **Grid Allowed Values**, except that you're not concerned with multiples of products per row, since each row only contains one product.

- **Products per Page on List Default Value**: As you can imagine, this is the default number of products that appear in a list view. As with any view default value, this can be a number larger than the smallest number in your list of allowed values.

- **Allow All Products per Page**: If your categories don't contain a very large number of products, you may want to allow customers to select All as one of the allowed values. Setting this value to **Yes** will automatically add All to the drop-down menu of allowed values.

- **Product Listing Sort by**: Customers can sort views by **Best Value**, **Name**, or **Price**. This selection determines the default sorting of views. **Position** is one of the more misunderstood concepts of Magento configurations, so allow me to explain. If you go to a category detail screen under **Products | Categories**, you'll find under the **Category Products** tab a list of products assigned to that category. The last column is labeled **Position**. By entering values into these fields, you dictate a manual sorting order for those products, in ascending order of the position value. For instance, if you want to feature products in a special order, you might enter position values of 10, 20, 30, and so on. The following screenshot shows how we can dictate the sorting order for the Jackets category so that the items are in ascending order according to the values entered into the last column.

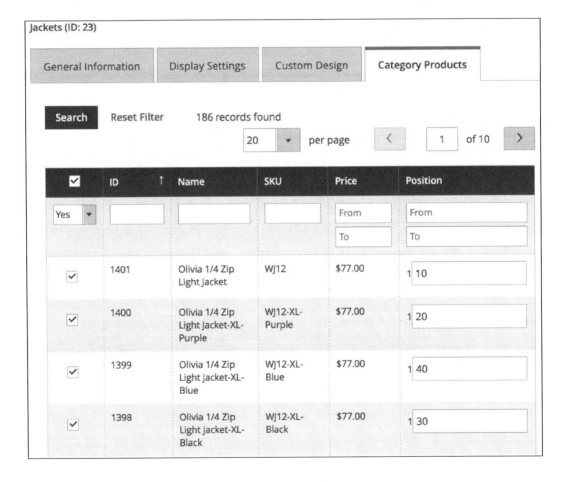

If you do not enter position values, **Position** sorts by the products' ID values. In this example, if I leave the position values at their default value of zero, these products would appear in this order: **Ottoman, Chair, Couch, Magento Red Furniture Set**.

- **Use Flat Catalog Category** and **Use Flat Catalog Product**: As discussed in *Chapter 9, Optimizing Magento*, flattening category and product records can speed up database lookups, thus decreasing page generation times.

- **Allow Dynamic Media URLs in Products and Categories**: If you want to insert images into product and category descriptions, you may want Magento to use dynamic URLs to preserve the image link regardless of changes you make to design themes. If you're set on your theme and where you want to store images, set this to **No**, as it can help reduce the amount of server processing time needed to render description content.

Product reviews

By default, Magento allows viewers to submit reviews for products. This panel determines whether non-registered customers — or guests — are allowed to submit reviews for products.

Product alerts

The alerts configured in this panel pertain to emails that can be sent to customers when product prices or stock availability changes. If you set **Allow Alert When Product Price Changes** to **Yes**, then customers will see a link labeled **Sign up for price alert** on each product page.

Product alerts run settings

If you have activated your cron jobs, Magento will process any customer-subscribed pricing and stock availability alerts according to the schedule you specify in this panel. You can also receive email alerts if an error in the processing occurs.

Product image placeholders

See the section *Placeholder Images* earlier in this checklist for information on uploading placeholder images.

Recently viewed/compared products

In this panel, you can set how customer-selected recently viewed and compared product lists are handled, especially if you are operating a multi-store installation.

Price

How you choose product price sharing — globally or by website — affects how currency conversions are applied to prices.

Layered navigation

In most cases, automatic calculation of price steps in the layered navigation sidebar will work fine. However, in some cases, you may want to set your own steps for each store.

Category top navigation

If you want to limit the depth of your top menu category navigation, enter the maximum level you wish. Zero (0) means all levels will be displayed.

Search engine optimizations

This panel contains several settings that can affect how well your site is indexed by search engines, such as Google, Yahoo! and Bing.

- **Popular Search Terms**: Enabling this feature adds a link to a page of search terms used in searches on your site. This helps search sites identify links generated by popular searches and can help in your rankings when those terms are used in the search engines.

- **Product URL Suffix** and **Category URL Suffix**: By default, product and catalog page URLs end in .html. You can specify any suffix you wish, but you may also want to have no suffix, as is the common practice for many websites.

- **Use Categories Path for Products URLs**: If you want URLs for products to contain the category name in the path, such as http://www.storedomain. com/furniture/living-room/ottoman, set this to **Yes**.

- **Create Permanent Redirect for old URLs if URL key changed**: During development and setup, I generally set this to **No**, as there is no reason to have Magento create a lot of redirects as you edit product URL keys. However, before launch, you should set this to **Yes** so that future updates will create redirects. These redirects mean that older links still showing in search engines will lead visitors to the correct pages.

- **Page Title Separator**: Enter the character you wish to use in URLs as a substitute for blank spaces. It is generally accepted that a hyphen (-) is better for SEO than an underscore (_).

- **Use Canonical Link Meta Tag for Categories** and **Use Canonical Link Meta Tag for Products**: Search engines — especially Google — can penalize you for duplicate content. In an e-commerce store, categories and products can be accessed through a variety of URLs. For instance, `http://www.storedomain.com/ottoman` and `http://www.storedomain.com/furniture/living room/ottoman` take the user to the very same page (Magento knows how to interpret both URLs). To Google, these are two different pages, both with the same content. Therefore, Google might penalize your site for having duplicate content, when, in fact, it's not. Canonical link meta tags are, as the name implies, meta tags in your page header that contain, for lack of a better term, the *definitive link* to the page. That is, if Google analyzes multiple URLs, but each one has the same value for the canonical link meta tag, then Google understands that these pages are really one in the same and treats them not as duplicate pages, but simply alternative link paths. An example of a canonical link meta tag, for our example ottoman, would be `<link rel="canonical" href="http://www.storedomain.com/ottoman" />`, and it would be the same regardless of the URL used to arrive at the ottoman page.

Catalog search

Your site will most likely have a site-wide search feature, with a search field somewhere on the page. Allowing your visitors to be able to search your site to find products is one more way you can increase the usability of your Magento site.

- **Minimal Query Length**: This represents the minimum number of characters that are required in order to do a search of your site. While the default value is 1, we usually set this to at least 3. Searching for one letter among all the possible categories and products of your site doesn't really make sense. Three may even be too small. Experiment and find the ideal minimum. In most Magento themes, the search field is auto complete, meaning that once the user starts typing into the field, Magento is immediately searching the database for possible matches, displaying them just below the field. This minimum value dictates how many letters are typed before Magento starts this searching process.

- **Maximum Query Length**: Enter the maximum number of characters you wish to allow for a query.

- **Maximum Query Words Count**: To keep searches fast and efficient, you should have some limit to the number of words that are used in a Like search.

RSS feeds

Go to **Stores | Configuration | Catalog | RSS Feeds** and enable any **RSS feeds** you want Magento to create.

Maintenance configurations

After setting up a new site, we know it's tempting to consider maintenance issues at a later time. However, before you know it, later becomes yesterday and you may find that not attending to basic maintenance tasks become tomorrow's "oh, shucks!"

Backups

Use the information in *Chapter 10, Advanced Techniques*, to re-confirm that you have set your backup systems in place. This is perhaps the most important pre-launch activity!

Summary

At this point, you should be ready to launch. Of course, the store owner or administrator may still need to add more products and content, but from a developer's point of view, if you have completed the steps in this checklist, your initial work is done.

Congratulations!

We would like to add one more item to the list, though: test. Test, test, test, and test again. Before you go live, have the store administrator, any backend users, and your colleagues go through all possible scenarios. Store owners are always eager to launch — usually yesterday — but you cannot overdo thorough testing. It's always better to catch problems before launch than after.

As you've no doubt realized — and one great reason you bought this book — Magento is powerful and complex. Many assume that since the community edition is free to use and PHP-based, that anyone with the knowledge of PHP can easily master Magento. We all know that's not really the case. Knowledge of how to apply Magento and the depth of Magento's features and interactions is what will truly turn a Magento novice into a Magento master.

Index

A

Apache
.htaccess file, modifying 33, 34
configuring 33
temporary URLs 35
virtual host declaration, modifying 35
vs Nginx 33
attributes
about 72
attribute properties, advanced 79
changing 75
labels, managing 80
options, managing 77
properties 76
storefront properties 80, 81
swatch, managing 77, 78
attribute sets
creating 81-84
attribute types
about 74, 75
selecting 75
Authorize.net direct post 152
automated currency conversions 46

B

backend orders
managing 140-143
orders, converting to invoices 143, 144
shipments, creating 144, 145
backups
backend backups 50-52
file structure backups 52
base currency 45, 46

base URLs
configuring 38, 39
blocks
using 189, 190
Braintree 151
branding 109
BrowserMob
URL 263
bundled products
creating 94-96
bundle product type 69, 70
Buy-One-Get-One (BOGO) 210

C

caching
about 258, 259
core caching 259
full page cache 260
impact 260
in Magento 2 261
managing 260
cart price rules
coupon codes, generating 221-223
creating 210, 211
new rule, adding 211-213
rule actions, defining 217-219
rule labels, modifying 220
rules conditions, defining 214-216
testing 223
catalog price rule
creating 205-209
catalogs
and categories 55
versus categories 26-28

categories
  and catalogs 55
  creating 56, 57
  planning 26, 27
  re-ordering 62
  special 62-64
  versus catalogs 26
categories, creating
  category products tab 61
  custom design tab 61
  general information tab 57-59
  settings tab, displaying 59, 60
CDNs (Content Delivery Networks)
  using 265
cloud server 18
CMS page
  creating 186-189
CMS page, customizing
  about 182
  content screen 184-186
  Home Page layout, modifying 182-184
configurable product
  creating 89-93
configurable product type 66-68
content management system (CMS) 179, 180
cron
  setting up, for back-up 284, 285
cron, Magento
  about 276
  compatible settings, creating 282
  frequency, setting 281
  jobs 276-278
  jobs, triggering 278-280
  schedules, tuning 281
  URL 280
crontabs 276
cross-sell products 104
currencies
  converting 45
  converting, automatically 46
customer groups
  about 203, 204
  creating 204
customers 4
customers segments 204

D

database, backing up
  about 283
  built-in back-up 283
  cron, setting up 284, 285
  MySQLDump, using 284
dedicated server 18
design configurations
  404 and error pages 296
  about 295
  favicon 296
  packing slips 295
  placeholder images 296
  transactional e-mails 295
design packages and themes
  default installation 117, 118
downloadable product
  creating 96
downloadable product type 71

E

e-commerce project
  scope, defining 2
  technical resources, assessing 5
  users, planning 3
Entity, Attribute and Value (EAV)
  about 252
  advantages 256
  attribute 253
  disadvantages 256
  entity 252, 253
  making flat 256, 257
  merging 254, 255
  value 254
extensions
  building 243
  files 243
  step five 246
  step four 246
  step one 244
  step six 247, 248
  step three 245
  step two 244, 245
  URL 238

F

fallback model 114
file structure backups 52
filtered navigation 60
Firebug plugin
  URL 126

G

GitHub
  URL 264
Global 10, 11
Global-Website-Store
  (GWS) methodology 9
Google Product feeds 277
grouped product
  creating 93, 94
grouped product type 69

H

hosting
  guidelines 18-20
  installation, effects 17
  types 17, 18
hosting partner
  URL 22
HTML
  using 193

I

Inchoo blog
  URL 243
indexing
  about 257, 258
  flat or no flat 258
  reindexing 258
indexing sitemaps
  URL 230
in-house hosting
  about 7
  servers 7, 8
inline translations 121, 122
inventory
  low stock notifications 98

managing 97, 98
product reports 98, 99

L

labels
  translating, manually 42-44
language files
  installing 40, 41
layered navigation 72
layouts
  controlling, expertly 130-132
  customizing 126-129
  default layout file, customizing 133, 134
  reference tag, using to relocate
    blocks 132, 133
localization
  used, for selling globally 40
local test installation
  setting up 8

M

MageMojo
  URL 22
Magento
  about 1, 2
  categories, planning 26, 27
  configuring 37
  currencies, converting automatically 46
  effects, of hosting on installation 17
  functionality extending, Magento
    plugins used 240-242
  installation process, considerations 22, 23
  module architecture 238, 239
  project, requisites 2
  sample data, installing 23
  strategies, for backups and security 50
Magento 2
  caching 261
  URL 243
Magento 2 Community 17
Magento Community
  language files, installing 40
Magento Community users 8
Magento Connect
  about 236
  free extensions 237, 238

searching 236, 237
URL 236
Magento developers
URL 5
Magento documentation
URL 243
Magento installation
requirements, checklist 3
Magento plugins
used, for extending Magento
functionality 240-242
Magento sales process 138, 139
Magento stores
cache, disabling 28, 29
Magento stores, setting up
localization, used for selling globally 40
Magento theme structure
about 110-113
parent theme, configuring in
theme.xml 115
theme files and directories 113, 114
Magento, upgrading
about 285
installation, upgrading 287-289
Marketplace keys, obtaining 286
Mail transfer agent (MTA) 8
maintenance configurations
about 308
backups 308
Marketplace keys
obtaining 286
meta fields
in Magento 231
using, for search engine visibility 230, 231
multiple businesses
used, for keeping finances separate 14
multiple domains
using, for effective market segmentation 12
multiple languages
used, for selling globally 14
multiple stores, planning
about 12
multiple businesses, used for keeping
finances separate 13
multiple domains, used for effective market
segmentation 12

multiple languages, used for selling
globally 14
MySQL
URL 264
MySQLDump
using 284
MySQL Workbench
URL 252

N

newsletters
about 223
customers, subscribing 224
issues, checking for 227
scheduling 226, 227
subscribers, managing 227
templates, creating 224, 226
Nginx
configuring 36
index.php file, modifying 36, 37
nginx.config file, modifying 36
Nginx server
using 264
non-product content 179

O

off-site payment systems
about 147
cons 148
pros 148
on-site payment systems
about 148
cons 149
pros 148

P

page link
adding 190, 191
HTML, using 193
widget, using 193
WYSIWYG, using 191, 192
pages
about 180-182
CMS page, customizing 182

payment methods
   about 145
   authorize.net direct post 152
   bank transfer payment 151
   Braintree 151
   cash on delivery payment 151
   check/money order 151
   Payment Card Industry Data Security
        Standard (PCI DSS) 146
   PCI compliance 146, 147
   purchase order 152
   zero subtotal checkout 151
payment systems
   classes 147
PayPal
   about 149
   all-in-one payment solutions 149
   payment gateways 150
   PayPal Express 150
PayPal Express 292
PCI Compliant
   avoiding 20, 21
PCI (Payment Card Industry) 20
PHP 5
phpAdmin 252
pipe delimited list 106
pre-launch checklist, Magento
   system configurations 292
pricing tools
   about 99
   autosettings 101, 102
   pricing, by customer group 99, 100
   quantity-based pricing 100, 101
products
   bundled products, creating 94-96
   complex product types 66
   configurable product, creating 89-93
   creating 85
   downloadable product, creating 96
   grouped product, creating 93, 94
   importing 105
   importing, shortcut 105-107
   managing, customer focused way 65
   new product screen 85
   simple product, creating 86-88
   simple product type 65, 66
   virtual product, creating 97

products configurations
   about 302
   catalog 303
   catalog search 307
   category top navigation 306
   layered navigation 306
   price 306
   product alerts 305
   product alerts run settings 305
   product image placeholders 305
   product reviews 305
   recently viewed/compared products 306
   RSS feeds 308
   search engine optimizations 306, 307
   storefront panel 303-305
product types, complex
   about 66
   bundle product type 69, 70
   configurable product type 66-68
   downloadable product type 71
   grouped product type 69
   virtual product type 71
promotions
   about 205
   cart price rules, creating 210, 211
   catalog price rule, creating 205-209

Q

quantity-based pricing 100, 101

R

related products 103

S

sales configurations
   about 297
   checkout 302
   company information 298
   contacts 298
   currency 299
   customers 299, 300
   general sales settings 299
   newsletters 301
   payment methods 301
   sales emails 300

shipping 301
store email addresses 298
tax rates and rules 300
terms and conditions 301
sales process
about 138
Magento sales process 138, 139
scope 292
search engine optimization
about 297
analytics 297
meta tags 297
sales configurations 297
sitemap 297
Search Engine Optimization (SEO) 228
search engines
meta fields, in Magento 231
optimizing 230
visibility, meta fields used 230
Secure Socket Layer (SSL) certificates 19
Secure Socket Layer (SSL) Encryption
Certificate 292
Send Newsletter crontab 281
SEO checklist
about 232
canonical URLs 232
category and product descriptions 232
meta description fields 232
meta keywords 232
meta title fields 232
XML Sitemap 232
server
CDNs (Content Delivery Networks),
using 265
deflation 262, 263
expires, enabling 263
MySQL cache, increasing 264
Nginx server, using 264
PHP memory, increasing 263
turning, for speed 261, 262
Varnish cache, using 264
SFTP (Secure File Transfer Protocol 52
shared server 17
shipping methods
about 152, 153
allowed countries 155
carrier methods 159

flat rate 156
free shipping 155
handling fee 154
method not available 155
origin 154
table rates 156, 157
sitemaps
adding 228-230
using 228
Sparse Matrix 252
SSL Certificate 292
staff 4
staging environment
about 267
basic staging set-up 268, 269
simple approach 268
static blocks 59
static files
overriding 115
stock keeping unit (SKU) 65
Store 11
store management screen 9
stores
setting up 29-33
store views
setting up 29
strategies
for backups 50
for security 50
system configurations
about 292
administrative base URL 293
base URLs 292, 293
caching 294
cron jobs 294
CSS files, merging 294
file download time, reducing 293
JavaScript files, merging 294
SSL 292
users and roles 294, 295

T

table rates, shipping methods
about 156, 157
quantity and price based rates 157
saving 158

settings 158, 159
uploading 159
taxes, managing
  about 160
  Magento manages taxes 160, 161
  tax rates, importing 166
  tax rules, creating 161-166
  value added tax configurations 166, 167
  VAT taxes, setting up 167-171
technical considerations
  about 6
  hosting provider 6
  in-house hosting 7
technical resources
  assessing 5
theme files
  overriding 116, 117
theme inheritance
  static files, overriding 115
  theme files, overriding 116, 117
themes
  customizing 126
theme variants
  applying 125
  selecting 125
  themes, assigning 124, 125
  working with 122, 123
third-party themes
  installing 119, 120
transactional e-mails
  about 172, 173
  e-mail header and footer,
      assigning 175, 176
  new e-mail template, creating 176, 177
  new header template, creating 174, 175

U

upsell products 104
URL rewrites 57
User-Agent Header
  URL 112

V

variables
  own variables, using 197, 198
  using 195, 196
variant 66
VCL (Varnish Configuration Language) 264
version control 269-275
virtual machine (VM) 18
virtual product
  creating 97
virtual product type 71

W

Web developer add-on
  URL 126
website
  setting up 29-33
widgets
  used, for inserting content onto site
      pages 199-201
  using 189-195
WYSIWYG
  using 191, 192

Made in the USA
Lexington, KY
22 November 2017